Jürgen Beyerer, Alexey Pak (Eds.)

Proceedings of the 2011 Joint Workshop of Fraunhofer IOSB and Institute for Anthropomatics, Vision and Fusion Laboratory

Karlsruher Schriften zur Anthropomatik
Band 11
Herausgeber: Prof. Dr.-Ing. Jürgen Beyerer

Lehrstuhl für Interaktive Echtzeitsysteme
Karlsruher Institut für Technologie

Fraunhofer-Institut für Optronik, Systemtechnik und
Bildauswertung IOSB Karlsruhe

Eine Übersicht über alle bisher in dieser Schriftenreihe erschienenen Bände finden Sie am Ende des Buchs.

Proceedings of the 2011 Joint Workshop of Fraunhofer IOSB and Institute for Anthropomatics, Vision and Fusion Laboratory

Edited by
Jürgen Beyerer
Alexey Pak

Impressum

Karlsruher Institut für Technologie (KIT)
KIT Scientific Publishing
Straße am Forum 2
D-76131 Karlsruhe
www.ksp.kit.edu

KIT – Universität des Landes Baden-Württemberg und nationales
Forschungszentrum in der Helmholtz-Gemeinschaft

KIT Scientific Publishing 2012
Print on Demand

ISSN: 1863-6489
ISBN: 978-3-86644-855-1

Preface

In the year 2011, the annual joint workshop of the Fraunhofer Institute of Optronics, System Technologies and Image Exploitation (IOSB) and the Vision and Fusion Laboratory (IES) of the Institute for Anthropomatics, Karlsruhe Institute of Technology (KIT) took place in Triberg-Nussbach, Germany. From July, 17 to July, 22 the workshop provided a forum for the doctoral students of both institutions to present the status of their research and facilitated unrestrained discussions of the potential further developments and the alternative solutions. The results presented at the workshop are collected in this book in form of technical reports. This volume thus constitutes a valuable insight in the status and the progress of the research program of the IES Laboratory and the Fraunhofer IOSB. The topics covered here include image processing, world modeling, signal processing, data fusion, and human-machine interaction.

The editors thank Yvonne Fischer and the other organizers of the workshop for their efforts that led to a pleasant and rewarding stay in the Black Forest (Schwarzwald). The editors also thank the doctoral students for writing and reviewing the technical reports as well as for responding to the comments and the suggestions of their colleagues.

Prof. Dr.-Ing. Jürgen Beyerer
Alexey Pak, PhD

Contents

Improving the Performance of Distant Object Classification with Advanced Pre-Processing

Michael Teutsch

Vision and Fusion Laboratory
Institute for Anthropomatics
Karlsruhe Institute of Technology (KIT), Germany
teutsch@kit.edu

Technical Report IES-2011-01

Abstract: Object classification is an important topic in many surveillance and reconnaissance applications. False detections can be suppressed, potentially suspicious objects identified, and finally different object types separated. However, robust classification is difficult to accomplish as objects do not operate cooperatively, object distance may be high, and various sensor-specific noise-effects are to be handled. Appropriate pre-processing can be very helpful for the classification process. This ranges from standard noise filters to advanced methods achieving scale and rotation invariance, which significantly supports the classifier performance and generality. In this work, several advanced and noise-resistant methods are presented with respect to three pre-processing tasks: scale invariance, rotation invariance, and precise object segmentation. The benefit of these methods is demonstrated using several bird's eye view real data examples coming from different imaging sensors.

1   Introduction

In many surveillance and reconnaissance applications, early automatic identification and verification of potentially dangerous situations and criminal activities play a key role. Classification of non-cooperative objects in high distance is an important but difficult topic in this field of research. With reliable classifiers, it is possible to reject confusion objects, distinguish suspicious from irrelevant objects, and discriminate between different object types. Besides the high distance there are challenges such as varying object background, sensor noise, sensor motion, or suppression of false positive detections. Powerful support for the classification process can be adequate advanced pre-processing generating invariances regarding object scale or rotation as well as performing accurate object segmentation. It is desirable to create a normalized object appearance, which makes it easier to train the classifier, because a smaller set of training samples is needed, and achieve a higher degree of generality.

This is common in the area of local image features such as SIFT [Low04] or SURF [BTG06], where scale-invariance is created using multi-scale analysis (e.g., Laplacian Pyramid), rotation-invariance is achieved considering dominant gradient direction in a local Region Of Interest (ROI), and even the influence of affine distortion can be diminished by image warping [MY09]. For objects in high distance the application of local image features is not suitable as the object appearance only covers several pixels in the image plane, which is sometimes even less than the ROI considered for one local feature. However, some ideas and methods can be adopted and adapted to provide pre-processing supporting the classification process. In this article, some adapted or new methods are presented and evaluated to find out about their potential benefit for classification. These methods are robust against strong sensor noise and scattered object appearance. The performance is evaluated on real image data coming from a visual-optical camera mounted on an Unmanned Aerial Vehicle (UAV) and a Synthetic Aperture Radar (SAR) sensor of TerraSAR-X satellite.

1.1   Related Work

The ideas of SIFT and SURF pre-processing have already been mentioned. However, the related work to be presented is about pre-processing for whole objects. Standard methods for object orientation estimation are Principal Component Analysis (PCA) [Gab09] and Hough Transform [SET$^+$11]. The assumption when using PCA is, that the object's orientation directly corresponds to the principal component as most vehicles (trucks, ships, etc.) are elongate in bird's eye view. With Hough Transform, the best straight lines along the object's major edges are detected. Their slope is used to estimate the orientation.

Object segmentation can be performed with advanced filtering and thresholding techniques [Gab09] as well as the supplemental use of row- and column-histograms, which are more robust against noise and gaps in the object appearance for example due to strong scattering [SET$^+$11]. In [LLLT10], the segmentation of aircrafts in infrared images is performed with Otsu thresholding, contour tracking, and a scan line filling algorithm to determine object blobs without holes and gaps. In infrared images, Fu et al. [FWH08] use the combination of Negative Selection algorithm and Otsu thresholding to segment objects with noise-affected and blurry edges. Object segmentation in SAR images is the topic in [SKT10]. With the application of a Wiener filter speckle noise is suppressed while edges are preserved at the same time.

1.2 Structure

The article provides the following organization: the different pre-processing methods are presented in Section 2. Some experimental results are demonstrated in Section 3 and a conclusion is given in Section 4.

2 Pre-processing Methods

In automatic image processing, there are many different approaches for pre-processing. Basic methods for image quality improvement and image restoration are noise smoothing filters such as Median- or Gauss-filter, sharpening algorithms, or super-resolution. However, this article is focused on advanced pre-processing methods supporting the special application of distant object classification in surveillance and reconnaissance image data. This means that objects appear very small in the image plane, often covering only a few pixels. Since these observed objects are not behaving cooperatively and trying to disguise themselves, special sensors and ways of observing have to be used, which leads to images affected by weak signal-to-noise-ratio (SNR) and difficult conditions such as sensor motion or bad weather.

There is a big variety of detection algorithms to find these objects, but this article concentrates on pre-processing algorithms, which are applied after detection and before classification. Three ways of pre-processing are discussed achieving scale-invariance, rotation-invariance, and object segmentation.

2.1 Scale-invariance

For achieving scale-invariance it is assumed that the sensor's Ground Sampling Distance (GSD) is available. This is the ratio of scale in the real world in meters to scale in the image plane in pixels. With a GSD of $0.5\,\frac{m}{pixel}$, $0.5\,m$ in the real world are encoded within one pixel of the image plane. With a smaller GSD, more object details appear and classification becomes easier as long as the whole object is visible in the image. The quality of GSD calculation is strongly depending on the quality of the underlying Digital Elevation Model (DEM). Furthermore, the sensor's altitude and calibration parameters are needed.

Scale-invariance is generated using the current input image (source image) with GSD and warping it to a new image (destination image) with a normalized reference GSD. Since the warping process will consider sub-pixel positions, inverse warping is performed. Thus, for each pixel position in the destination image, the sub-pixel position in the source image is calculated and the pixel value is determined with bi-linear interpolation. This leads to the following formalization:

$$x_{src} = \frac{GSD_{ref}}{GSD_x} \cdot x_{dst}$$
$$y_{src} = \frac{GSD_{ref}}{GSD_y} \cdot y_{dst}$$

where (x_{src}, y_{src}) denotes a pixel position in the source and (x_{dst}, y_{dst}) in the destination image. GSD_{ref} is the reference and GSD_x and GSD_y are the horizontal and vertical Ground Sampling Distance, respectively. In general, GSD_x and GSD_y are different and dependent on the sensor incidence angle.

In Fig. 2.1, two examples of UAV-based urban surveillance and one of SAR satellite-based maritime surveillance are shown. In the SAR example, which is on the bottom, it is clearly visible, that $GSD_x \neq GSD_y$. The normalization of vehicles and building sizes is well visible in the urban scene observed by an UAV.

2.2   Rotation-invariance

Since only bird's eye view images are considered in this report, it is sufficient to consider rotations just around the axis that is perpendicular to the image plane. This way, the task of achieving rotation-invariance becomes easier but is still challenging as object appearance is small in the image and might be affected by noise. The difficulty of this task increases significantly, if rotations around all coordinate axes are possible, which cause the necessity of Hessian warping for appearance normalization [MY09]. Two different approaches are presented which use different prior knowledge: the motion vector in the first and the assumption that the object's longest edge corresponds to its orientation in the second case.

2.2.1   Rotation Compensation using the Motion Vector

Object motion vectors are estimated by precise sub-pixel image registration between two or more consecutive images in video data. This is a very robust method eliminating most false positive object detections especially if some kind of object tracking

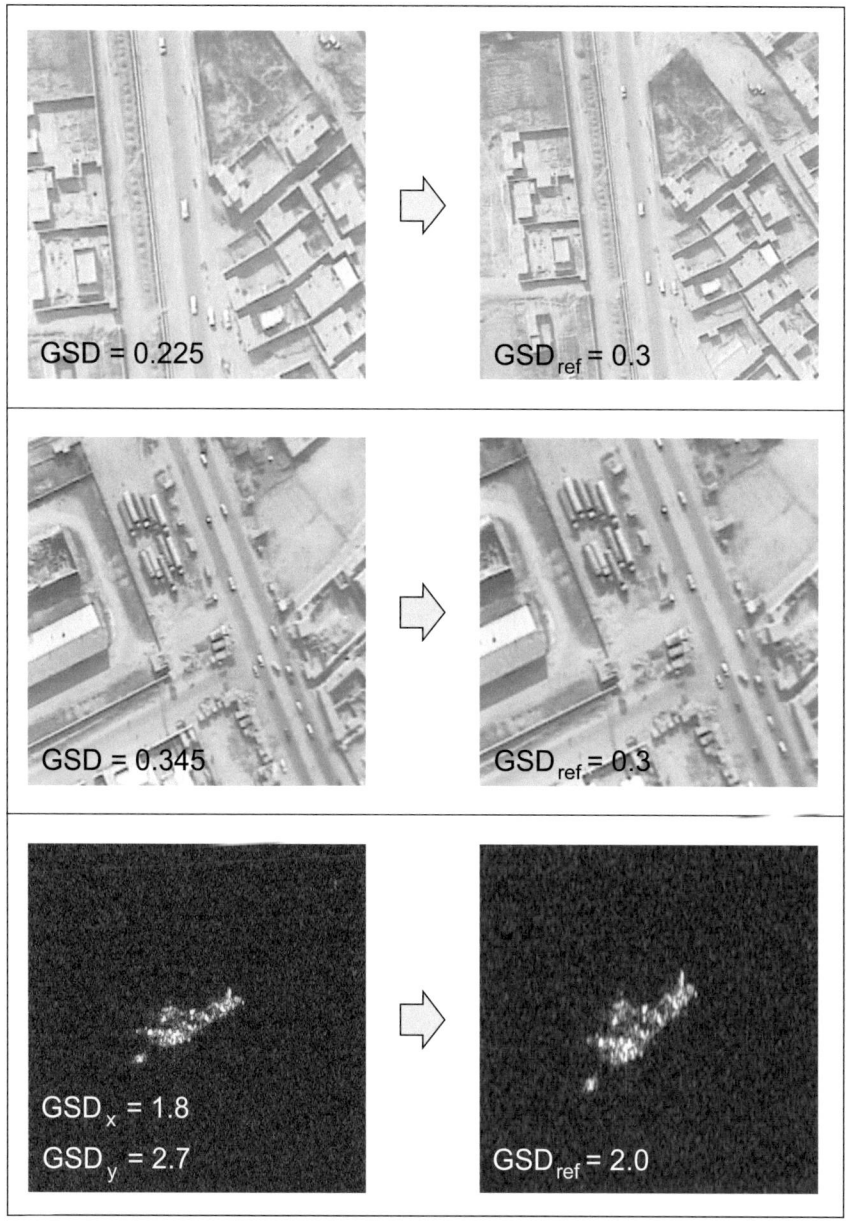

Figure 2.1: Example for achieving scale invariance using GSD.

is introduced. Normally, the differences in the scene depth itself are rather small compared to the observing camera distance. Hence, the scene may be approximated by a ground plane and a homography [HZ04] can be estimated as global transformation. There are two popular approaches for image registration which base either on subtraction of consecutive images (image difference) [KSS+01, HEKS08] or detection of point correspondences between two or more images [SGK00, YMKC07]. The result is a homography describing the background motion. All vectors that are outliers from this homography are coming from moving objects. Thus, they are not only detected, but also information about their motion direction and velocity is available. Rotation-invariance is generated by rotating the ROI image, which contains the object around the motion angle to get an object appearance where the object is always moving upwards. The principle of image warping is the same as for scale-invariance, so again the source pixel position for a given destination pixel position is determined and the pixel value is bi-linearly interpolated at this sub-pixel position. This leads to the following formalization:

$$\alpha = \text{atan2}(1,0) - \text{atan2}(v_y, v_x)$$
$$x_{src} = \cos(-\alpha) \cdot (x_{dst} - x_c) - \sin(-\alpha) \cdot (y_{dst} - y_c) + x_c$$
$$y_{src} = \sin(-\alpha) \cdot (x_{dst} - x_c) + \cos(-\alpha) \cdot (y_{dst} - y_c) + y_c$$

where α denotes the motion angle, (v_x, v_y) is the motion vector, $(1,0)$ is the reference vector pointing upwards, (x_c, y_c) is the rotation center, (x_{src}, y_{src}) is a source and (x_{dst}, y_{dst}) a destination pixel position. α is calculated with the arctangent-function atan2 and the rotation is performed inversely with negative α to find the source pixel position to given destination position. Rotation center is the found point correspondence due to the assumption that this is the object position. If motion angle and GSD are known a priori, combined warping is possible using the following equations:

$$x_{src} = s_x \cdot \cos(-\alpha) \cdot (x_{dst} - x_c) - s_y \cdot \sin(-\alpha) \cdot (y_{dst} - y_c) + x_c$$
$$y_{src} = s_x \cdot \sin(-\alpha) \cdot (x_{dst} - x_c) + s_y \cdot \cos(-\alpha) \cdot (y_{dst} - y_c) + y_c$$
$$\text{with} \quad s_x = \frac{GSD_{ref}}{GSD_x} \quad \text{and} \quad s_y = \frac{GSD_{ref}}{GSD_y}.$$

In Fig. 2.2, combined warping is demonstrated with two example objects (bus and truck) with different GSDs and orientations.

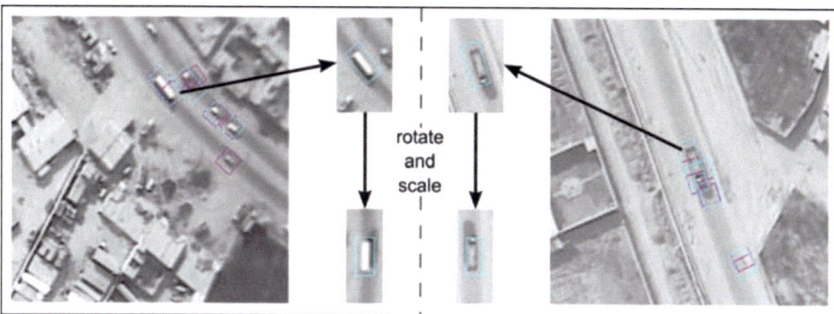

Figure 2.2: Example for combined scale and rotation compensation using GSD and motion vector. The two example objects (bus and truck) had different GSD and orientation [TKH11].

2.2.2 Rotation Compensation using longest Edge Detection

It is assumed that the longest object edge directly corresponds to the object orientation, which is obviously the case for most vehicles and ships. Up to now, Hough Transform [SET+11] and PCA [Gab09] are common methods to detect the longest object edge. However, both methods are rather prone to noise effects.

An approach which is more robust towards noise is detecting the preferred gradient orientation in the object ROI. All gradient orientations are stored in a Histogram of Oriented Gradients (HOG) and the maximum should directly point out the dominant gradient direction located at the longest edges. Again, this idea is inspired by [Low04] where the preferred gradient orientation is used to generate rotation-invariance for local image features. The problem in the application discussed in this report is, that the object ROI contains a lot of noise, which is also mapped to the HOG and makes it more difficult to detect the maximum. Canny edge detection [Can86] can be used to find pixel positions with high gradient magnitude, collecting only these pixels for the HOG. However, a novel approach is presented here which is more sufficient to handle the strong noise effects appearing especially in SAR images.

The proposed method is demonstrated in Fig. 2.3. In the center of Fig. 2.3 (a) an example ship object sensed by TerraSAR-X satellite can be seen. The object appearance is severely disturbed by speckle noise, typical SAR artifacts (e.g., sidelobe effects), and confusion objects (other ships) near to the desired object. The application of structure-emphasizing filtering [TS11b] is displayed in Fig. 2.3 (b). This filter is based on Local Binary Patterns (LBP) [OPM02] and suitable to find structured areas with significant edges and corners in the image. It is more

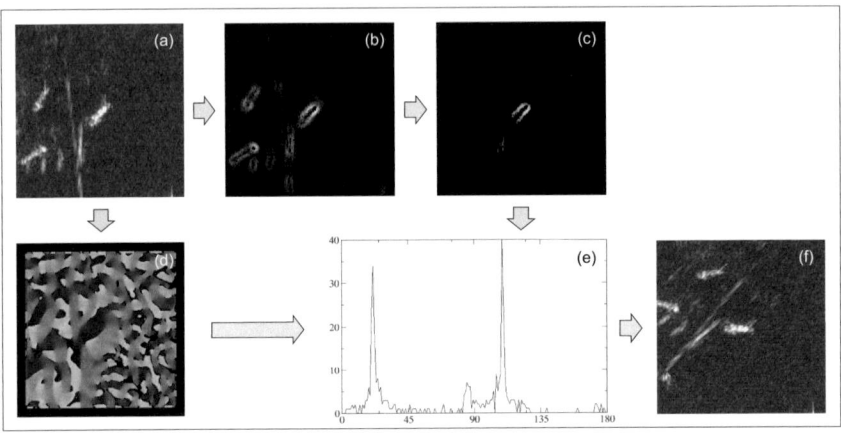

Figure 2.3: Rotation compensation using longest edge detection [TS11a].

robust towards speckle noise than finding strong gradient magnitudes with Canny edge detection [TS11b]. Standard thresholding and clustering methods lead to the exclusion of most artifacts and confusion objects as seen in Fig. 2.3 (c). The calculated gradient directions discretized in 180 orientation steps of $2°$ each are visualized in Fig. 2.3 (d). Therefore, Canny algorithm [Can86] can be used. In the HOG (Fig. 2.3 (e)), the horizontal axis corresponds to the discretized gradient directions and the vertical axis to the number of pixels with specific gradient direction. Due to successful noise suppression, only the gradient directions with high magnitudes (Fig. 2.3 (c)) are accumulated and the two longest object edges are clearly visible as maxima in the HOG.

2.3 Object Segmentation

After object detection, a ROI is determined around each object hypothesis. This ROI can be an oriented bounding-box closely surrounding the object as demonstrated in Fig. 2.2 or an image region where the object is barely in the center as seen in Fig. 2.3 (a). Further variations are possible, of course, but this report focuses on the just mentioned ones, which already cover most potential cases. The bounding-box example in Fig. 2.2 is already suitable for subsequent classification, but for the SAR example, further pre-processing is necessary. The image ROI contains too much background, which would disturb the classifier training process and influence generalization abilities negatively. Thus, the aim of object segmentation is to determine a bounding-box fitting better to the object contours. Two different

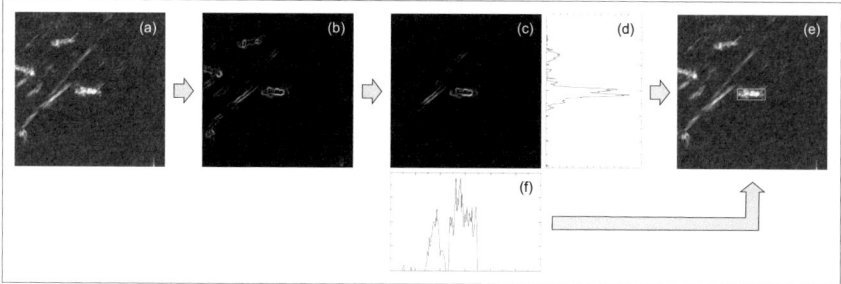

Figure 2.4: Object segmentation with LBP and row-/column histograms [TS11a].

approaches are presented, both with the secondary objective to be as robust as possible against noise or gaps in the object appearance.

2.3.1 Object Segmentation with LBPs and Histograms

It is assumed that an object hypothesis has already been rotation compensated, for example using the LBP-filter presented in subsection 2.2.2. Now, the LBP-filter is applied again but with different parameters to emphasize detailed instead of rough structure. This process is demonstrated in Fig. 2.4 (b). Again, standard clustering and thresholding techniques are used to suppress artifacts and confusion objects as seen in Fig. 2.4 (c). The bright object pixels are accumulated row- and column-wise in two histograms: the row (Fig. 2.4 (d)) and the column histogram (Fig. 2.4 (f)). By detecting the borders of connected areas in the histograms, the object borders are directly determined. The result is shown in Fig. 2.4 (e). Strong noise effects were successfully suppressed. The application of row-/column-histograms for object segmentation in SAR satellite images has also been proposed in [SET+11] but without prior LBP-filtering. This is suitable if no confusion objects or artifacts are close to the object hypothesis. If there is such kind of noise, LBP-filtering generated more robust results [TS11b].

2.3.2 Object Segmentation using Relative Connectivity

A totally different segmentation approach is presented in [TS11c]. The principle of relative connectivity was introduced in [Yip94] and used to perform a Hough Transform detecting start and end points of potential line segments instead of straight lines given a set of edge points. This approach is called Line Patterns Hough Transform (LPHT). The idea is to detect sets of points connected by a fixed relative displacement and store this information in the LPHT accumulator. Edge point positions (x, y) are detected using a binary decision function B, position-related pixel intensity value $I(x, y)$, and intensity threshold t:

$$B(x, y) = \begin{cases} 1, & \text{if } I(x, y) \geq t \\ 0, & \text{if } I(x, y) < t. \end{cases}$$

For a set of n collinear and equidistant points $P_i(x_i, y_i)$ with $\forall i \in \{1, \ldots, n\}$: $B(x_i, y_i) = 1$, the relative displacement $(\Delta x, \Delta y)$ is given by

$$\Delta x = x_2 - x_1$$
$$\Delta y = y_2 - y_1.$$

For being a start point, P_1 has to satisfy the constraint

$$B(x_1, y_1) = 1 \quad \text{and} \quad B(x_1 - \Delta x, y_1 - \Delta y) = 0.$$

The definition of P_n being an end point is done analogously

$$B(x_n, y_n) = 1 \quad \text{and} \quad B(x_n + \Delta x, y_n + \Delta y) = 0.$$

n is the connectivity number, since

$$B(x_n + \Delta x, y_n + \Delta y) = B(x_1 + n \cdot \Delta x, y_1 + n \cdot \Delta y) = 0$$

and

$$B(x_1 + i \cdot \Delta x, y_1 + i \cdot \Delta y) = 1 \quad \forall i \in \{0, \ldots, n-1\}.$$

To store this found relative connectivity, n is entered to the Line Patterns Hough accumulator at start and end point position (x_1, y_1) and (x_n, y_n).

Unfortunately, this approach is time-consuming with a complexity of $O(M \cdot N \cdot \log M \cdot \log N)$ for an image dimension of $M \times N$. However, this complexity can be reduced to $O(M \cdot \log M)$, if not the whole 2D image is considered for calculating the LPHT accumulator, but only row-wise 1D calculation in a few desired directions. This idea is shown in Fig. 2.5, where the relative connectivity was calculated in four diagonal directions. With going through the image diagonally, the typical SAR-related paraxial blooming effects are successfully suppressed. The object border areas appear in the LPHT accumulator nearly without noise or background and by standard edge pixel determination, the object contour is extracted as seen in the segmentation result of Fig. 2.5.

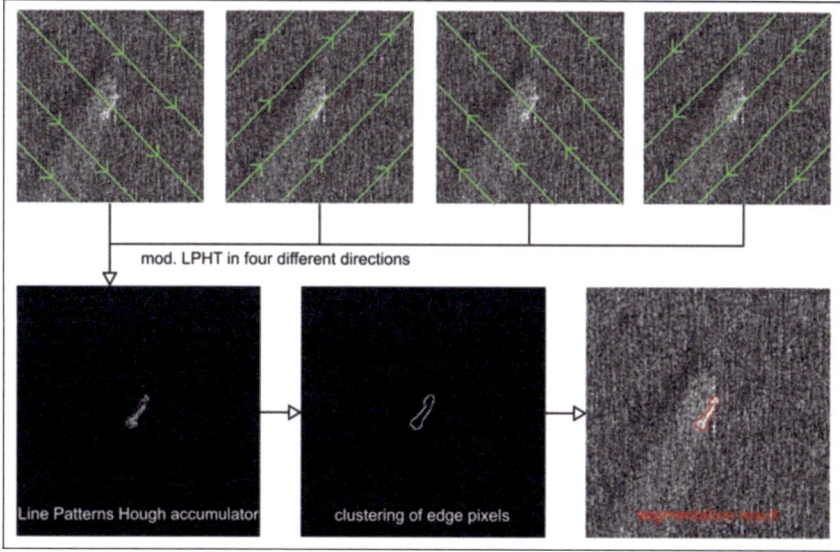

mod. LPHT in four different directions

Line Patterns Hough accumulator   clustering of edge pixels

Figure 2.5: Object segmentation using relative connectivity [TS11c].

3   Results and Applications

In two example applications, the presented approaches have been implemented and evaluated empirically. In noisy images coming from different sensors, object hypotheses are to be pre-processed for better classification performance. Classification aims to separate real detections from clutter appearances on the one hand and to distinguish between different object types on the other.

3.1   Urban Surveillance with UAVs

The German small sized UAV LUNA is used for urban surveillance in this application. Flying in an altitude of about $400\,\mathrm{m}$ and equipped with a standard visual-optical camera pointing perpendicularly to the ground, the aim is to detect and classify moving objects. Main challenges are the ego-motion of the camera and the high object distance. Algorithms have been developed to guarantee robust and fast image stabilization and registration as well as moving target detection and tracking [HEKS08, TKH11]. Classification is used to separate vehicles and people. This is a non-trivial task since each object covers only few pixels in the image. Due to highly robust object tracking methods, considering the separation of clutter and

Table 3.1: Classification rates for different classifiers and optional GSD consideration.

classifier	3-NN		9-NN	
GSD	no	yes	no	yes
correct classification rate	94.71 %	95.56 %	94.62 %	96.08 %
false positives rate	0.29 %	0.88 %	0.07 %	0.09 %
false negatives rate	5.00 %	3.56 %	5.31 %	3.83 %

real objects is not necessary. The classification framework consists of two stages:
training and evaluation. During training, a big set of image processing features is
tested for separability towards the given classification task and the best ones are
concatenated to a feature vector or rather descriptor. With these low-dimensional
descriptors, standard classifiers such as k-Nearest-Neighbor (k-NN), Support Vector
Machine (SVM), or Normal Bayes are trained. In the evaluation stage, a set of
samples, which were skipped for classifier training, is used to find out about the
classifier performance. This evaluation was done for different classifiers as well as
with and without GSD consideration. Since k-NN classifier performed better than
SVM or Bayes in this application, the demonstrated results are focused only on
k-NN and the influences of considered GSD.

Choosing different k was affecting the classification rates as seen in table 3.1. All
samples have been rotation-compensated using the motion vector. Besides the
different classifiers also GSD consideration was evaluated. The positive effect of
scale-normalization using GSD is clearly noticeable in the classification rates as
GSD consideration increases the rates of both classifiers by $1.0\,\%$ to $1.5\,\%$. This
is a significant improvement since correct classification rates around $95\,\%$ were
already achieved before. Object segmentation was no topic in this application as the
resulting bounding-boxes of moving target detection were already sufficient. Some
examples for object classification are shown in Fig. 3.1. The red bounding-boxes
denote vehicles, the yellow people. Not detected vehicles and people are supposably
not moving.

3.2   Maritime Surveillance with TerraSAR-X

In the second example application, German satellite TerraSAR-X is used for wide
maritime surveillance. SAR images are the result of active, radar-based sensing.
Thus, it is possible to observe the earth independently of light or weather conditions,
which is a big advantage to other optical sensors. However, on the other hand,

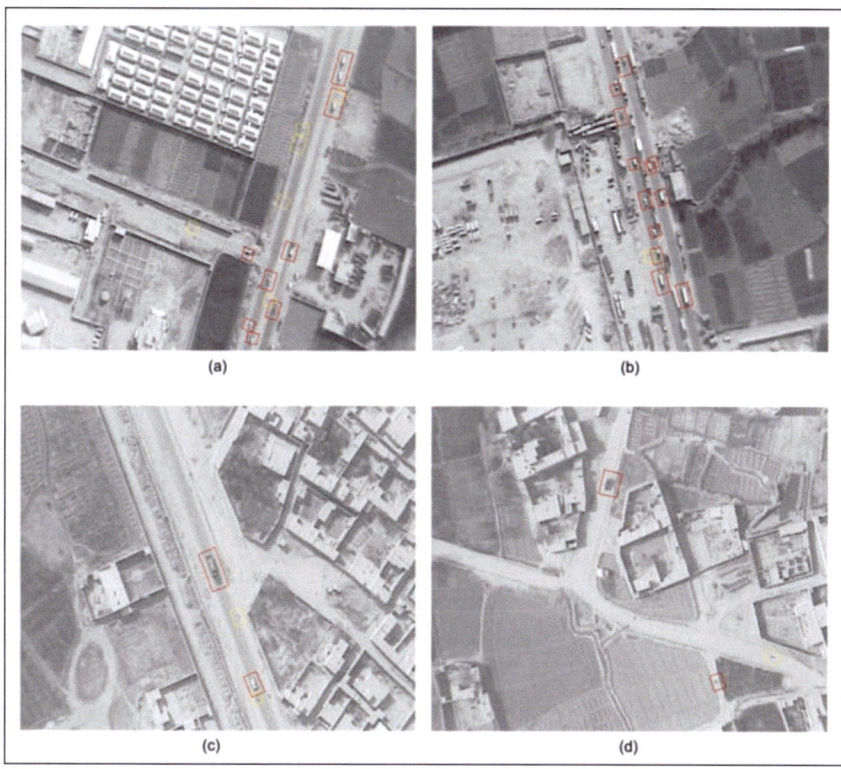

Figure 3.1: Object classification for urban surveillance with UAVs [TKH11].

Table 3.2: Rotation-compensation error compared to sensed-truth.

method	rotation estimation error	
	median	mean
LBP + HOG + PCA	5.99 °	12.16 °
LBP + HOG	6.71 °	12.99 °
LBP + PCA	12.09 °	24.38 °
HOG	10.68 °	23.36 °
PCA	16.26 °	29.92 °

SAR image processing is difficult due to strong noise and clutter effects as seen in section 2.

The benefit of considering rotation- and scale-normalization for classification has already been demonstrated in section 3.1. In this application example, the focus lies on the performance evaluation of the proposed pre-processing approaches in presence of noise. The sensor model of TerraSAR-X is highly precise, so it is not necessary to evaluate the quality of GSD. However, scale-normalization is very important here as horizontal and vertical GSD are generally different. In the following, rotation compensation using longest edge detection and object segmentation with LBPs and histograms are applied and evaluated. Therefore, 756 object hypotheses coming from 17 different TerraSAR-X images have been manually labeled for orientation and length. As no ground-truth was available, the outcome of this labeling process is interpreted as sensed-truth. The results of the rotation-compensation evaluation are demonstrated in table 3.2.

The rotation-compensation error distribution is not Gaussian, so the median error is taken as main evaluation basis. PCA is currently one of the standard approaches to orientation estimation, but has a median error of $16.26°$. With the HOG approach applied directly to the image ROI without LBP-filtering, the median error stays high with $10.68°$. When introducing LBP-filtering, the median errors for both approaches are reduced significantly but the best performance is reached with a fusion of all three algorithms. In few cases where the object appearance is strongly scattered, the HOG approach produces high errors. But these cases can be detected and with application of PCA, the result is better. For all other cases, HOGs are used. The resulting median error is $5.99°$.

For the evaluation of object segmentation, the estimated object length was compared to the sensed-truth. The median error was 19.62 m. As also potential clutter objects as well as many other artifacts and noisy samples were considered besides the

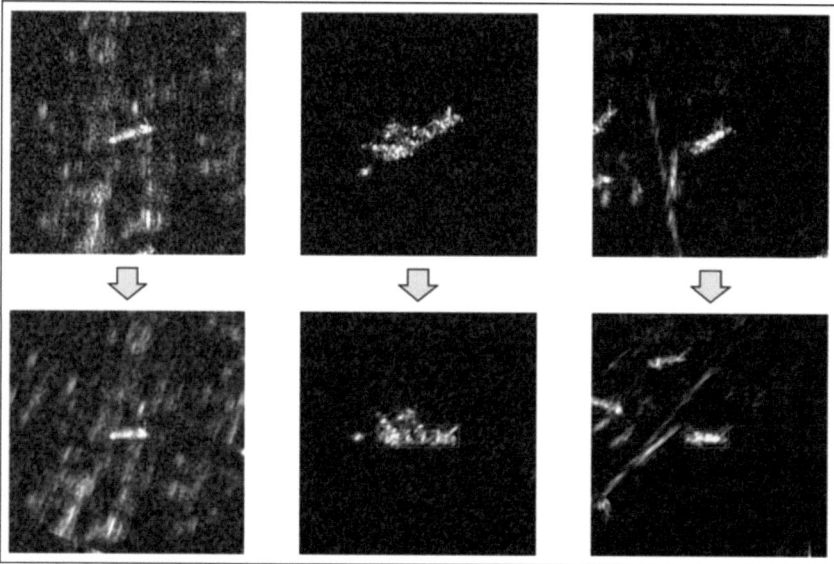

Figure 3.2: Rotation-compensation and object segmentation for maritime surveil-lance with TerraSAR-X.

good-quality object appearances, the results are promising. Some examples are visualized in Fig. 3.2. By using full-polarimetric SAR images [TS11a], these results can be improved to $5.3°$ median rotation-compensation error and 17.3 m median object length estimation error.

4   Conclusions

Appropriate pre-processing approaches for scale- and rotation-normalization as well as precise object segmentation influence subsequent classification significantly. Several different algorithms are presented to solve these tasks with the constraint to be robust against noise and other clutter effects. The considered data set consists of visual-optical and SAR images taken in bird's eye view coming from an UAV and TerraSAR-X satellite. The improvement of classification performance was demonstrated in an application scenario where a small UAV is used for urban surveillance. Object hypotheses delivered from a moving target detection algorithm were classified for either being vehicle or people. Rotation- and scale-normalization with the proposed approaches increased the correct classification rate by about

1.5 %. The robustness of the presented pre-processing algorithms was evaluated in a second application scenario for maritime surveillance with TerraSAR-X satellite. Rotation-compensation with LBP-filtering and HOGs achieved better results than current state-of-the-art approaches.

5 Acknowledgements

The research on TerraSAR-X data was supported with funds from the German Bundesministerium für Wirtschaft und Technologie (BMWi) and the DLR Space Agency under Fkz. 50EE0807. The TerraSAR-X images have been provided by DLR under the proposal COA1018.

Bibliography

[BTG06]   Herbert Bay, Tinne Tuytelaars, and Luc Van Gool. SURF: Speeded Up Robust Features. In *Proceedings of the 9th European Conference on Computer Vision (ECCV)*, Graz, Austria, 2006.

[Can86]   John Canny. A Computational Approach to Edge Detection. *IEEE Transactions on Pattern Analysis and Machine Intelligence*, 8(6):679–698, 1986.

[FWH08]   Dongmei Fu, Xiaochen Wang, and Xiaoping Han. An Extraction of Infrared Occluded-object Based On Maximum Variance and Negative Selection. In *Proceedings of the 2008 International Workshop on Education Technology and Training & 2008 International Working on Geoscience and Remote Sensing*, Shanghai, China, December 2008.

[Gab09]   Matthias Gabel. Untersuchung von Schiffssignaturen in TerraSAR-X-Bildern. Diploma thesis, KIT Karlsruhe and Fraunhofer IOSB Karlsruhe, Germany, December 2009.

[HEKS08] Norbert Heinze, Martin Esswein, Wolfgang Krüger, and Günter Saur. Automatic image exploitation system for small UAVs. In *Proceedings of SPIE Vol. 6946, Airborne intelligence, surveillance, reconnaissance (ISR) systems and applications V*, Orlando, FL, USA, March 2008.

[HZ04]   Richard Hartley and Andrew Zisserman. *Multiple-View Geometry in Computer Vision*. Cambridge University Press, March 2004.

[KSS+01] Rakesh Kumar, Harpreet Sawhney, Supun Samarasekera, Steve Hsu, Hai Tao, Yanlin Guo, Keith Hanna, Arthur Pope, Richard Wildes, David Hirvonen, Michael Hansen, and Peter Burt. Aerial video surveillance and exploitation. *Proceedings of the IEEE*, 89(10):1518–1539, October 2001.

[LLLT10] Jingfu Li, Zhijun Long, Yanze Li, and Rongfang Tang. A Modified Segmentation Algorithm for Infrared Image. In *Proceedings of the 2010 International Conference on Optoelectronics and Image Processing (ICOIP)*, Haiko, Hainan, China, November 2010.

[Low04]   David G. Lowe. Distinctive Image Features from Scale-Invariant Keypoints. *International Journal of Computer Vision*, 60(2):91–110, 2004.

[MY09]   Jean-Michel Morel and Guoshen Yu. ASIFT: A New Framework for Fully Affine Invariant Image Comparison. *SIAM Journal on Imaging Sciences*, 2(2):438–469, 2009.

[OPM02]   Timo Ojala, Matti Pietikäinen, and Topi Mäenpää. Multiresolution Gray-Scale and Rotation Invariant Texture Classification with Local Binary Patterns. *IEEE Transactions on Pattern Analysis and Machine Intelligence*, 24(7):971–987, July 2002.

[SET⁺11]   Günter Saur, Stephane Estable, Frank Teufel, Stefan Knabe, Michael Teutsch, and Matthias Gabel. Detection and Classification of man-made Offshore Objects in TerraSAR-X and RapidEye Imagery: Selected Results of the DeMarine-DEKO Project. In *Proceedings of IEEE OCEANS*, Santander, Spain, June 2011.

[SGK00]   Harpreet S. Sawhney, Yanlin Guo, and Rakesh Kumar. Independent motion detection in 3D scenes. *IEEE Transactions on Pattern Analysis and Machine Intelligence*, 22(10):1191–1199, October 2000.

[SKT10]   P. Subashini, M. Krishnaveni, and Suresh Kumar Thakur. Coupling optimal method of segmentation with restoration for target detection in SAR images. In *Proceedings of the 2nd International Conference on Computer and Automation Engineering (ICCAE)*, Singapore, February 2010.

[TKH11]   Michael Teutsch, Wolfgang Krüger, and Norbert Heinze. Detection and classification of moving objects from UAVs with optical sensors. In *Proceedings of SPIE Vol. 8050*, Orlando, FL, USA, April 2011.

[TS11a]   Michael Teutsch and Günter Saur. Comparison of using single- or multi-polarimetric TerraSAR-X images for segmentation and classification of man-made maritime objects. In *Proceedings of SPIE Vol. 8180*, Prague, Czech Republic, September 2011.

[TS11b]   Michael Teutsch and Günter Saur. Segmentation and Classification of Man-made Maritime Objects in TerraSAR-X Images. In *Proceedings of the IEEE International Geoscience and Remote Sensing Symposium (IGARSS)*, Vancouver, Canada, July 2011.

[TS11c]   Michael Teutsch and Thomas Schamm. Fast Line and Object Segmentation in Noisy and Cluttered Environments Using Relative Connectivity. In *International Conference on Image Processing, Computer Vision, and Pattern Recognition (IPCV)*, Las Vegas, NV, USA, July 2011.

[Yip94]   Raymond K. K. Yip. Line Patterns Hough Transform for Line Segment Detection. In *Proceedings of the 1994 IEEE Region 10's Ninth Annual International Conference (TENCON'94)*, pages 319–323, August 1994.

[YMKC07]   Chang Yuan, Gerard Medioni, Jinman Kang, and Isaac Cohen. Detecting motion regions in the presence of a strong parallax from a moving camera by multiview geometric constraints. *IEEE Transactions on Pattern Analysis and Machine Intelligence*, 29(9):1627–1641, 2007.

Modeling and Recognizing Situations in the Maritime Domain

Yvonne Fischer

Vision and Fusion Laboratory
Institute for Anthropomatics
Karlsruhe Institute of Technology (KIT), Germany
yvonne.fischer@kit.edu

Technical Report IES-2011-02

Abstract: In today's surveillance systems, there is a need for enhancing the situation awareness of an operator. Supporting the situation assessment process can be done by extending the system with a module for automatic interpretation of the observed environment. In this article the information flow in an intelligent surveillance system is described and the separation of the real world and the world model, which is used for the representation of the real world in the system, is clarified. The focus of this article is on modeling situations of interest in surveillance applications and inferring them from sensor observations. For the representation in the system, concepts of objects, scenes, relations, and situations are introduced. Situations are modeled as nodes in a dynamic Bayesian network, in which the evidences are based on the content of the world model. Several methods for inferring situations of interest are suggested, which make use of the underlying network modeling. Due to this modeling, we get a probability of all the situations in the network in every time step. By collecting more evidences over time, the probability of a specific situation is either increasing or decreasing. Finally, we give an example of a situation of interest in the maritime domain and show how the probability of the situation of interest evolves over time.

1 Introduction

During the operation of complex systems that include human decision making, the processes of acquiring and interpreting information from the environment forms the basis for the state of knowledge of a decision maker. This mental state is often referred to as situation awareness [Sha07], whereas the process to achieve and maintain that state is referred to as situation assessment. In today's surveillance system, the situation assessment process is highly supported through various hetero-geneous sensors and appropriate signal processing methods for extracting as much information as possible about the surveyed environment and its elements. Using these methods is, of course, an essential capability for every surveillance system in order to be able to observe a designated area and to detect and track objects inside this area. The approach of collecting as much sensor data as possible and extracting as much information as possible from it is termed bottom-up, or also known as data-driven processing.

However, this approach is not useful for the situation awareness of an operator, because his workload in interpreting all this information will be too high. The challenge of intelligent surveillance systems is therefore not only to collect as much sensor data as possible, but also to detect and assess complex situations that evolve over time as an automatic support to an operator's situation assessment process, and therefore enhancing his situation awareness. The approach of defining and presenting only relevant information about events and activities is termed top-down processing. However, there is a need for concepts and methods supporting higher level situation awareness, i.e., methods that are able to infer real situations from observed elements in the environment and to project their status in the near future.

The paper is structured as follows. In Section 2, an overview of related work is given. As this article follows the top-down approach, the information flow in an intelligent surveillance system is highlighted in Section 3. In Section 4, the methods of modeling situations of interest and inferring their existence are explained. In Section 5, an example in the maritime domain is given.

2   Related Work

Working with a system that uses heterogeneous sensors, the theories of multi-sensor data fusion [ASSC02] offer a powerful technique for supporting the situation as-sessment process. A lot of research has been done in combining object observations coming from different sensors [MRV10], and also in the development of real-time methods for tracking moving objects [DSR10]. Regarding data fusion in surveil-lance systems, the *object-oriented world model (OOWM)* is an approach to represent relevant information extracted from sensor signals, fused into a single comprehen-sive, dynamic model of the monitored area. It was developed in [BEVB09] and is a data fusion architecture based on the JDL (Joint Directors of Laboratories) data fusion process model [Gam88]. Detailed description of the architecture and an example of an indoor surveillance application has been published in [MMH02]. The OOWM has also been applied for wide area maritime surveillance [WV07].

First ideas of modeling situations in surveillance applications have been presented in our previous work in [FBB11]. For the situation assessment process, probabilistic methods like hidden Markov models can be used, see for example [MDPB09]. In [GGS06], Markov random fields are used to model contextual relationships and maximum a posteriori labeling is used to infer intentions of observed elements.

However, most of the methods used for situation assessment are based on machine learning algorithms and they result in models that humans are not able to understand. They are also strongly dependent on training data, which are not always available, especially not for critical situations. The contribution of this work is the modeling approach from a top-down perspective, which tries to model situations from a human perspective, i.e., which situations an operator wants to detect, and how to link them to methods for automatic interpretation.

3 Information Flow in Surveillance Systems

In surveillance applications, a spatio-temporal section of the real world, a so-called *world of interest*, is considered. The general information flow for intelligent surveillance systems is visualized in Figure 3.1, wherein information aggregates are represented by boxes and processes are represented by circles. The information flow can also be applied for autonomous systems as described in [BKFB12].The information flow is as follows.

First of all, all elements in the real world are termed *entities*. By the term entity, not only physical objects are meant, as entities can also be non-physical elements in the real world like relations or the name of a vessel. Thus, entities can represent observable or unobservable elements.

Sensor systems for observing the real world can be of extremely heterogeneous types, e.g., video cameras, infrared cameras, radar equipment, or radio-frequency identification (RFID) chips. Even human beings can act like a sensor by observing entities of the real world. Observing the world of interest with sensors results in sensor data, for example a radar image or a video stream. Sensor data is then analyzed by means of knowledge and the resulting information is transferred to the world model. Analyzing sensor data includes for example the detection and localization of moving vessels at sea from a video stream. Knowledge contains all information that is necessary for analyzing sensor data, for example specific signal-processing methods and algorithms used for the detection, localization and tracking of vessels in video streams.

The world model is a representation of entities in the world of interest and consists therefore of *representatives*. Every representative has a corresponding entity in the

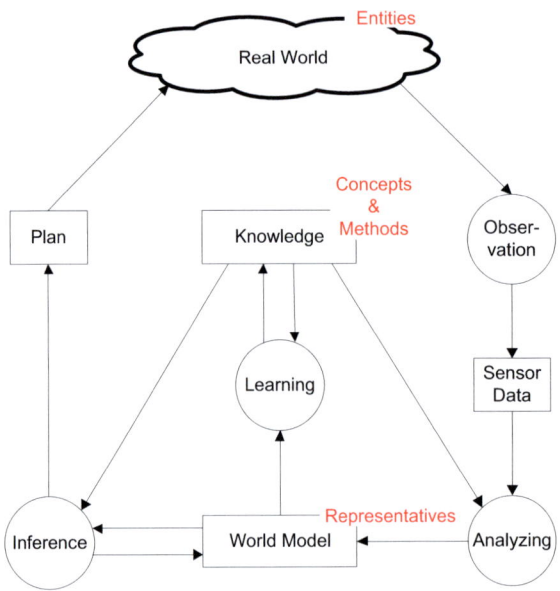

Figure 3.1: Information flow in a surveillance system represented by information aggregates *(boxes)* and processes *(circles)*.

real world. The mapping between entities in the world of interest and representatives in the world model is structure-preserving and can therefore be interpreted as a homomorphism. Specific mappings are defined by *concepts* and are part of the knowledge. Concepts are for example used in the analyzing process by defining how an observed vessel is represented in the world model. As the world of interest is highly dynamic and changes over time, the history of the representatives is also stored in the world model. However, as mentioned before, some entities cannot be observed directly. Therefore an inference process is reasoning about unobservable (and also unobserved) entities by means of knowledge. A simple inference process is for example the calculation of an object's velocity from the previous and current position. A more complex inference process would be to estimate if the intention of an observed vessel is benign or adversarial. Doing this way, the world model is always being updated and supplemented with new information by predefined inference processes.

Summing up, knowledge contains all information for analyzing sensor data, updating the world model and supplementing it with new information. Concepts are used for the representation of real-world entities in the world model. Characteristics of the knowledge are of course extremely dependent on the application domain. Additionally, knowledge is not static. The content of the world model can be used for acquiring new knowledge by a learning process, for example structure or parameter learning in graphical models.

To close the loop of the information flow, the result of an inference process can also include a plan of how to act further in the real world. This could be an action plan for an agent, for example to call the police, or a sensor management plan, for example a request for more detailed information from a specific sensor.

4 Modeling and Inferring Situations of Interest

Two problems are faced in this section: First, several concepts have to be defined, which means to define how the real-world entities can be represented in the world model. Second, the inference process has to be defined, which means to define how to reason about non-observable entities like situations or intentions from observed entities.

4.1 Concepts of world modeling

In this section, some basic concepts that can easily be used for the representation of real-world entities are defined. Addressed concepts here are objects, scenes, attributive relations, and situations. However, the world model can easily be extended by defining new concepts, e.g., for activities and events.

The concept of an *object* is defined as a physical entity of the real world. Regarding its spatial position, an object can be mobile, e.g., a vessel, or stationary, e.g., a land border. An object has several attributes, which can be divided into properties and states. Properties are time-invariant attributes, e.g., the length or the name of a vessel. State values can change over time and are therefore time-variant, e.g., the position or the velocity of a vessel. As the representation in the world model also has a memory, which means that the past states of an object are stored, the complete history of the observed object is always available. Furthermore, the representation of an object in the world model does not only include observed attributes, but also inferred ones. For example, based on observed positions of a vessel, the velocity can be inferred. Furthermore, attribute values can be quantitative or qualitative. For example, the absolute position and velocity of a vessel are quantitative attributes, and the attribute value that a vessel is made of wood is a qualitative one.

The concept of a *scene* is defined as the set of all observed and inferred object information at a point in time. A scene can therefore be interpreted as a snapshot of all objects and their attributes. To include the time aspect, a sequence of scenes can be defined, when the scenes are considered at several discrete points in time. However, a scene does not include any type of relations in an explicit way. This means, that it is for example not explicitly modeled that two vessels are close to each other. But implicitly, of course, this relation can be inferred by the positions of the two vessels. The concept of an object and a scene is visualized in Figure 4.1.

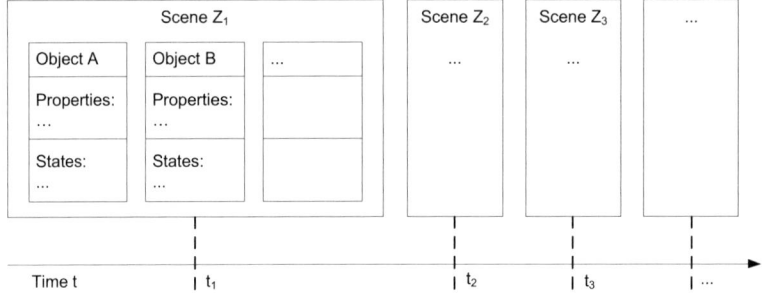

Figure 4.1: The concept of an object and a scene.

The *configuration space* is defined by all possibly occurring objects and their attributes. Thus, a scene, which is represented in the world model, can be identified by exactly one point in the configuration space. A sequence of scenes can be interpreted as a trajectory through the configuration space defined by a series of points in time.

The concept of *attributive relations* is defined as a statement about dependencies between at least two different attribute values of one or more objects. Similar to the attribute values of an object, relational values can be quantitative, e.g., the distance of two objects, or they can be qualitative, e.g., two objects are close to each other. Mostly, relational values are inferred, but some can also be observed, e.g., a measured distance by a laser. A relation can also exist between representatives of the same object in different scenes, e.g., the distance an object has covered between the two scenes.

The concept of a *group* is defined as set of object representatives that have the same values for a specific attribute. It is therefore a special case of an attributive relation and can also be interpreted as an equivalence-relation on a specific attribute value. Examples for groups are vessels that have the same size or vessels that are all in a certain area.

The concept of a *situation* is defined as a statement about a subset of the configuration space, which is either true or false. A specific situation of interest exists, if its statement was inferred to be true. Situations are therefore characterized by qualitative attribute values and their truth is inferred based on information in the world model. This means that situations have a higher level of abstraction and the level of detail included in the quantitative attribute values of objects and relations is getting lost. The simplest situation is a statement about qualitative attribute value of an object, e.g., that a vessel is made of wood. There are also situations, which can only be inferred by observing the real world over a period of time, e.g., the situation that a vessel is taking a straight course.

But although situations are also characterized by information collected over a time-period, they only exist at a point in time. Their existence in the next time point has to be verified again. However, there are a lot of dependencies between different situations. First of all, situations can be inferred from other situations, e.g., if a vessel is heading in a certain direction and has a lot of people on board, the inferred situation could be that the vessel is carrying refugees on board. Furthermore, several situations can exist in parallel or the existence of one situation can exclude the existence of another situation. Mathematically, a situation at a time t can be modeled as a binary random variable S_t, such that

$$S_t(\omega) = \begin{cases} 1 & \text{if } \omega \text{ is true,} \\ 0 & \text{if } \omega \text{ is false,} \end{cases}$$

and ω is the statement of the situation of interest. Then, we are interested in the probability, that ω is true, and thus that the situation S_t exists at time t. We write this existence probability as $P(S_t = 1)$, or $P(S_t)$ in short.

For calculating this probability, the aforementioned dependencies between other situations have to be modeled. The following two cases can be distinguished:

- Directly inferred situations: the existence probability $P(S_t)$ can be inferred directly from the information content of a scene (or other concepts like relations or groups);

- Indirectly inferred situations: the existence probability $P(S_t)$ depends on the existence probability of other situations.

This also includes, that the existence probability of an indirectly inferred situation in future can for example be supported by the earlier existence of the situation itself, and the existence probability of a directly inferred situation cannot be supported over time. This concept of a network of situations is visualized in Figure 4.2.

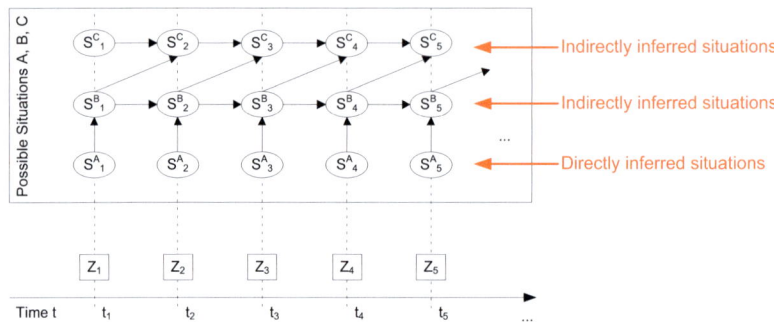

Figure 4.2: A network of situations, divided into directly and indirectly inferred situations.

4.2   Inferring Situations of Interest

Due to this modeling, the network of situations can be interpreted as a probabilistic graphical model, namely a dynamic Bayesian network (DBN). In a simple Bayesian network, the basic idea is to decompose the joint probability of various random variables into a factorized form. Random variables are depicted as nodes and conditional probabilities as directed edges. The joint probability can then be factorized as

$$P(X_1, \dots, X_n) = \prod_{i=1}^{n} P(X_i | Pa(X_i)), \qquad (4.1)$$

where $Pa(X_i)$ is the set of parents of the node X_i. If $Pa(X_i)$ is an empty set, then X_i is a root node and $P(X_i | Pa(X_i)) = P(X_i)$ denotes its prior probability.

A DBN [DSR10] is defined as a pair $(B_0, 2TBN)$, where

- B_0 defines the prior distribution $P(\boldsymbol{X}_0)$ over the set $\boldsymbol{X}_0$ of random variables, and

- $2TBN$ defines a Bayesian network over two time slices with

$$P(\boldsymbol{X}_t | \boldsymbol{X}_{t-1}) = \prod_{i=1}^{n} P(X_t^i | Pa(X_t^i)), \qquad (4.2)$$

where X_t^i is a node at time slice t and $Pa(X_t^i)$ is the set of parent nodes, which can be in the time slice t or in the time slice $t - 1$.

Note that in the definition of a $2TBN$, $Pa(X_t^i)$ is never empty, i.e., every node in time slice t has at least one parent node and therefore the left side of equation (4.1) differs from the left side of equation (4.2). An example of a $2TBN$ with 3 nodes in each time slice is shown in Figure 4.3. The joint probability distribution of a DBN can then be formulated as

$$P(\boldsymbol{X}_{0:T}) = P(\boldsymbol{X}_0) \cdot \prod_{t=1}^{T} \prod_{i=1}^{n} P(X_t^i | Pa(X_t^i)).$$

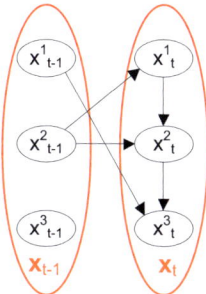

Figure 4.3: A example of a $2TBN$ defining dependencies between two time slices and dependencies between nodes in time slice t. Note that a $2TBN$ does not define the dependencies between nodes in time slice $t - 1$.

As we want to model a network of situations by a DBN, the structure of the network has to fulfill the following assumptions:

- Stationarity: the dependencies within a time slice t and the dependencies between the time slices $t - 1$ and t do not depend on t.

- 1st order Markov assumption: the parents of a node are in the same time slice or in the previous time slice.

- Temporal evolution: dependencies between two time slices are only allowed forward in time, i.e., from past to future.

- Time slice structure: the structure of one time slice is a simple Bayesian network, i.e., without cycles.

For modeling the situational network, the set of situations are divided into the set of directly inferable situations E and the set of indirectly inferable situations S, as described above. The state transition between two time slices satisfies the Markov assumption

$$P(S_t|S_{0:t-1}) = P(S_t|S_{t-1}),$$

and the dependencies between directly and indirectly inferred situations are modeled by

$$P(E_t|S_{0:t}, E_{0:t-1}) = P(E_t|S_t).$$

Due to this dependency, it is assumed that the values of the directly inferred situations are only dependent on the values of the indirectly inferred situations. The joint probability can then be calculated recursively by

$$P(S_{0:T}, E_{1:T}) = P(S_0) \cdot \prod_{t=1}^{T} P(S_t|S_{t-1})P(E_t|S_t).$$

By modeling the network of situations in this way, the following inference calculations are possible:

- Filtering: $P(S_t|E_{1:t})$ gives a solution to the existence probability of a set of situations S at the current time,

- Prediction: $P(S_{t+k}|E_{1:t})$ (with $k > 0$) gives a solution to the existence probability of a set of situations S in the (near) future,

- Smoothing: $P(S_k|E_{1:t})$ (with $0 < k < t$) gives a solution to the existence probability of a set of situations S in the past,

- Most likely explanation: $\operatorname{argmax}_{S_{1:t}} P(S_{1:t}|E_{1:t})$ gives a solution to the most likely sequence of situations $S_{1:t}$.

Due to this modeling, the existence probability of a set of indirectly inferable situations can be calculated in a recursive way at each point in time. A situation is represented in the world model, if the corresponding existence probability is larger than an instantiation-threshold. If the existence probability in the next time step is below a deletion-threshold, it is assumed that the situation doesn't exist any longer and its representation is removed from the world model. This way, it is tried to keep an up-to-date representation of the existing situations of the real world.

5 Application Scenario in the Maritime Domain

For a representation of the world model, the OOWM system as described in [WV07] was adapted to the maritime domain. The graphical user interface of the OOWM is depicted in Figure 5.1. It shows observed vessels at the Mediterranean Sea between the African coast and the island of Lampedusa. Sensor observations are simulated in the system, but they are assumed to be generated by coastal radar systems or signals from the automatic identification system (AIS). In Figure 5.1, an observed vessel is selected and its observed attributes can be seen on the left side of the user interface. These are exactly the attributes that are stored in the world model and are used for inferring situations of interest.

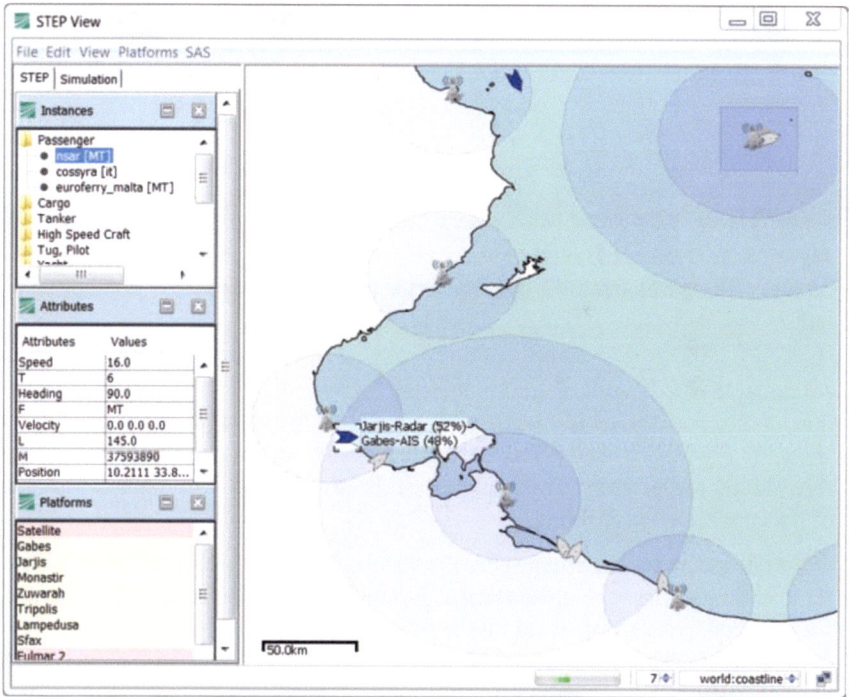

Figure 5.1: The OOWM system applied to the maritime domain.

In the Mediterranean Sea, a situation of interest is a vessel that is carrying refugees on board. Based on various statements by maritime experts, these vessels have the following (observable) characteristics: They start from the African coast (Tunisia or Libya), are heading towards Lampedusa, take a direct course, and do not send any

AIS-Signal for identification. They are either wooden boats or motor-boats, where the wooden boats are slower and smaller than the motor-boats, and the motor-boats often go the border, put the refugees into the water and make an emergency call.

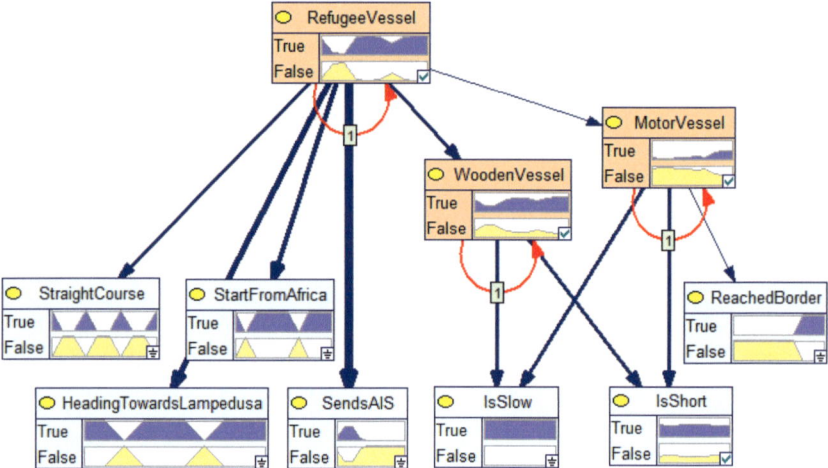

Figure 5.2: Dynamic Bayesian Network with 3 situations of interest (colored in orange). Temporal arcs over one time slice are marked with a "1" and colored in red.

An example of a dynamic Bayesian network representing the 3 situations of interest that an observed vessel is a refugee vessel, a wooden vessel, or a motor-vessel is shown in Figure 5.2. The 3 temporal arcs are pointing to the situations of interest themselves, respectively. The thickness of the arcs show the strength of influence of the conditional probabilities.

The evidence nodes have been set to the values listed in Table 5.1, where the empty set means no evidence. Note that this is just one possible combination that has been chosen for one observed vessel for the seven variables over ten time steps. For one time point, there are seven variables that can take three values (true, false, $\emptyset$), and therefore there are $3^7 = 2187$ possible combinations. For a time series of ten time points, the number of possible combinations is $(3^7)^{10}$, which is about $2, 5 \cdot 10^{33}$. In this simple example one can already see how the number of possible time series is exploding.

The resulting existence probabilities (calculated by filtering) for the three situations of interest (refugee vessel) over ten time steps are visualized in Figure 5.3. It can clearly be seen that due to the evidence that has been collected over time, the

Table 5.1: Evidences set over 10 time steps.

Time	Straight Course	Towards Lampedusa	From Africa	Sends AIS	Slow Slow	Short Short	Reached Border
1	True	True	True	∅	True	∅	False
2	False	True	False	∅	True	∅	False
3	False	False	True	∅	True	∅	False
4	True	True	True	∅	True	∅	False
5	False	True	True	False	True	∅	False
6	False	True	True	False	True	∅	False
7	True	False	False	False	True	∅	False
8	False	True	True	False	True	∅	True
9	False	True	True	False	True	∅	True
10	True	True	True	False	True	∅	True

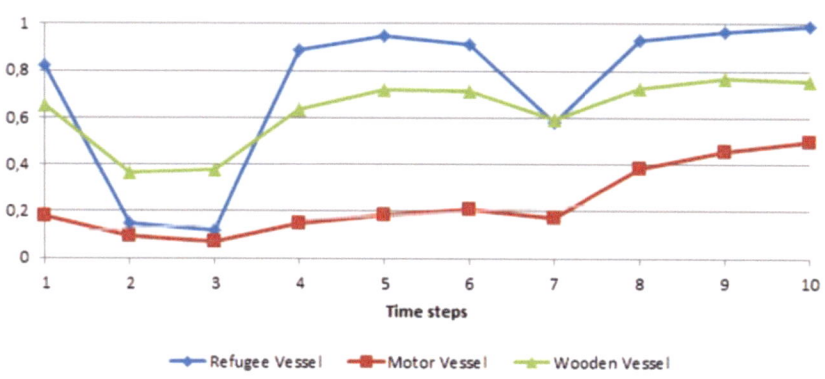

Figure 5.3: Resulting existence probabilities for the three situations of interest.

existence probability of situation that the observed vessel is a refugee vessel is increasing over time. After ten time steps, it is also more likely that the vessel is a wooden vessel rather than a motor vessel. The drop of the existence probability is due to the influence of the observed variables "Towards Lampedusa" and "Starts from Africa". Both of them are observed as false in this time step, which might indicate that the vessel is not a refugee vessel. To avoid such strong changes in the resulting probabilities, the temporal influence could be increased.

The challenges of designing the situational network are to model the structure and to determine the parameters, i.e., the conditional probabilities. Finally, the resulting probabilities for different configurations have to be interpreted (e.g., for the specification of the instantiation- and the deletion-threshold), which is often not straightforward.

6   Conclusion and Future Work

In this article the information flow in an intelligent surveillance system was highlighted and it was described how situations of interest in surveillance applications can be modeled by concepts. For modeling a network of situations, the framework of dynamic Bayesian networks is suggested, in which the values of the directly inferable nodes are based on the content of the world model. This modeling fulfills the requirements resulting from the definition of situations and allows the application of efficient inference methods. An example of a situation of interest in the maritime domain was given. By extending the surveillance system with such a module for automatic interpretation of the observed environment it is able to support the situation assessment process of an operator and thus enhances his situation awareness.

Future work includes an experimental evaluation of the proposed method and an investigation on supporting the human operator in designing a situational network without having a detailed knowledge of the underlying method. Also the real-time capability of the proposed method when using a large amount of data has to be investigated.

Bibliography

[BEVB09]   A. Bauer, T. Emter, H. Vagts, and J. Beyerer. Object oriented world model for surveillance systems. In *Future Security: 4th Security Research Conference*, pages 339–345. Fraunhofer Press, 2009.

[BGB+10]   M. Baum, I. Gheta, A. Belkin, J. Beyerer, and U. D. Hanebeck. Data association in a world model for autonomous systems. In *Proc. of the 2010 IEEE International Conference on Multisensor Fusion and Integration for Intelligent Systems (MFI 2010)*, pages 187–192, 2010.

[BKFB12]   A. Belkin, A. Kuwertz, Y. Fischer, and J. Beyerer. World modeling for autonomous systems. In Christos Kalloniatis, editor, *Information System*. InTech – Open Access Publisher, 2012. Accepted for publication.

[DSR10]   A. Dore, M. Soto, and C. S. Regazzoni. Bayesian tracking for video analytics: An overview. *IEEE Signal processing magazine*, 27(5):46–55, 2010.

[End95]   M. R. Endsley. Towards a theory of situation awareness in dynamic systems. *Human Factors*, 37(11):32–64, 1995.

[FB10]   Y. Fischer and A. Bauer. Object-oriented sensor data fusion for wide maritime surveillance. In *2nd International Conference on Waterside Security,IEEE,(WSS 2010)*, pages 1–6, 2010.

[FBB11]   Y. Fischer, A. Bauer, and J. Beyerer. A conceptual framework for automatic situation assessment. In *IEEE First International Multi-Disciplinary Conference on Cognitive Methods in Situation Awareness and Decision Support (CogSIMA 2011)*, pages 234–239, 2011.

[GGS06]   R. Glinton, J. Giampapa, and K. Sycara. A markov random field model of context for high-level information fusion. In *9th International Conference on Information Fusion*, pages 1–8, 2006.

[HM04]   D. L. Hall and S. A. H. McMullen. *Mathematical Techniques in Multisensor Data Fusion*. Artech House, Inc., 2004.

[MDPB09]   D. Meyer-Delius, C. Plageman, and W. Burgard. Probabilistic situation recognition for vehicular traffic scenarios. In *Proceedings of the 2009 IEEE International Conference on Robotics and Automation*, pages 459–464, 2009.

[MRV10]   J. Moßgraber, F. Reinert, and H. Vagts. An architecture for a task-oriented surveillance system: A service- and event-based approach. In *Fifth International Conference on Systems (ICONS 2010)*, pages 146–151, 2010.

[SBW99]   A. N. Steinberg, C. L. Bowman, and F. E. White. Revisions to the JDL data fusion model. In *Sensor Fusion: Architectures, Algorithms, and Applications, Proceedings of the SPIE Vol. 3719*, pages 430–441, 1999.

Navigation using 3D features from side-scan sonar data for a deep-sea AUV

Philipp Woock

Vision and Fusion Laboratory
Institute for Anthropomatics
Karlsruhe Institute of Technology (KIT), Germany
woock@ies.uni-karlsruhe.de

Technical Report IES-2011-03

Abstract:

Simultaneous navigation and mapping (SLAM) of an autonomous underwater vehicle (AUV) based on side-scan sonar data has significant peculiarities that make standard SLAM techniques inapplicable. In particular, recognition of already visited places (loop closure) which is an important tool improving the navigation accuracy cannot be done with the raw sonar data. This and other navigation tasks can be more conveniently performed based on the 3D seafloor shape (elevation map). In this report we first present an extension of a well-known sonar data reconstruction method to account for nontrivial AUV motion, and then discuss various algorithms useful in the context of SLAM processing elevation data.

1 Introduction

Mankind is in need of more and more natural resources so that areas of easily obtainable raw materials on land are mostly explored. In the oceans and especially in the deep-sea huge amounts of raw materials (metals, gas hydrates) can be found. Unfortunately, knowledge about the deep sea is still scarce. Autonomous underwater vehicles (AUVs) are a way to acquire seafloor maps automatically with comparably low effort. However, the quality of the map is strongly dependent on the navigation capabilities of an AUV. The latter can be improved by employing Simultaneous Localization and Mapping (SLAM) methods.

Our goal is to establish whether sonar-based SLAM may serve as a reliable navigation tool for vehicles operating autonomously for several hours.

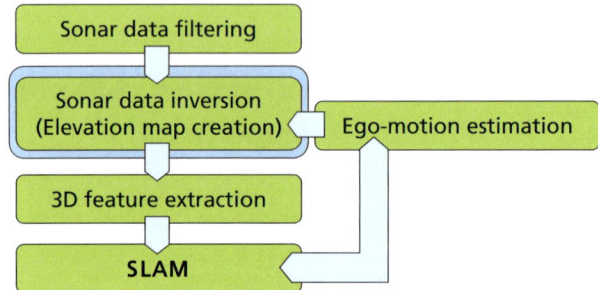

Figure 1.1: Workflow of a sonar-based SLAM navigation

In all SLAM methods, re-visiting a location and detecting it as such (loop closure) is used to limit the positional error growth in the current motion and map estimates. Given that the data association at the loop closure is correct, the growth of motion and map errors is limited. The aiding sensor in this case is an imaging side-scan sonar and re-visits are to be found based on that sonar data.

The outline of a workflow how this can be achieved is given in Figure 1.1.

2 Side-scan sonar data processing

Side-scan sonar data is recorded as echo amplitude over time, which poses certain challenges interpreting the data spatially. For example, it leads to an effect called "sonar shadow": when a certain area is ensonified by an AUV for a second time upon a re-visit, it is very likely that the traveling direction of the AUV is different from the first visit. That in turn leads to sonar shadows cast differently and simple image matching techniques are unlikely to succeed as the same surface may have a varied appearance when viewed from a different angle. For a detailed summary of side-scan sonar signal interpretation and the related navigation issues see [Woo10], [WF10], and [Woo11b].

In addition to that, side-scan sonar data is usually processed by stacking the data lines on top of each other to form a sonar image. For an AUV that does not move in a straight line, this creates distortions in the image accruing from the resulting irregular sampling of the seafloor. Those distortions make image matching even more difficult.

In addition to the inherent ambiguity of sonar data, the motion and the rotation of AUV lead to irregular seafloor sampling. Since our prototype vehicle buit in the joint Fraunhofer project TIETeK[1] is equipped with an inertial measurement unit (IMU), we incorporate the ego-motion information to compensate for these distortions.

This paper first recaps an existing side-scan sonar data inversion technique for stacked sonar data lines. Then, this method is extended to take non-straight non-uniform vehicle motion into account. In the following section various 3D-features are presented and their underlying principles are discussed.

2.1 Sonar inversion

The literature on 3D geometry reconstruction from side-scan sonar data is rather scarce. To the best of our knowledge, the method of Coiras et al. [CPL07] describes the most relevant method for 3D geometry reconstruction using side-scan sonar data. Using a 2D sonar image created from stacked sonar lines, they try to iteratively estimate the surface model parameters for each pixel individually that would yield the recorded sonar echo. The model parameters are restricted to surface shape $Z(x, y)$, reflectivity (mostly depending on sediment type) and the sensors' antenna beam form. Regularization constraints for the reflectivity and beam form are imposed by means of the full 2D image.

A strong sonar response may therefore originate from either the surface being inclined towards the sensor, the surface consisting of well-reflecting materials, or a strong ensonification by the sensor. The surface inclination with respect to the sensor is calculated for each surface patch by the angle between surface normal and the line of sight between the sensor and the given surface patch.

The estimation process starts with a flat surface and the original sonar image as reflectivity map as well as a homogeneous antenna beam form and then creates a virtual measurement given these parameters. The difference between the recorded measurement and the virtual measurement shows where the model does not yet match the environment. Parameters are adjusted accordingly and a new virtual measurement is generated. This is done until the virtual measurement is close enough to the recorded measurement (see Figure 2.1).

To obtain a reasonable parameter estimation from the model, it is necessary to restrict the freedom of the model by the so-called regularization. These regularization constraints employ additional knowledge about the parameters and enforce them in the estimation process, e.g. , it is unlikely that the sediment type changes extremely frequently on a small patch of ground. It can also be assumed that the beam form of the sensor changes only very slowly throughout the duration of a mission. An

---

[1]http://www.tietek.de

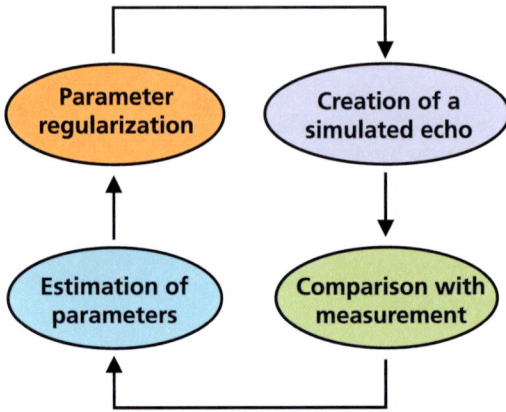

Figure 2.1: Iterative estimation process of the seabed surface shape.

assumption also made in [CPL07] is that in shadowed areas the surface reflectivity is not different from the adjacent non-shadowed parts. To establish this constraint, a separate detection of shadowed areas is used. Additional constraints can also be imposed on the surface shape (e.g. , regarding surface smoothness), however those constraints need to be carefully chosen to still allow the necessary variation to represent the environment correctly while at the same time the estimation of any implausible parameter sets is avoided, like for example an overly spiky seafloor shape.

The estimation of the parameters is done in a hierarchical fashion using parameter pyramids containing subsampled versions of the parameter sets. This helps to avoid local minima in the parameter estimation process while at the same time the subsampling employed to obtain the lower resolution stages also aids the convergence stability as noise is mainly smoothed out.

2.2   Related work

Further work of this group [CG09] was aimed mainly at SAS (synthetic aperture sonar) systems and due to its cylindrical coordinate system was not that suitable for doing SLAM in a cartesian framework. However, the idea of treating the seafloor as deformable mesh is worth considering also in the cartesian case.

The method of Bikonis [BSM08] is using a shape-from-shading approach but is relying on proper shadow zone detection, which can be unreliable. Other research

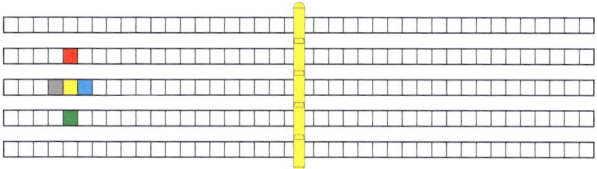

Figure 3.1: Nearest neighbors in stacked pixel grid image.

on SLAM with side-scan sonar sensors is treating the sonar data as an image with data association done by hand [RRPL04].

3 Sonar inversion for a moving vehicle

The method described in 2.1 implicitly makes an assumption that is not necessarily true: by stacking the individual lines to an image, a neighborhood relationship in the resulting pixel grid is introduced among different sonar scan lines. Such a relationship is only true for an AUV that is going straight ahead at a constant speed. If the vehicle performs another movement, like a turn for example, the sonar data recorded in this turn does not stem from surface parts directly adjacent to the parts ensonified by the previous sonar measurement. This is the reason why distortion is introduced to a map by simple stacking of sonar lines. Using the neighboring pixels for a query in the stacked representation means that values are used which are not necessarily closest to the query pixel in reality. Additionally, the neighborhood order could be flipped upside down on a vehicle turn. Figures 3.1 and 3.2 illustrate this problem. The currently processed sample is colored yellow. The red sample, which is a top neighbor in the pixel grid, is a bottom neighbor in reality. Additionally, neither the red or the green sample are the closest neighbors like the pixel grid suggests. The magenta colored samples are the closest ones in reality.

3.1 Inversion in consideration of true spatial point neighborhoods

The inversion method therefore needs to be extended to treat non-straight non-uniform vehicle motion and the resulting irregular sampling of the seabed correctly. To accomplish this, the vehicle's IMU (inertial measurement unit) data are used to correctly reference the sonar scan lines to each other. With that information the true neighborhood information can be obtained.

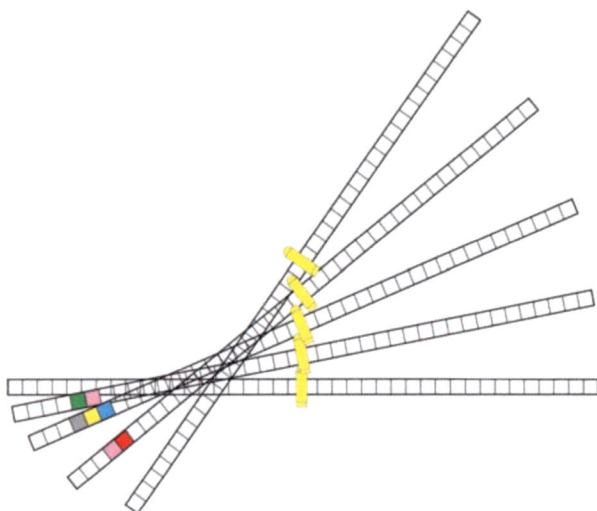

Figure 3.2: Nearest neighbors on a curved trajectory. The nearest neighbors from the pixel grid are wrongly ordered in reality and are not necessarily the nearest.

The extension is quite straightforward and does not change the basic working principle of the method. The original method uses surface gradients $\frac{\partial Z}{\partial x}$ and $\frac{\partial Z}{\partial y}$ in the estimation of echo intensity. The local coordinate frame for each scan line is x in across track direction, y is along track direction and z is pointing up. Therefore, the gradient $\frac{\partial Z}{\partial x}$ is estimated within each scan line whereas the gradient $\frac{\partial Z}{\partial y}$ is taken across different scan lines in the pixel grid of the sonar image. This is where the extension has its main difference: the $\frac{\partial Z}{\partial y}$ gradient is estimated from surface points in the true seafloor surface neighborhood.

The extension initializes the surface as flat lines, each line at the depth of the detected first bottom return (FBR) (see [WF10] for further reading about the FBR) and inserts the estimation scan lines according to the vehicle position and orientation into a point cloud. Depending on the vehicle pitch motion, the initial estimated line is placed not exactly beneath the vehicle but according to the lever arm consisting of the pitch angle and the the altitude (see Figure 3.3). Vehicle roll motion is more difficult to handle as this affects the sonar propagation direction (see Figure 3.4 and 3.4). There may be areas right beneath the the vehicle where multiple echoes are received (so-called layover). When this information is discarded and the roll angle increases, the angles necessary for calculation of ground-range correction (φ and $\varphi\prime$) deviate more from $90°$. More detailed reading about the changes to ground range correction can be found in [Woo11a].

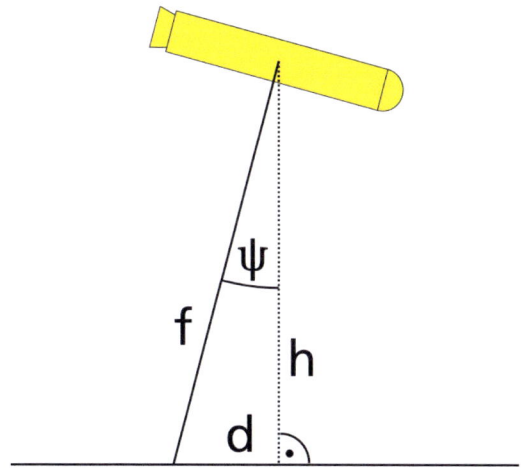

Figure 3.3: Vehicle pitch angle.

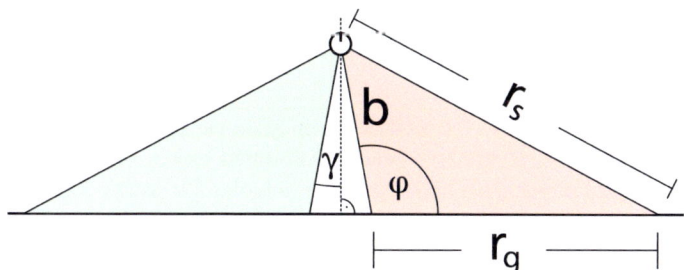

Figure 3.4: Sonar sensor beams without roll motion. r_s denotes slant range coordinates, r_g denotes ground range coordinates, γ denotes the mounting angle of the side-scan sonar sensor and b denotes the first bottom return (FBR).

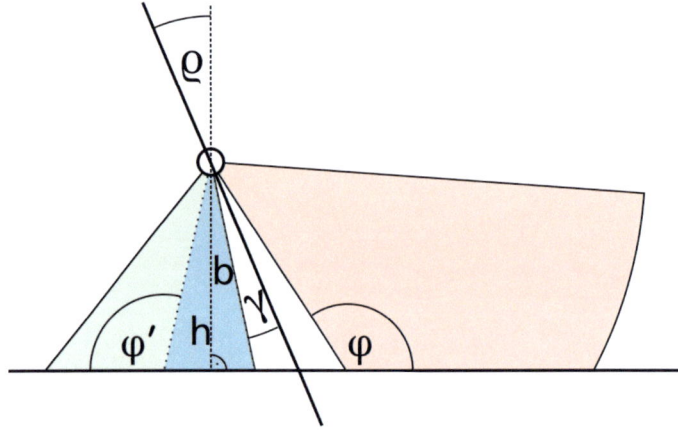

Figure 3.5: Sonar sensor beams undergoing roll motion with roll angle ϱ. For the ground range correction the angles φ and $\varphi\prime$ have to be taken into account. The area where layover occurs is colored with blue.

For each point the x-gradient is calculated just like in the unmodified case by finite differences within the same scan line. This is done because the nearest neighbors in the local x direction almost always lie within the line independent of how the line is oriented in space. The y-gradient is calculated by estimating a surface normal out of the nearest k neighbors that do not belong to the same line (see Figure 3.6). The reasoning behind that decision is that by using simply all the nearest neighbors, by far the most neighbors would stem from the same sonar line where the query point lies due to the sampling density within a sonar line being much higher than between lines. However, it may still happen that all k nearest neighbors stem from only one of the other lines.

The second reason is that the immediate neighbors from the same line already contribute to the x-gradient and would be counted twice. Figure 3.7 shows that choosing a fixed radius instead of k-nearest neighbors is worse due to the varying sample density where k-nearest neighbors algorithm inherently is able to adapt to.

Depending on how many neighbors are used for the normal vector calculation a certain smoothing effect is observed. Using only relatively few neighbors, the estimated surface normal is relatively unstable as it is strongly influenced by outliers, whereas using too many neighboring points for the estimation may smooth out surface details.

The estimated surface normal vector needs then be projected onto a plane perpendicular to the query line in order to remove the gradient component in x direction

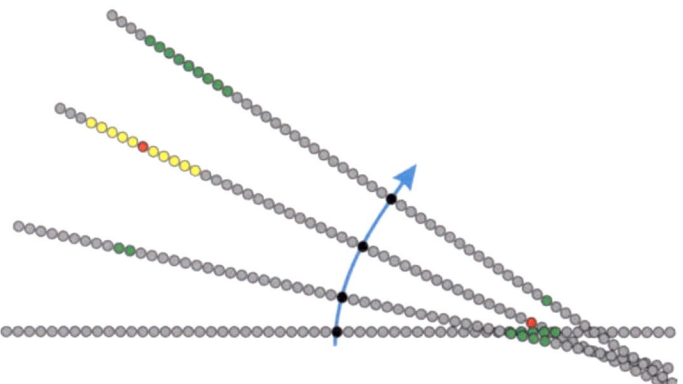

Figure 3.6: Choosing k nearest neighbors can cope with different sampling densities. The yellow marked samples would indicate the nearest neighbors to the left query point if the line where the query point (red) originates was not omitted from the query surface.

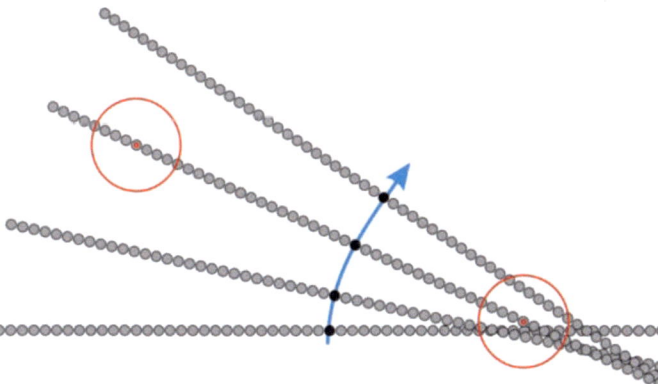

Figure 3.7: Choosing neighbors in an area described by a fixed radius will not work as the sampling density of the area is highly variable. There may easily be zero points in a given distance that belong to a different line than the query point.

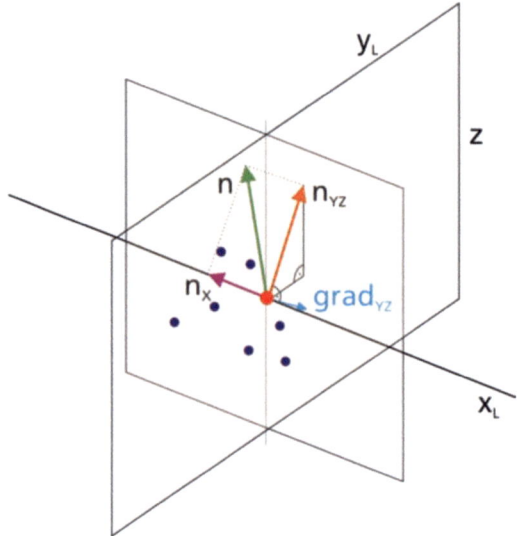

Figure 3.8: Projecting the surface normal vector into the local yz-plane to obtain the y-gradient.

(which is already covered by the in-line gradient calculation). From that vector, the sought-after surface gradient in y direction is obtained (see Figure 3.8). The result of the estimation is a patch of the environment elevation map located at the current vehicle position estimate.

3.2 Sliding window approach

As computation power is limited, the estimation of the surface gradients is becoming increasingly lengthy as the mission duration grows. Therefore, a sliding window approach in combination with a fixed lag is proposed. That way, a fixed number of measurement lines is treated in each step which keeps the computational burden of the inversion step constant. As new measurements arrive, older lines are dropped from the sliding window and the estimation is executed again. Of course it is not necessary to perform a re-estimation for every single new line as the other measurements stays the same and therefore the normal estimation also for the most part remains the same. Only if a new measurement comes to lie in the neighborhood, the normal estimation changes.

Besides that, the fact that due to the fixed lag the query line does not lie on the boundary avoids unstable surface normal estimation in most cases as the surface

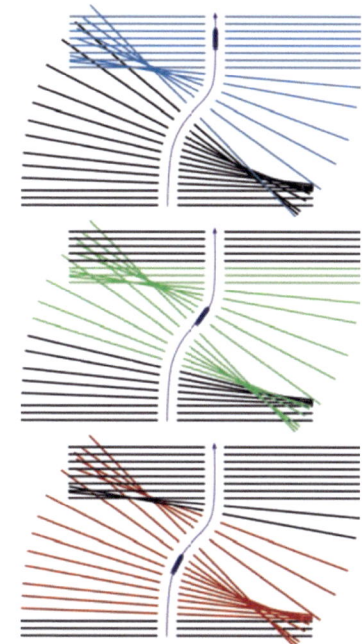

Figure 3.9: Sliding window on vehicle progression at different time steps.

normal vector cannot be estimated well on boundary points. Yet, not all of the available information on a certain location is used. This is illustrated in the top image of Figure 3.9 where older lines are not considered even though they could contribute to the estimation. A specific selection of only those lines that lie in a certain area would highly increase the complexity as a search over all measurements of the mission would be necessary. At the moment, we have not implemented this feature due to high computational cost, but in further versions with non-line-based surface parameterization one could perhaps implement it efficiently.

4   Three-dimensional features

On the estimated elevation map environmental features can be extracted that describe salient points or regions. Points or regions where the feature description closely matches earlier occurrences build a so-called loop closure. However, it is of utmost importance that the match stems from an actual re-visit of the same area. Unfortunately, it may also happen that the feature descriptor of two different

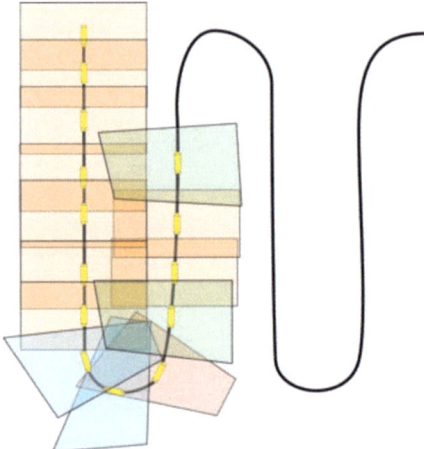

Figure 3.10: Overlapping submaps as a basis for SLAM estimation. Depending on the vehicle motion the covered area of each submap can be shaped differently.

regions is very similar and it would be fatal to introduce a loop closure there as no re-visit has happened. This is a case where a SLAM approach will no longer be able to create accurate map or localization estimates. Finding robust feature descriptors that are unique for a certain location is therefore key to successfully running a SLAM system. A more detailed study on loop closure in an AUV context can be found in [LHW+10].

A robust matching mechanism does not try to match single features but several features at once. Hence, using a sliding window approach lends itself well to a SLAM method which uses feature-based submaps. While the association of single features is rather unstable, matching a set of features of a submap to a set of features of another submap provides a much more robust SLAM estimation.

4.1   Short survey on terrain identification features

There is a multitude of three-dimensional features that may be suited to be used in a SLAM context. An overview and a description of several features found in literature is given in this section, however they have not yet been investigated for their robustness.

It can be argued that techniques to identify human fingerprints may also be well suited for recognition of places in submarine terrain. However, in fingerprint research the identification task is mostly treated as a 2D problem where common image processing techniques are employed. In spite of this, using a 3D terrain map with elevation values interpreted as intensity values, fingerprint matching techniques may indeed be applied to the recognition problem.

In [ZYZ05] a descriptor is presented that is invariant regarding translation and rotation. Given an underwater vehicle moving relative to the seafloor these should be the transformations experienced most often in real data. The presented matching technique does not only use single minutiae of the fingerprint to perform the matching but rather a whole set that is matched at a time. This leads to a more robust estimation of the matching pairs.

Rusu et al. presented point histogram features (PFH) [RMBB08] and later a slimmed version called fast point histogram features (FPFH) [RBB09]. They generalize the mean curvature over k neighbors and in this way obtain a discriminative point descriptor. The FPFH descriptor is slightly different from the PFH descriptor but can be computed much faster and is easily parallelizable. The faster computation is traded for worse predictability of the descriptor's coverage area though. The descriptor can be calculated for every point whereas for matching purposes only points with a unique descriptor should be used.

In [CHH99] the focus is on large data sets. Their method is based on Spin Images [Joh97]. They describe that on differently meshed versions of a terrain the spin images at the mesh points change considerably. They propose to interpolate the meshed surface and create the spin images on the interpolated surface. That way the spin images resemble each other much more. The downside is that the surface interpolation is quite costly from a computing perspective. One has to keep in mind that as an unmeshed point cloud is given there should be quite some computing overhead.

Sun and Abidi [SA01] present another descriptor for points: They use geodesic circles around an interest point and project them onto the tangential plane in that point. This yields a kind of fingerprint for this point. Salient points have a great radius variation in their fingerprint. They show that for different views of the same point the feature descriptor is very similar. In order to use this descriptor on point cloud data, a geodesic measure needs to be obtained first. This in turn calls for a triangulation of the point cloud which is computationally expensive.

Point Signatures [CJ96] is a well-established descriptor that intersects a ball around an interest point on a surface to obtain a space curve. Subsequently, a plane is fitted through the space curve and the plane is moved along its normal vector until the interest point lies on the plane. After projecting the space curve to the shifted plane the projected curve is sampled clockwise at the point farthest away from the interest point. This is called signature of the point and it can deal with discontinuities while being invariant regarding translation and rotation.

4.2   Terrain estimation

In [HBHH10] a method is presented to learn a continuous surface function by
kernel functions. The method was originally created for 3D laser scanner data and
has the advantage of not only estimating a surface but also calculating uncertainty
bounds for the estimated surface. As the method is especially suited for variable
point density, a kernel-based surface representation could also be suitable for the
surface reconstructed from side-scan sonar data.

5   Conclusion

In this paper it is shown how an autonomous underwater vehicle can navigate based
on side-scan sonar data. The importance of correct spatial referencing of sonar data
and the implications for the sonar data inversion have been illustrated. It has also
been described how a suitable SLAM framework may be designed and an overview
of different surface features to employ in the SLAM context has been given.

The next step consists of finding 3D features that are robust against different
sampling patterns of the surface.

Bibliography

[BSM08]   K. Bikonis, A. Stepnowski, and M. Moszynski. Computer Vision Techniques Applied for
         Reconstruction of Seafloor 3D Images from Side Scan and Synthetic Aperture Sonars
         Data. In Prof. Dick Botteldooren, editor, *Journal of the European Acoustics Association
         (EAA), Acoustics '08 Paris*, volume 94, May/June 2008.

[CG09]   Enrique Coiras and Johannes Groen. 3D target shape from SAS images based on a
         deformable mesh. In *Proceedings of the 3rd International Conference on Underwater
         Acoustic Measurements (UAM), Nafplion, Greece*, 2009.

[CHH99]   O. Carmichael, D. Huber, and M. Hebert. Large data sets and confusing scenes in 3-D
         surface matching and recognition. In *Proc. Second Int 3-D Digital Imaging and Modeling
         Conf*, pages 358–367, 1999.

[CJ96]   Chin Seng Chua and Ray Jarvis. 3D free-form surface registration and object recognition.
         International Journal of Computer Vision, 17:77–99, 1996. 10.1007/BF00127819.

[CPL07]   Enrique Coiras, Yvan Petillot, and David M. Lane. Multiresolution 3-D Reconstruction
         From Side-Scan Sonar Images. *IEEE Transactions on Image Processing*, 16(2):382–390,
         February 2007. Heriot-Watt University Edinburgh.

[HBHH10] Raia Hadsell, J. Andrew (Drew) Bagnell, Daniel Huber, and Martial Hebert. Space-
         carving kernels for accurate rough terrain estimation. *International Journal of Robotics
         Research*, 29(1), July 2010.

[Joh97]   Andrew Edie Johnson. *Spin-images: A representation for 3-d surface matching*. PhD thesis, Carnegie Mellon University, 1997.

[LHW⁺10]   Jing Luo, Bo He, Peixun Wang, Ke Yang, and Chunyun Ren. Data association for AUV localization and map building. In *Proc. Int Measuring Technology and Mechatronics Automation (ICMTMA) Conf*, volume 1, pages 886–889, 2010.

[RBB09]   Radu Bogdan Rusu, Nico Blodow, and Michael Beetz. Fast Point Feature Histograms (FPFH) for 3D Registration. In *Proceedings of the IEEE International Conference on Robotics and Automation (ICRA)*, Kobe, Japan, May 12-17 2009.

[RMBB08]   Radu Bogdan Rusu, Zoltan Csaba Marton, Nico Blodow, and Michael Beetz. Persistent Point Feature Histograms for 3D Point Clouds. In *Proceedings of the 10th International Conference on Intelligent Autonomous Systems (IAS-10)*, Baden-Baden, Germany, July 23-25 2008.

[RRPL04]   Ioseba Tena Ruiz, Sébastien de Raucourt, Yvan Petillot, and David M. Lane. Concurrent Mapping and Localization Using Sidescan Sonar. *IEEE Journal of Oceanic Engineering*, 29(2):442–456, April 2004.

[SA01]   Y. Sun and M. A. Abidi. Surface matching by 3D point's fingerprint. In *Proc. Eighth IEEE Int. Conf. Computer Vision ICCV 2001*, volume 2, pages 263–269, 2001.

[WF10]   Philipp Woock and Christian Frey. Deep-sea AUV navigation using side-scan sonar images and SLAM. In *Proceedings of the IEEE Oceans Conference 2010*, may 2010.

[Woo10]   Philipp Woock. Deep sea navigation using SLAM. *Proceedings of the 2009 Joint Workshop of Fraunhofer IOSB and Institute for Anthropomatics, Vision and Fusion Laboratory*, 4, 2010.

[Woo11a]   Philipp Woock. Deep-sea seafloor shape reconstruction from side-scan sonar data for AUV navigation. In *OCEANS, 2011 IEEE - Spain*, pages 1 –7, June 2011.

[Woo11b]   Philipp Woock. Side-scan sonar based SLAM for the deep sea. *Proceedings of the 2010 Joint Workshop of Fraunhofer IOSB and Institute for Anthropomatics, Vision and Fusion Laboratory*, 7, 2011.

[ZYZ05]   En Zhu, Jianping Yin, and Guomin Zhang. Fingerprint matching based on global alignment of multiple reference minutiae. *Pattern Recognition*, 38(10):1685   1694, 2005.

Requirements for reputation in decentralized smart sensor networks

Hauke Vagts

Vision and Fusion Laboratory
Institute for Anthropomatics
Karlsruhe Institute of Technology (KIT), Germany
vagts@kit.edu

Technical Report IES-2011-04

Abstract: In the recent years, sensors have improved to the point where they process data autonomously, instead of delivering raw information, e.g., a smart camera may send events such as a person falling instead of the video stream. Modern sensors also offer standardized interfaces and their output can be combined to execute a specific task. For saving costs, monitoring bigger areas or enhancing the quality of each task, a number of sensors may be shared between multiple parties. The key challenge to the distributed use of smart sensors is assessing trust. When a sensor is used, especially after a long break or for the first time, it is essential to know whether it can be trusted, i.e., it must be determined, if the information is authentic and has the quality sufficient for the specific purpose. This report discusses the requirements to the reputation of sensors and presents the resulting model for building trust.

1 Introduction

A *sensor network* consists of a multitude of sensors that belong to several partners. These sensors can be placed locally or highly distributed [Sha07, ASSC02]. Output of conventional sensors is raw information, e.g., a video stream or a temperature. *Smart sensors* process the gathered information before submitting it, e.g., a face detector. Multiple sensors can also be combined and accessed via one specified interface, e.g., a multi-camera tracker that just provides the current position data of a specific object. In general, modern sensors can offer all kind of information. Networks of such sensors are not used for military purposes only, but also in robotics, environmental monitoring, automotive industry, etc. Improvement of sensors, algorithms and applications goes hand in hand with the extended use.

This directly leads to security issues. Sensors and operators, i.e., their accessing services must be authenticated and authorized. Furthermore, in most cases, communication should be treated as confidential. However, well-known techniques can be utilized to achieve authenticity, integrity and confidentiality, e.g., asymmetric cryptography and a Public Key Infrastructure.

It remains an open question, in which way trust can be established in sensors and systems of the different operators. If an operator wants to take advantage of his partner's sensors, he must know, whether he can trust the data or not, i.e., he must determine the quality of the requested information for reasonable usage. Even if it is proven that data d belongs to a partner P or to a sensor s_P of P, no statement can be made about the quality of d or whether s_P is intentionally corrupted or not. The behavior of a sensor can change quickly. When someone is interacting with a sensor, the trust in it can be calculated based on the experiences made. In many events, this is not possible and the recommendations of others must be used, similar to online shops, where recommendations from other people can be viewed. In a similar way entities can be assessed in sensor networks. An *entity* is either a single sensor or an entire system of a partner, e.g. a surveillance system. Entities are rated to calculate reputation and trust. Based on this calculation, partners can choose other sensors or partners to build up a network for specific use. Multiple approaches exist for calculating reputation in different areas, e.g., peer-to-peer networks. The requirements in smart sensor networks are different.

This work highlights the requirements for calculating trust in smart sensor environments and discusses a resulting model for building trust.

2 Terms and definitions

Sensor networks, usually discussed in scientific papers, consist of low-energy devices that transmit their information in ad-hoc networks. Bandwidth and energy problems are in the focus of research and not much data is transmitted. However, the smart sensor networks discussed in this work are different.

2.1 Smart Sensor networks

Smart sensor networks can be used for various purposes. The most typical scenario for the use of sensor networks is surveillance. Conventional surveillance systems are based on cameras, video still being the predominant information source. However, modern surveillance systems, also referenced as smart or intelligent surveillance

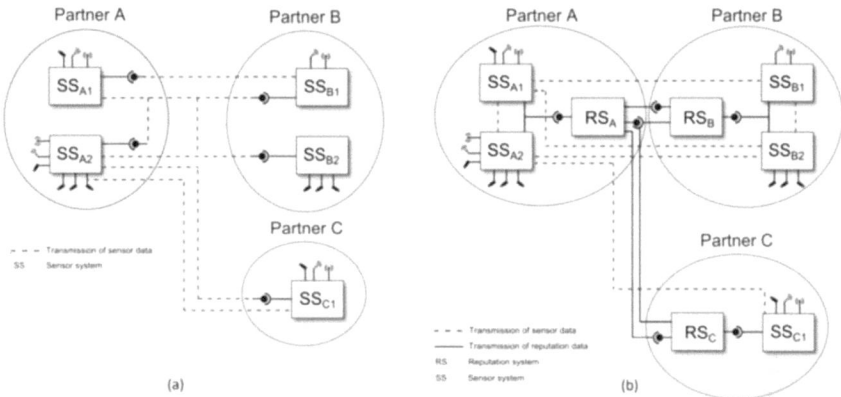

Figure 2.1: Subfigure (a) shows a typical scenario with three partners and five smart sensor systems. Subfigure (b) is showing the same scenario with reputations systems.

systems, can implement different types of sensors and process information at a high level, e.g., [MRV10].

Figure 2.1 is showing an example scenario. A partner can host multiple networks at different locations. In each network, different sensors are used to gather information, e.g., acoustic sensors, cameras and RFID readers. In (a) three operators (A-C) host sensor networks. At each location of the partner, a system is installed that stores and processes local sensor data. Each local system consists of *low-level services* that encapsulate the (smart) sensors and offer a standardized interface, e.g., described by WSDL. A coordination module manages the sensors and delivers their information to a central information storage, where it is accessed by *high-level services*. These high-level services are combined to perform a specific task. For instance, such a deployment can be installed in a branch bank. Cameras collect information about customers and deliver it to the storage. High-level services can then search for suspicious behavior to prevent robbery or manipulation of an ATM. Other services might analyze the data for statistical purposes, such as, detecting which counters have the longest lines.

Figure 2.1 show the same scenario, but with reputation systems. Every partner hosts one reputation system for all his systems. The reputation system manages all information about the existing surveillance systems and connected sensors. Only the address of the reputation system must be available to perform all tasks related to reputation.

2.2 Trust

Reputation and trust are used differently in literature [Gam88, MMH02, WV07]. A popular definition is from Gambetta: "Trust (or, symmetrically, distrust) is a particular level of the subjective probability with which an entity assesses that another entity or group of entities will perform a particular action [...]." This work uses the following definitions.

Definition 1 (Trust) Trust is based on the direct experience made in the past. It is the subjective expectation about the credibility and quality of data from another entity

As trust is based on direct experience, it is only a subjective opinion of the observer.

Definition 2 (Direct experience) A direct experience is based on interaction between two entities. During an interaction data is exchanged that is required for fulfilling a specific task.

With the number of parties the objectivity of a reputation is increasing. Recommendation is specified as follows.

Definition 3 (Reputation) Reputation is the average trust in a data source. The calculation is based on the own trust, if existing, and the recommendations of third parties.

Definition 4 (Recommendation) A recommendation is the propagation of the own trust in an entity.

Definition 5 (Evaluator) The reputation system that is sending a recommendation is denoted as evaluator.

Finally the trustworthiness is defined as following.

Definition 6 (Trustworthiness) A data source is trustworthy, if it achieves a certain level of reputation.

3   Requirements

Each operator can have different requirements and conditions. Hence, he must be able to calculate his own threshold for trustworthiness. As a result no central repository for trust exists.

Requirement 1 Each operator must be allowed to to set his own threshold for trustworthiness.

Two more requirements directly result from the independency of the operator. When calculating reputation, an operator must be able to weight the recommendations from his partners. This might be due previous experiences or due to existing relations in the business world. Similarly, the transitivity must be limited, if a partner passes a request when he cannot answer. When building a trust chain and believing in the recommendation of another entity, only direct trust must be passed [JP05]. If recommendations contain indirect experiences, experiences might be included more than once in a reputation calculation. This could lead to an unintended results. Only flow models, e.g., PageRank [PBMW99], avoid this issues by normalization. When combining smart sensors for a specific task, no regular flow can be assumed and a centralized model is not sufficient as well.

Requirement 2 An operator must be able to weight the recommendations of his partners.

Requirement 3 An operator must be able to limit the number of involved entities when passing a request.

Requirement 4 Indirect trust cannot be included in recommendations.

Sensor data can be used for different purposes. Hence, the model must be general enough to calculate trust in each of these contexts. It is also desirable to calculate trust in an evaluator, i.e., in the trust in his recommendations.

Requirement 5 Reputation and Trust must be computable in different contexts.

Some trust models allow a binary rating of data, which is not sufficient for smart sensor networks. As the assessment of the data quality is difficult in many cases, a reasonable amount of values is enough. However, in theory it can be specified more accurately, if more values are used.

Requirement 6 *The values for rating transactions, i.e., for rating the data quality, must be sufficient.*

In a sensor data processing system, data is stored in a central storage. In many cases, data of the different sources is fused to enhance the quality. Operators can also share information of storages instead of sensors. The storage is filled with sensor information. Hence, trust in the data should change, if the trust in the underlying sensors is calculated. Trust for sensors can only be calculated, if the information is directly received from the sensor or if it is received from the storage and it can be traced that the information belongs to a specific sensor.

Requirement 7 *Trust must be computable for sensors and systems.*

Trust can change with each transaction. Hence, it must be updatable with each rating. The behavior of sensors can change quickly, e.g., due to a malfunction. It is highly dependent on external conditions. Future behavior is hard to predict. Trust that is based on old experiences must be aged, i.e., when calculating a current trust value; the old trust must be weighted according to its age.

Requirement 8 *Trust must quickly adapt to changes. Old trust values become obsolete.*

Ratings can be within a specific range, depending in the satisfaction, not only "postive" "or negative". It is possible that always (slightly) positive ratings are made. The should converge to the specific value that represents the light trust, but not to the global maximum value, i.e., the maximum trust. Vice versa, the same should be fulfilled with only negative rankings. A prerequirement is that the global maximum value is known in advance and is constant. Including aging of older trust values in some approaches can have an impact on the value.

Requirement 9 *Global maximum and minimum values must exist, be known and constant over time.*

Requirement 10 *The trust value must not converge to the global maximum or minimum value, when only positive, negative ratings are made,respectively.*

Multiple approaches have been evaluated and further details can be found in [VCB11]. The model presented in [YSS04] provides a solid base and can be extended to fulfill the requirements specified above.

4   A model for calculating trust

The requirements named above lead to the following trust model. It consists of functions for calculating *ratings, trust* and *reputation*. Depending on these ratings, the trust of entities will be updated. Furthermore, a function is needed to update the trust value after inactivity of entities without an incoming rating. The existing trust values are exchanged as recommendation between reputation systems. This recommendation represents the opinion of the evaluator and is used for reputation calculation. Finally, the trustworthiness of the entities can be determined by their reputation. In this paper, the values for rating, trust and reputation are in the interval [0,1]. I neutral rating is represented by 0.5.

4.1   Calculating the rating for a smart sensor system

A smart sensor systems hosts multiple sensors and all of them transmit their information to the central data storage. Hence, a rating for a specific sensor also updates the rating of the entire system. The calculation considers the existing trust in the systems and new rating for the sensor. the number of sensors in a system l is known.

$$b^i(S) = \frac{l-1}{l} \cdot v^{i-1}(ss) + \frac{1}{l} \cdot b^i(s)$$

The rating for a sensor s is denoted with $b^i(s) \in [0,1]$ and for a sensor system S with $b^i(S) \in [0,1]$ at time t_i. The trust in S at time t_{i-1} is denoted with $v^{i-1}(S) \in [0,1]$.

4.2   Calculating the rating for reputation systems

Reputation systems calculate the ratings for evaluators based on their recommendations and for sensor systems based on the ratings for their sensors. They also update their trust values and exchange these as recommendations with other reputation systems. Each recommendation is rated by its recipient. After the next transaction, each recommendation can be compared with the own perception of the entity. The comparison reflects the credibility of the recommendation.

$$b^i(R) = 1 - |(b^i(q) - r(R,s))|$$

The rating of a sensor s at time t_i is denoted with $b^i(s)$ and the reputation system R with $b^i(R) \in [0,1]$. A recommendation from a reputation system R for a smart sensor is specified as $r(R,s) \in [0,1]$.

4.3 Updating trust by an incoming rating

It is impossible to predict the behavior of sensors. The behavior of a sensor can, e.g., be influenced by the weather. Additionally, the failure or defect of a sensor can influence the quality of the published sensor data. For this reason calculation and update of trust need a mathematical function, which is qualified for unpredictable behavior of sensors. In addition, there is a need to consider the old trust value and the new rating while calculating the trust. This can be reached by weighting the existing trust value and the rating. However, the weight of the incoming rating depends on the time difference between the last trust calculation and the new rating. In the meantime, changes might occur, in weather or other environmental factors. The larger this time difference, the more weight has the new rating in the calculation.

$$v^i(s) = \alpha \cdot v^{i-1}(s) + (1 - \alpha) \cdot b^i(s)$$

The model is based on exponential smoothing, as no assumptions about trends could me bade. The weighting of the new ratings can be modeled by a smoothing factor α, which results in the following function, where $v^i(e) \in [0, 1]$ is the trust in an entity s, i.e., a sensor or an entire system. To allow a weighting related to time, α is replaced by a function

$$\alpha = e^{-\frac{\Delta t}{T_p} \cdot \lambda} \cdot \sigma$$

that considers the temporal difference $\Delta t \geq 0$, i.e., the time between the last and the current rating. The function contains an aging factor $\sigma \in [0, 1]$. T_p is the length of a time period and is given by an organization. To scale σ with the exponential function another parameter $\lambda \in [0, 1]$ is used. This results in the following function for updating trust. The parameter σ leads to a starting weight different to 1. In general the weight increases with higher T_p and decreases with λ.

$$v^i(s) = e^{-\frac{\Delta t}{T_p} \cdot \lambda} \cdot \sigma \cdot v^{i-1}(s) + (1 - e^{-\frac{\Delta t}{T_p} \cdot \lambda} \cdot \sigma) \cdot b^i(s)$$

4.4 Updating trust after inactivity

Trust is dynamic and also requires updating without incoming ratings and must therefore be independent from them. Intuitively trust decreases over time with the growing uncertainty. However, it is hard to predict the aging of trust, depending on more optimistic or pessimistic general attitude, you can chose a different function. A neutral one would be linear, achieving the trust value zero after a defined time difference. Let $\eta > 0$ denote the number of time periods, in which the trust can be considered up-to-date, i.e., bigger than zero.

$$v^i(e) = \begin{cases} v^{i-1}(e) \cdot \left(1 - \frac{\Delta t}{T_p} \cdot \frac{1}{\eta}\right), & \text{for } \frac{\Delta t}{T_p} < \eta \\ 0, & \text{else.} \end{cases}$$

It can also be assumed that trust is constant, i.e., not decreasing for a certain period. Such a period could be the estimated time until the next rating. If no rating is received within such a period the value should drop to the next lower level. Therefor the function $f = 1 - \frac{\Delta t}{T_p} \cdot \frac{1}{\eta}$, in the equation above, should be replaced by $f^* = 1 - \lfloor \frac{\Delta t}{T_p} \rfloor \cdot \frac{1}{\eta}$. The rounding of $\frac{\Delta t}{T_p}$ ensures that the trust is constant for a time period.

4.5 Reputation

Reputation is the average trust of the direct neighbors of an entity. These trust values of its neighbors are weighted by the trust of the requesters in the evaluators. If any trust values exist, the local trust of the requester in the entity will be considered.

Reputation calculation requires a factor for weighting recommendations of some individual evaluators. These evaluators keep a special relationship with the requester. Only recommendations of direct evaluators can be weighted additionally. This additional weight is defined as $g(R_i, R_j) \geq 1$, where R_i represents the source and R_j represents the destination reputation system. A trust chain χ_n consists of IDs of the reputation systems, which are passed through. The reputation is calculated as follows:

$$r^i(q_z) = \sum_{n=0}^{M} \left(r_{\chi_n}(R_k, s_z) \cdot \left(\frac{v_{\chi_n}(R_k)}{\sum_{m=0}^{M} v_{\chi_m}(R_k)} \right) \right)$$

Where M denotes the number of recommendations. The trust v_χ in an entity rs_k via the trust chain χ_n is calculated as follows:

$$v_{\chi_n}(R_l) = \prod_{i=0}^{l} v_{\chi_n}(R_i, R_{i+1}) \cdot g(R_i, R_{i+1}) \,,$$

with

$$0 \leq l < k, \chi_{0:k} = (id(R_0), id(R_1), ..., id(R_k))$$

A recommendation made by a repuation system R_k via a trust chain χ_n to the entity s_z is denoted with $r_{\chi_n}(R_k, s_z) \in [0, 1]$, whereby $z = k + 1$. The system R_k is a direct neighbor of the target entity s_z and $rR0$ is requesting reputation system. The own trust in s_z is included in the recommendation by $\chi_{0:0} = (R_0)$ with $g(R_0, R_0)$. If R_{i+1} is not a direct neighbor of the requesting system, then $g(R_i, R_{i+1}) = 1$. Only recommendations of a direct neighbor or the trust in the own trust in the target entity can be weighted manually.

4.6 Determining the trustworthiness

An entity is trustworthy if its reputation excesses a certain threshold, otherwise the entity is untrustworthy. The threshold is individually defined by the organization. A reputations score containing a high number of opinions can be seen as more reliable in general.

5 Conclusion

This work presented the requirements for calculating trust and reputation in a smart sensor networks. The proposed model extends the work [YSS04] to be sufficient for the use in smart sensor networks. Even if simulations with test ratings look very promising the model is not validated with a real system, which is a general issues of all existing trust models. This is basically due to missing rating function that rate data/results automatically. Future research must focus on such rating functions, and they must be developed for different sensors of different modalities.

Bibliography

[ASSC02]   I.F. Akyildiz, Weilian Su, Y. Sankarasubramaniam, and E. Cayirci. A survey on sensor networks. *Communications Magazine, IEEE*, 40(8):102 – 114, aug. 2002.

[Gam88]   Diego Gambetta. *Trust: Making and Breaking Cooperative Relations*, chapter Can We Trust Trust?, pages 213–237. Basil Blackwell, 1988.

[JP05]   Audun Jøsang and Simon Pope. Semantic constraints for trust transitivity. In *Proceedings of the 2nd Asia-Pacific conference on Conceptual modelling - Volume 43*, APCCM '05, pages 59–68, Darlinghurst, Australia, Australia, 2005. Australian Computer Society, Inc.

[MMH02]   L. Mui, M. Mohtashemi, and A. Halberstadt. A computational model of trust and reputation for e-businesses. Hawaii International Conference on System Sciences, 2002.

[MRV10]   Jurgen Mossgraber, Frank Reinert, and Hauke Vagts. An architecture for a task-oriented surveillance system: A service- and event-based approach. *Proc. Fifth International Conference on Systems ICONS*, 0:146–151, 2010.

[PBMW99]   Lawrence Page, Sergey Brin, Rajeev Motwani, and Terry Winograd. The pagerank citation ranking: Bringing order to the web. Technical Report 1999-66, Stanford InfoLab, November 1999. Previous number = SIDL-WP-1999-0120.

[Sha07]   Pravin Shankar. Sensor networks - a survey. Rutgers University, http://paul.
            rutgers.edu/~spravin/sensornw-survey-spravin.pdf, May 2007.

[VCB11]   H. Vagts, T. Cosar, and J. Beyerer. Establishing trust in decentralized smart sensor networks.
            volume 8063, page 806306. SPIE, 2011.

[WV07]   Yao Wang and Julita Vassileva. A Review on Trust and Reputation for Web Service Selec-
            tion. In *ICDCSW '07: Proceedings of the 27th International Conference on Distributed
            Computing Systems Workshops*, volume 0, pages 25+, Washington, DC, USA, 2007. IEEE
            Computer Society.

[YSS04]   Bin Yu, M.P. Singh, and K. Sycara. Developing trust in large-scale peer-to-peer systems.
            In *Multi-Agent Security and Survivability, 2004 IEEE First Symposium on*, pages 1 – 10,
            August 2004.

Principles of Underwater Vision

Thomas Stephan

Vision and Fusion Laboratory
Institute for Anthropomatics
Karlsruhe Institute of Technology (KIT), Germany
thomas.stephan@ies.uka.de

Technical Report IES-2011-05

Abstract: Optical imaging under water represents an unresolved problem until today. Poor visibility, blurred images and a minor signal-to-noise-ratio are the consequences of absorption, scattering and marine-snow dominating the properties of water. This technical report depicts the reasons for poor image qualities of such imaging systems and provides a mathematical model of radiative transfer under water. With respect to computational performance two efficient approximations of radiative transfer are presented and their advantages and disadvantages discussed. Furthermore computational imaging under water will be discussed from the perspective of image restoration.

1 Introduction

The inspection of offshore parks, dam walls and other infrastructure under water can be expensive in terms of time and money. The reason therefore lies in the fact that such constructions must be still inspected manually by divers. Under water buildings have to be surveyed visually to find small cracks, spallings or other deficiencies. This inspection task is time-consuming and claiming for the inspection diver.

Automation of underwater inspection depends on established water-proved imaging systems. Most used under water imaging systems are based on acoustic sensors. The disadvantage of such acoustic systems is the loss of the complete visual impression. All information which lies in texture and surface reflectance get lost. Therefore acoustic sensors are mostly insufficient for visual inspection tasks under water.

Imaging systems based on optical sensors possess a vast potential for underwater applications. The bandwidth from visual imaging systems reach from inspection of underwater buildings via marine biological applications through to exploration of seafloor. The reason for the lack of established optical systems lies in the technical difficulties of underwater image acquisition and processing. Lightening, highly degraded images and therefore computational imaging play an important role in such visual imaging systems.

1.1   Problem of underwater imaging

The increase of camera based automation in industry, surveillance and research in the last decade is conspicuous. This development makes a stop at all underwater tasks. The reason for this circumstance apart from technical problem of water-resistance and energy supply are poor visibility and hence highly degraded images. Degradation of imaging results are basically caused by three factors.

Absorption   The energy of a light ray traversing a column of water is attenuated by water and small particles within the water. This mechanism is called absorption.

By loss of energy of light rays crossing water, effects low intensities of imaged scene objects. Light attenuation by absorption causes also changes of imaged colors. Because of dependency of absorption on wavelength of light, attenuation of light varies with its wavelength. Some ranges of the spectrum get more attenuated than others. Thus imaged objects appear with a change of color. Figure 1.1 illustrates the results of absorption and scattering.

Scattering   Absorption is not the only form of light-water interaction. Light rays interact with water and its inherent particles also in form of scattering. Scattered photons get deflected into another direction. Thus a single light ray in a designated direction gets attenuated by scattering but the energy within the light field does not get lost.

Scattering causes two effects with respect to imaging. First, rays coming from an object surface get fanned out and consequently the image gets blurred. On the other hand light rays reach the optical sensor which were never reflected by the object surface but scattered by water. In consequence of this circumstance the resulting image receives an additional intensity amount consisting no information about the scene objects. This additional image intensity appears as bright haze (see figure 1.1).

Particles   Particles located in water degrade the quality of optical imaging. As seen, small particles are an issue for absorption and scattering. However, big particles – particles which are much bigger than the wavelength of the interacting light ray – degrade the quality of images in other way. Parts of scene objects are covered by such particles.

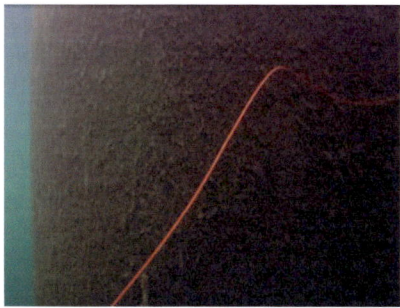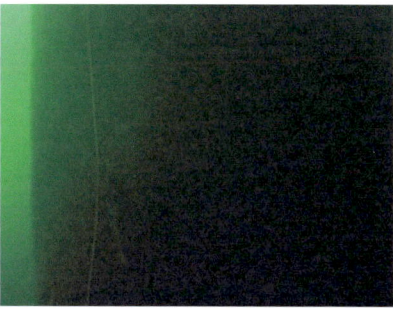

Figure 1.1: The right image is captured just below the water surface. The minor column of water that light rays have to traverse barely causes a change of color. Thus, the orange color of the electric cable points out clearly. On the other hand, the right image illustrates the color shift for a bigger water column. Light traverse water and red parts of light spectrum get lost by absorption. Thus, the orange color does not appear clearly.

Particles within water diminish the signal-to-noise-ratio (SNR). For all image restoration tasks the signal-to-noise-ratio limits the possible quality of restored image. As a last consequence the density of large particles determines the capabilities of optical underwater imaging systems.

1.2   Contribution

This technical report gives an insight into the theme of the theoretics of physical principles of light propagation (section 2), of underwater image processing and image restoration (section 4). Therefore, difficulties and their reasons of underwater imaging will be explained, the general phenomena of radiative interaction will be depicted (section 2.2) and the modeling of radiative transfer under water will be discussed (section 3). Finally, some innovative ideas for underwater imaging will be outlined (4.1).

2   Radiative Transfer

2.1   Radiometry – Quantities

For understanding radiative transfer, some physical quantities have to be explained. These are in detail the radiant flux, the radiance, the irradiance and the radiant intensity.

2.1.1   Radiant Flux

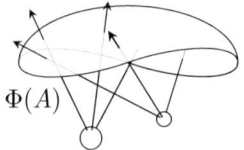

$\Phi(A)$

Figure 2.1: Illustration of the radiant flux

The radiant flux Φ is the measure of the power of radiation passing a surface A. Its unit is Watt $[W]$. If the surface A equals to a sphere around a light source, the corresponding radiant flux gives the emitted power of the light source. The figure beside illustrates the quantity of radiant flux $\Phi(A)$.

2.1.2   Radiance

A quantity of radiometry is the radiance. It gives the best association to a single light ray at a certain position in a certain direction. The radiance L is the area-projection of the density of power coming from an area element dA radiated into a solid angle element $d\omega$. The figure beside illustrates the quantity of radiance.

The relation between radiance and the radiant flux Φ is given by the integral over all solid angles and the area A.

$$\Phi = \int_{\Omega} \int_{A} L(\vec{r}, \vec{x}) \cos(\theta) \, dA \, d\omega \quad ,$$

where $\vec{x} \in A$ denotes the position of radiance, $\vec{r}$ denotes the direction of radiance with its elevation angle θ and $\omega \in \Omega$ denotes the solid angle corresponding to the

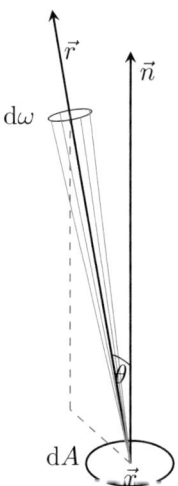

Figure 2.2: Illustration of outgoing radiance from an area element dA in direction $\vec{r}$ through a solid angle element $d\omega$.

direction $\vec{r}$. Hence the unit of radiance is written as Watt per square meter and steradian $[\frac{W}{m^2 sr}]$

2.1.3 Irradiance

The quantity of irradiance $E(\vec{x})$ describes the density of radiant flux Φ per area. Thus irradiance can be written as:

$$E(\vec{x}) = \frac{\mathrm{d}\Phi}{\mathrm{d}A},$$

with its unit $[\frac{W}{m^2}]$. The relation between radiance $L(\vec{x}, \vec{r})$ and irradiance $E(\vec{x})$ is given by the integral over all solid angles

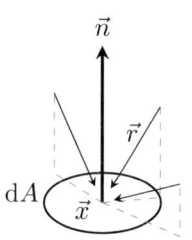

$$E(\vec{x}) = \int_{\Omega} L(\vec{x}, \vec{r}) \cos(\theta)\, \mathrm{d}\omega,$$

where θ is the angle between the normal vector $\vec{n}$ of the surface and the direction of the incident radiance $\vec{r}$. The solid angle element $\mathrm{d}\omega$ corresponds to the direction $\vec{r}$ of the incident radiance $L(\vec{x}, \vec{r})$.

To provide a surface independent representation of irradiance, it can be defined [Mob94] a vector irradiance $\vec{E}(\vec{x})$ with

Figure 2.3: Illustration incoming irradiance at an area element $\mathrm{d}A$

$$\vec{E}(\vec{x}) = \int_{\Omega} L(\vec{x}, \vec{r}) \vec{r}\, \mathrm{d}\omega$$

The direction $\vec{r}$ can be written in component form as a sum of basis vectors as

$$\vec{r} = (\vec{r}^T \vec{e}_x)\vec{e}_x + (\vec{r}^T \vec{e}_y)\vec{e}_y + (\vec{r}^T \vec{e}_z)\vec{e}_z ,$$

where, for example, $\vec{r}^T \vec{e}_x = \cos(\theta_x)$ gives the cosine of the angle between the vector $\vec{r}$ and the basis vector $\vec{e}_x$. Thus the vector irradiance can be written as

$$\vec{E}(\vec{x}) = \left[\int_{\Omega} L(\vec{x}, \vec{r}) \cos(\theta_x)\, \mathrm{d}\omega \right] \vec{e}_x$$
$$+ \left[\int_{\Omega} L(\vec{x}, \vec{r}) \cos(\theta_y)\, \mathrm{d}\omega \right] \vec{e}_y$$
$$+ \left[\int_{\Omega} L(\vec{x}, \vec{r}) \cos(\theta_z)\, \mathrm{d}\omega \right] \vec{e}_z .$$

Hence the irradiance at a surface point $\vec{x}$ with the normal vector $\vec{n}$ can be written as $\vec{n}^T \vec{E}(\vec{x})$. The illustration in the above figure depicts the quantity of irradiance at an area element $\mathrm{d}A$

2.1.4 Radiant Intensity

Whereas irradiance is the density of radiated power related to an area element $\mathrm{d}A$, the radiant intensity $I(\vec{r})$ is the density of radiated power related to a solid angle element $\mathrm{d}\omega$. Thus the radiant intensity can be defined as:

$$I(\vec{r}) = \frac{\mathrm{d}\Phi}{\mathrm{d}\omega} \,,$$

with its unit Watt per steradian $\left[\frac{W}{sr}\right]$. Hence the relations between radiance and radiant intensity are given as

$$I(\vec{x}) = \int_A L(\vec{x}, \vec{r}) \cos(\theta) \, \mathrm{d}\vec{x},$$

where θ is the angle between the normal vector of the surface and the direction of the outgoing radiance.

The concept of radiant intensity is useful to describe point sources, but it has not found much application in modeling radiative transfer under water except in the definition of the volume scattering function [Mob94].

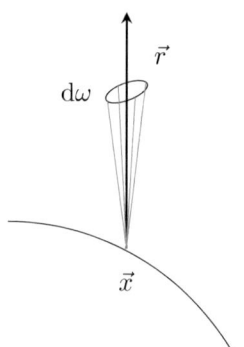

Figure 2.4: Illustration outgoing radiant intensity into an solid angle element $\mathrm{d}\omega$

2.2 Medium-induced effects on radiance

Light rays more precisely radiation interacts with its surrounding. That may be volumes or surfaces of objects. These interactions can be divided into different effects.

2.2.1 Absorption

Absorption is caused by annihilation of photons of the radiance beam and conversion of radiant energy to nonradiant energy. The change in radiance while crossing a volume element at $\vec{x}$ in direction $\vec{r}$ due to absorption is proportional to the incident radiance. Thus absorption can be described by

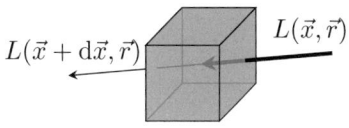

$$\vec{r}^{T} \nabla_{\vec{x}} L\left(\vec{x}, \vec{r}\right) = -a(\vec{x}) L\left(\vec{x}, \vec{r}\right)$$

Here $d\vec{x} = \vec{r}^{T} \nabla_{\vec{x}}$ denotes the directional derivative at $\vec{x}$ in direction $\vec{r}$. The proportionality constant $a(\vec{x})$ is called the absorption coefficient.

2.2.2 Emission

Emission can be caused e.g. by emitting light sources or by bioluminescence. Energy in terms of nonradiant energy will be converted and emitted in the form of radiant energy.

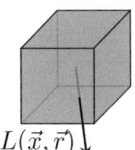

The dependencies of emission on direction, location and other quantities can be very complex. In this report, emission will be simply included as a generic source function S that represents creation of radiance along path $\vec{r}^{T} \nabla_{\vec{x}}$ in direction $\vec{r}$. Thus emission can be written as

$$\vec{r}^{T} \nabla_{\vec{x}} L\left(\vec{x}, \vec{r}\right) = S\left(\vec{x}, \vec{r}\right)$$

without specifying the mathematical form of the source function S.

2.2.3 Refraction

Refraction is the change of direction of a radiance. The phenomenon of refraction occurs essentially on surfaces but can also appear in volumes. It is caused by a change of the medium and its inherent light speed. On surfaces the ratio of sines of the angle

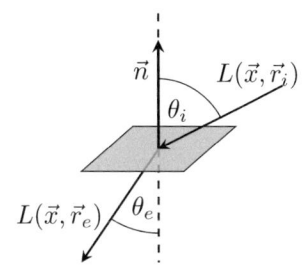

of incidence and refraction is equivalent to the ratio of phase velocities or the opposite ratio of the indices of refraction:

$$\frac{\sin(\theta_i)}{\sin(\theta_e)} = \frac{v_i}{v_e} = \frac{n_e}{n_i}$$

The angle θ is the angle between the corresponding light beam with direction $\vec{r}$ and the normal $\vec{n}$ of the surface.

2.2.4   Scattering

A photon can be deflected by a particle into direction $\vec{r}$ divergent from origin direction $\vec{r'}$. This process is called scattering. First of all scattering causes a decrease of radiance from direction $\vec{r'}$. The decrease in radiance while crossing a volume element $\vec{x}$ in direction $\vec{r'}$ due to scattering is proportional to the incident radiance. Thus loss of radiance due to scattering can be described by

$$\vec{r'}^T \nabla_{\vec{x}} L\left(\vec{x}, \vec{r'}\right) = -b(\vec{x}) L\left(\vec{x}, \vec{r'}\right)$$

Here $b(\vec{x})$ denotes the scattering coefficient.

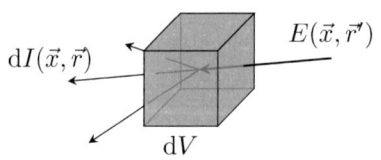

As discussed in 1.1 it should not be assumed that this reduction in radiance is lost to the radiation field. The part of the energy lost from an incident light beam will reappear as scattered radiation in other directions. The distribution of angles of scattered radiation can be described by the volume scattering function $\beta\left(\vec{x}, \vec{r}\right)$, which is defined [Mob94] as

$$\beta(\vec{x}, \vec{r'} \rightarrow \vec{r}) = \frac{dI(\vec{x}, \vec{r})}{E(\vec{x}, \vec{r'})\, dV} \,,$$

where dV denotes a volume element of scattering medium. The relation between volume scattering function $\beta(\vec{x}, \vec{r})$ and the corresponding scattering coefficient b can be described by

$$b(\vec{x}) = \int_{\Omega} \beta\left(\vec{x}, \vec{r}\right) d\omega$$

as a consequence of conservation of energy in radiation field by scattering. Here $\omega \in \Omega$ denotes the solid angle corresponding to the direction $\vec{r}$.

In summary, increase of radiance at location $\vec{x}$ in direction $\vec{r}$ by scattering can be written as

$$\vec{r}^{\,T}\nabla_{\vec{x}}L\left(\vec{x},\vec{r}\right) = \int_{\Omega}\beta\left(\vec{x},\vec{r}'\to\vec{r}\right)L\left(\vec{x},\vec{r}'\right)\mathrm{d}\omega'\ ,$$

where $\vec{r}'\to\vec{r}$ represents the change of direction from $\vec{r}'$ to $\vec{r}$.

2.2.5 Reflection

Reflection is the change of the direction of a radiant beam on a surface. The law of specular reflection say that the angle of the incident radiance respective to the surface normal equals to the angle of the reflected radiance.

Most objects do not have perfectly reflecting surfaces. Thus the angle of the reflected radiance differs from the incident angle. This phenomenon is called diffuse reflection. The properties of objects respect to their reflection can be described by the **B**idirectional **R**eflectance **D**istribution **F**unction called BRDF. The BRDF is defined as

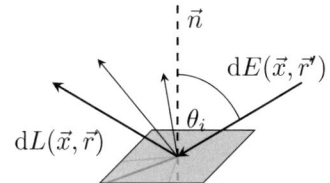

$$\mathrm{BRDF}(\vec{x},\vec{r}',\vec{r}) = \frac{\mathrm{d}L\left(\vec{x},\vec{r}\right)}{\mathrm{d}E\left(\vec{x},\vec{r}'\right)} = \frac{\mathrm{d}L\left(\vec{x},\vec{r}\right)}{\mathrm{d}L\left(\vec{x},\vec{r}'\right)\cos(\theta')\,\mathrm{d}\omega'}\,,$$

where $E\left(\vec{x},\vec{r}'\right)$ is the incident irradiance, θ' is the angle between surface normal and direction $\vec{r}'$ and ω' is the solid angle corresponding to the incident direction $\vec{r}'$. Thus the reflected radiance in direction $\vec{r}$ can be written as

$$L\left(\vec{x},\vec{r}\right) = \int_{\Omega}\mathrm{BRDF}\left(\vec{x},\vec{r}',\vec{r}\right)L\left(\vec{x},\vec{r}'\right)\cos(\theta')\,\mathrm{d}\omega'\ .$$

2.2.6 Other interactions

There are also other interaction of light field with surfaces and volumes, for instance stimulated emission, polarization, diffraction and photon-effects. These interactions do not play an important role for modeling macroscopic effects of radiative interactions with water. [Cha60], [Ish78] and [Mob94] give a deeper insight into the subject matter of radiative transfer.

2.3   Derivation of radiative transfer equation

So far different interactions of radiation with its surrounding have been described. To simplify the model of underwater radiative transfer, it is assumed that interactions of irradiance with surfaced can be described by the BRDF (section 2.2.5) and interactions of radiance with water consists of absorption, scattering and emission (section 2.2.1 - 2.2.5). From this assumptions the radiative transfer equation can be derived [Cha60],[Mob94]:

$$\vec{r}^{T} \nabla_{\vec{x}} L\left(\vec{x}, \vec{r}\right) = - \left(a(\vec{x}) + b(\vec{x})\right) L\left(\vec{x}, \vec{r}\right) \cdot$$
$$\int_{\Omega} \beta\left(\vec{x}, \vec{r}' \rightarrow \vec{r}\right) L\left(\vec{x}, \vec{r}'\right) \mathrm{d}\omega_i +$$
$$S(\vec{x}, \vec{r})$$

The sum of the absorption coefficient and the scattering coefficient $c(\vec{x}) = a(\vec{x}) + b(\vec{x})$ is sometimes called total attenuation.

3   Approximations of Radiative Transfer

The radiative transfer equation derived in section 2.3 has only analytical solutions in very special cases. The physical simulation of correct radiative transfer is extremely expensive in terms of time and memory. Thus for most applications of computational imaging evaluations of radiative transfer have to be much faster than such simulations. As a consequence, radiative transfer must be approximated. However, inverse problems like image restorations (see section 4) need accurate results.
Hereafter some approximations of radiative transfer will be described and their qualities discussed.

3.1   Approximation of Narasimhan et.al.

Narasimhan et.al. have proposed an approximation in [NN09]. They derive an analytic solution of the radiative transfer equation for special assumptions on the surrounding media and the used light source. The solution is mathematically determined by an infinite sum of orthonormal Legendre polynomials. The approximation consists of termination the infinite sum after finite computation steps. The assumptions of the approach are:

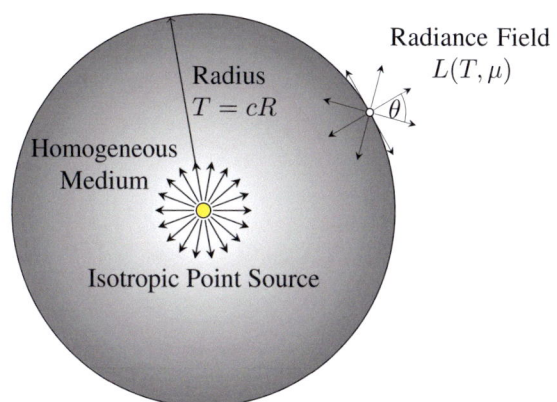

Figure 3.1: An isotropic point source illuminating the medium. The light field in the medium depends on radial optical thickness T and the angle θ from the radial direction [NN09]

Isotropic Point Source The emitted radiant intensity of the given point source is constant for all solid angles. Thus the radiant intensity at source location is given by $I(\vec{0}, \vec{r}) = I_0$.

Homogeneous Medium The surrounding medium is homogeneous. Thus the volume scattering function is denoted by $\beta(\vec{x}, \vec{r}) = \beta(\vec{r})$

Symmetrical Medium The surrounding medium is assumed to be symmetrical, i.e. the volume scattering function only depends on the elevation angle θ. Thus the volume scattering function can be denoted as $\beta(\vec{r}) = \beta(\theta)$.
As a consequence of isotropic point source, homogeneous and symmetric medium the given scene can be described straight forward in polar coordinates with its light source in the origin.

Special Volume Scattering Function It is assumed, that the volume scattering function is characterized by the Henyey-Greenstein phase function

$$\beta(\cos(\theta)) = \frac{1 - q^2}{(1 + q^2 - 2q\cos(\theta))^{\frac{3}{2}}},$$

where $q \in [0, 1]$ is a function parameter and is called *forward scattering parameter*. For $q = 0$ medium becomes isotropic scattered. The more q increase volume scattering function becomes more peaked forward [NN09].

No Absorption It is assumed that absorption can be neglected.

An illustration of the scene properties is given in fig.3.1. The complete solution of radiative transfer can written by:

$$L(T, \mu) = \sum_{m=0}^{\infty} \left(g_m(T) + g_{m+1}(T) \right) \mathrm{LP}_m(\mu),$$

where

$$g_m(T) = I_0 e^{\gamma_m T - \alpha_m \log(T)},$$
$$\alpha_m = m + 1,$$
$$\gamma_m = \frac{2m+1}{m} \left(1 - q^{m-1} \right).$$

The parameter $T = cR$ is called optical thickness, $\mu = \cos(\theta)$ is the cosine of the elevation angle and $\mathrm{LP}_m(\cdot)$ denotes the m-th Legendre-Polynom.

The advantage of this approach is the analytical correctness of simulation results. The disadvantage consists in symmetry of scene and light source. If there are objects located in scene, the condition of symmetry most often is violated.

3.2   Small-Angle Approximation

Another approach of an approximation of radiative transfer has been derived by *Willard H. Wells* in his paper "Loss of Resolution in Water as a Result of Multiple Small-Angle Scattering" [Wel69]. Wells does not model the radiative transfer in itself, but the perspective imaging caused by a projection of a point light source through a pinhole camera. In the approach of Wells a simple linear shift-invariant system was derived so that imaging in scattered media can be calculated by a simple convolution of the signal function with a specified point spread function (PSF). The approach of *Wells* requires restrictive assumptions.

Small-Angle Assumption Sines of small angles can be approximated by the angles itself $\sin \theta \approx \theta$. *Wells* assume strongly peaked scattering in forward direction. Thus the angle of deflected power of scattered light is assumed to be very small.

Symmetric Medium Radiance is assumed to scatter rotationally symmetrically. Thus the volume scattering function only depends on the elevation angle θ

No Absorption It is assumed that absorption could be neglected.

Homogeneous Medium The properties of medium are assumed to be location-invariant.

The bigger the water inherent particles the smaller is the angle of scattered radiance. Induced by this circumstance Wells derive a PSF and a corresponding modulation transfer function (MTF) in frequency domain characterizing the radiative transfer. The MTF can be explicitly written by:

$$F(\nu, R) = e^{(Q(\nu R) - b_t)R} ,$$

where

$$Q(\Psi) = 2\pi \int_0^{\Theta_0} u(\theta) J_0(2\pi \Psi \theta) \, d\theta,$$

$$u(\theta) = \int_0^{\theta} \beta(\vartheta) \, d\vartheta,$$

$$b_t = \int_0^{\Omega} \beta(\theta) \, d\omega = 2\pi \int_0^{\Theta_0} \beta(\theta) \sin(\theta) \, d\theta,$$

where ν denotes the frequency in frequency domain, R denotes the distant to the imaged object and J_0 is the Bessel function of the first kind and the first order. The integration limit Θ_0 is the maximum angle to be regarded as small-angle scattering. The resulting image on image plane can be calculated in frequency domain by multiplying the Fourier-transformed signal function with the depicted MTF of radiative transfer.

The insufficiencies of this approximation root in the restrictive assumptions of small-angle scattering. The phenomenon of backscattering cannot be explained by this approach. Nevertheless, Wells approach of small-angle approximation has its usage in under water simulation because of its efficient computation.

4   Outlook on possible Image Restoration Strategies

Imaging under water is characterized by a high amount of image degradation by absorption, scattering and particles (see section 1). To increase the visible quality of resulting images there are two different strategies: image enhancement and image restoration. The goal of image enhancement is to increase the subjective visible quality of images. The tools of image enhancement are most often heuristically. Whereas image restoration denotes the increase of image quality with respect to an objective quality criterion like least-square minimization.

Basis of image restoration is the signal and the transfer model. The signal $s(\cdot)$ describes the perfect image information without any degradations. Image signals have to pass the transfer model $h(\cdot)$, which can be the model of camera projection or radiative transfer. In most cases transfer model degrade the quality of image in terms of contrast reduction, blurring or geometrical distortion. Thus a noiseless imaging process can be written as function g with

$$g : \mathbb{R}^2 \rightarrow \mathbb{R}^Q$$
$$\vec{x} \mapsto g(\vec{x}) = (h \circ s)(\vec{x}),$$

where Q is the number of color channels. In general imaging is subjected to noise. Thus imaging can be described as stochastic process with $g(\vec{x}, e)$, where e is an elementary event of a random experiment. Purpose of image restoration is an Estimation $\hat{s}(\cdot)$ of the origin signal $s(\cdot)$. Thus image restoration $r(\cdot)$ can be written as

$$\hat{s}(\vec{x}) = r(g(\vec{x}, e)) = (r \circ h \circ s)(\vec{x}, e)$$

If transfer model can be described as a linear shift-invariant system (LSI), estimation of signal leads to the classical approaches of the *Inverse Filter* and the *Wiener Filter* [Jäh05].

4.1 Under Water Image Restoration

There are different tasks to develop an accurate image restoration approach for an underwater imaging system. Before developing an image restoration filter $r(\cdot)$ one have to decide for a signal model $s(\cdot)$ and a transfer model $h(\cdot)$. This must be done accurately. The quality of restored image basically depends on the choice of these two models.

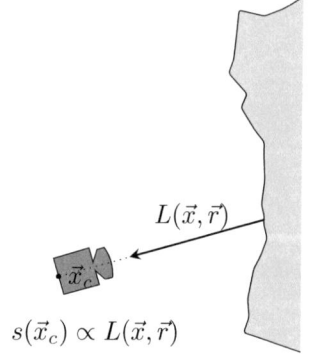

$$s(\vec{x}_c) \propto L(\vec{x}, \vec{r})$$

4.1.1 Signal Model

First of all a signal model must be chosen. Most image restoration approaches takes as signal an ideally pinhole camera projection, so that the signal $s(\cdot)$ is proportional to the radiance at object surfaces with direction to the center of projection.

Figure 4.1: Illustration of simple signal model. The signal $s(\vec{x}_c)$ is modeled proportional to the radiance on corresponding object surface. Here $\vec{x}_c$ denotes a point on image plane and $\vec{x}$ denotes the corresponding point on object surface.

The figure beside illustrates the geometrical properties of the posed simple signal model. Thereby the signal $s(\vec{x}_c)$ is modeled proportional to the radiance on the corresponding object surface. Here $\vec{x}_c \in \mathbb{R}^2$ denotes a point on image plane.

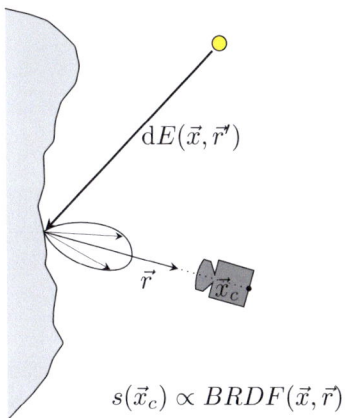

$$dE(\vec{x}, \vec{r'})$$

$$\vec{r} \quad \vec{x}_c$$

$$s(\vec{x}_c) \propto BRDF(\vec{x}, \vec{r})$$

Figure 4.2: The signal $s(\vec{x}_c)$ is modeled proportional to the reflectance of the corresponding object surface. Here $\vec{x}_c$ denotes a point on image plane and $\vec{x}$ denotes the corresponding point on object surface.

In context of *Under Water Vision* this signal model is insufficient. Light which comes from a light source and pass the medium water changes in color, thus the spectral radiance $L_\lambda(\vec{x}, \vec{r})$ on object surface depends on the column of water between light source and surface. Hence in reality radiance of object surfaces under water often appears green or blue, because of the high absorption of red parts of color spectrum.

Intuitively the signal has to represent the 'real' color of object surface. In terms of radiometry the color or more precise the spectral reflectance of surface is specified by its BRDF. Thus an accurate signal model in context of *Under Water Vision* has to represent the spectral reflectance, i.e. the BRDF of object surface.

The figure beside illustrates the geometrical properties of the reflectance signal model. The object surface at an object point $\vec{x}$ is irradiated by one or more light sources. The reflected radiance depends on the BRDF at the point $\vec{x}$. An under water adapted signal model have to represent the BRDF of the object surface.

4.1.2 Transfer Model

An important part for future work is the derivation of an efficient computable transfer model, which approximates the radiative transfer (see section 2). There is a tradeoff between accuracy and computational performance in modeling radiative transfer. The principles of radiative transfer and their approximations are described in section 2.

Another aspect of transfer model is its dependency on parameters like object geometry and water properties, i.e. absorption coefficient, scattering coefficient and volume scattering function. All these parameters must be estimated to get an accurate image restoration filter.

Figure 4.3: Image of an alley of trees at a hazy day (left image) and the estimated depth image from dark channel prior.

4.1.3 Depth Estimation

The distance between object surface and camera is crucial for degradation effects like contrast reduction, color shifting and image blur. To restore image content, depth estimation, i.e. an estimation of the distance to the object surface has to be done. In context of *Under Water Vision*, there are different approaches to be possible for depth estimation.

The first approach mentioned here is depth estimation by disparity. One scene point can be projected at different image points in different image planes of different cameras. The distance to the scene point can be calculated by the disparity of the image points by known location camera relations, i.e. by known extrinsic and intrinsic camera parameters. The main difficulty of depth estimation by disparity is to find corresponding image points.

Another approach of Kaiming He et.al. [HST10] takes local contrast hints into account. They estimate the depth of objects by using the brightening nature of backscattering and a so called dark channel prior. He et. al. assume that in every image patch one dark scene point is imaged. With this assumption, they developed an image restoration by haze removal approach with depth estimation as byproduct. Figure 4.3 shows exemplary results of their depth estimation.

Future approaches can be developed towards information fusion by merging results of both, depth by disparity and depth by using dark channel prior.

4.1.4 Estimation of Water Properties

Effects of blurring and contrast reduction depend on distance between camera and object as well as on water properties. As described in section 2 absorption

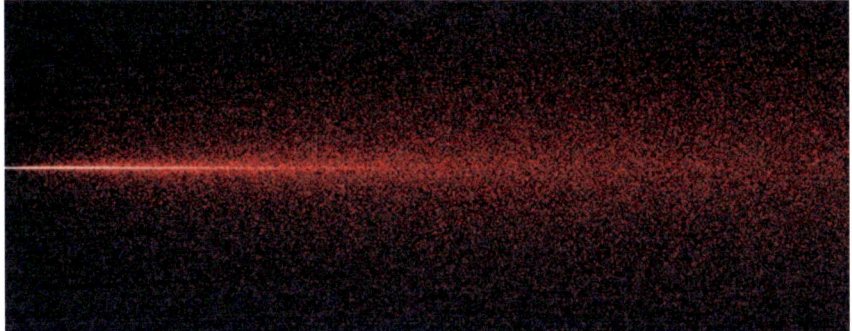

Figure 4.4: Simulation of spread laser beam by scattering.

and scattering plays an important role for radiative transfer and thus for image degradation.

An idea to a future approach is the property estimation by appearance of different laser beams. Laser beams are attenuated by absorption and spread by scattering. Thus it is obvious to assume, that these properties can be estimated by the appearance of an imaged laser beams. Figure 4.4 shows a simulation of a spread laser beam by a scattering media.

5   Summary

The thematic of *Under Water Vision* is highly complex and interesting. The exploit of the potential of optical imaging systems is the task presented in this report. The work of restoring images and therefore the increasing of visibility under water is in an early phase. But the possibilities of computational imaging for underwater tasks are wide and promising. The way forward in context of *Under Water Vision* is to pursue the depicted ideas of system modeling, depth estimation and the estimation of the water properties.

Bibliography

[Cha60]   Subrahmanyan Chandrasekhar. *Radiative transfer*. Dover, New York, 1960.

[HST10]   Kaiming He, Jian Sun, and Xiaoou Tang. Single Image Haze Removal Using Dark Channel Prior. *IEEE Transactions on Pattern Analysis and Machine Intelligence*, 2010.

[Ish78]   Akira Ishimaru. *Wave propagation and scattering in random media*. Academic Pr., New York, 1978.

[Jäh05]   Bernd Jähne. *Digitale Bildverarbeitung*. Springer, Berlin, 6., überarbeitete und erw edition, 2005.

[Mob94]   Curtis D. Mobley. *Light and water: Radiative transfer in natural waters*. Academic Press, San Diego, 1994.

[NN09]   Srinivasa G. Narasimhan and Shree K. Nayar. Analytic Rendering of Multiple Scattering in Participating Media, 15.10.2009.

[Wel69]   Willard H. Wells. Loss of Resolution in Water as a Result of Multiple Small-Angle Scattering. *Journal of the Optical Society of America*, 59(6):686, 1969.

Catadioptric illumination device for capturing hemispherical illumination series

Robin Gruna

Vision and Fusion Laboratory
Institute for Anthropomatics
Karlsruhe Institute of Technology (KIT), Germany
robin.gruna@kit.edu

Technical Report IES-2011-06

Abstract: The choice of an appropriate illumination design is one of the most important steps in creating successful machine vision systems for automated inspection tasks. In a widely used technique, inspection images are captured under angular-varying illumination directions over the hemisphere, which yields a set of images referred to as illumination series. However, these approaches are restricted in that they use rather simple illumination patterns like point- or sector-shaped illumination patterns on the hemisphere. In this report, we present a catadioptric illumination device that is able to illuminate small objects with arbitrary complex illumination patterns. To this end, we model and utilize a parabolic projection from the sphere to the plane, which allows to use an ordinary digital projector as computational light source. In order to be able to control the spectrum of the illumination, we also investigate the photometric properties of the utilized projector-camera system.

1 Introduction

Imaging and analyzing objects under different illumination directions has long been an active research area in both machine vision and computer graphics. While computer graphics aim to synthesize realistic images from appearance models, machine vision addresses the problem of deducing properties of a scene based on its appearance. Therefore, many algorithms from both disciplines rely on an accurate analysis of how light over an illuminating hemisphere reflects off surfaces and how the appearance of a scene depends on different illumination conditions. However, most of the existing approaches from the literature use rather simple and unspecific illumination patterns like point- or sector-shaped patterns on an illuminating hemisphere [LPL07][WGSD09][JSJ10][GB11].

In this technical report, we present an acquisition device to image objects under extended and arbitrary complex illumination patterns over the hemisphere. We restrict ourselves to the case of a distant illuminating light field, i.e., the incident illumination only varies directionally and thus is spatially constant across the illuminated object. Thus, we define the illuminating light field as function

$$L \colon \Omega^+ \to \mathbb{R}^+$$

over the upper illuminating hemisphere $\Omega^+ := [0, \pi/2] \times [0, 2\pi)$, which describes the incident radiance ($[L] = \mathrm{W/sr \cdot m^2}$) reaching the object from direction $\boldsymbol{\omega} := (\theta, \phi) \in \Omega^+$. The device utilizes a parabolic mirror to direct illumination patterns emitted by a digital projector onto the object to be investigated (see Figure 2.1). At the same time, the appearance of the object is captured with a color camera with fixed viewpoint.

2 Catadioptric Illumination Device

In order to capture illumination series with extended illumination patterns over the hemisphere, we developed a catadioptric illumination device which is shown schematically in Figure 2.1a. The device is able to image small objects with a diameter up to 20 mm under arbitrary hemispherical illumination patterns. To this end, the object is placed at the focal point of a parabolic mirror and is illuminated by a digital light projector. At the same time, we capture high dynamic range images of the object from a fixed camera position. Jehle et al. [JSJ10] use a very similar device in their work. However, our device, developed independently, differs in a wax coating of the parabolic mirror to obtain a more homogeneous illumination of the object under study.

The projector serves as programmable light source that allows controlling the relative radiance along the emitted light rays independently. Assuming a pinhole model for the projector, each projector pixel can be thought of as source of individual light rays that diverge from the optical center of the projector. By placing the projector at the focal point of the Fresnel lens, the diverging light rays from the projector are converted into parallel rays so that an orthographic light field is obtained.

The parabolic reflector is then used to transform the orthographic light field beyond the Fresnel lens. By ensuring that the light field is parallel to the optical axis of the reflector, the light rays are reflected so that they intersect at the focal point F of the parabolic reflector. Since the parabolic reflector can be described by a regular paraboloid, and incident and reflected light rays are coplanar with the optical axis, only a planar cross-section of the reflector must be considered (see Figure 2.1b).

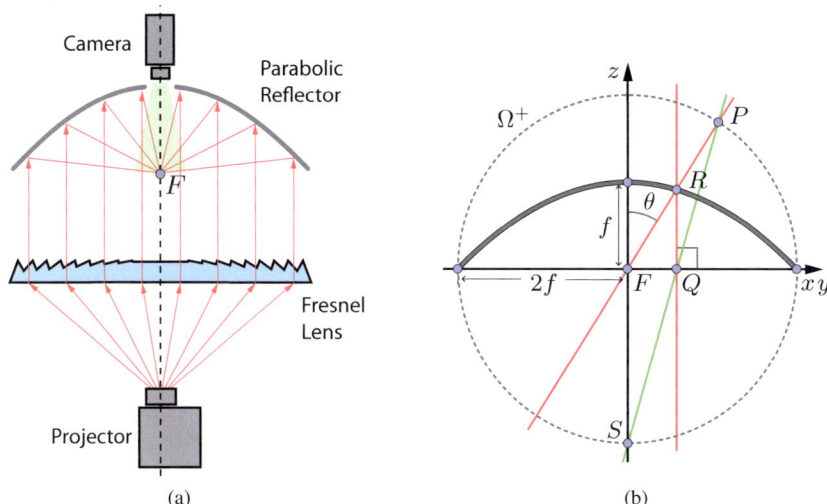

Figure 2.1: (a) Catadioptric illumination device for illuminating small objects with arbitrary hemispherical illumination patterns. A digital LCD projector, a Fresnel lens, a parabolic reflector with a center hole and a digital camera are aligned along their optical axes. By placing the optical center of the projector at the focal point of the Fresnel lens, all emitted light rays intersect at the focal point F of the reflector. (b) Schematic x-z-section through the parabolic reflector's center F. A ray QR parallel to the parabola's axis is reflected to the ray RF incident to the focal point F of the parabola. A point P on the hemisphere Ω^+ can be mapped to the corresponding point Q on the projector image plane (x-y-plane) by *parabolic projection* (red lines) or via *stereographic projection* (green line) from the sphere's south pole S.

We establish a Cartesian coordinate system with its origin at the focal point F of the parabolic reflector and its z-axis aligned with the optical axis of the device, pointing into the direction of the camera. Hence, the surface of the parabolic mirror can be described by the graph

$$\left\{ (x, y, z) \colon f - \frac{x^2 + y^2}{4f} - z = 0 \right\},$$

where f denotes the focal length of the reflector.

A x-z-slice through the parabolic reflector is schematically illustrated in Figure 2.1b. We refer to the x-y-plane as the *projector image plane* of the orthographic projection system and identify points in this plane by projector pixel coordinates. A light ray from the projector pixel Q parallel to the optical axis is reflected at R and passes through the focal point F. In order to illustrate the fact that the illumination device is able to produce arbitrary hemispherical illumination patterns $L(\boldsymbol{\omega})$, we consider the upper hemisphere of illumination directions Ω^+ that has radius $2f$ and is centered at F. Then there is a one-to-one correspondence between the ray QR, originating in the projector image plane, to the virtual light ray PF, originating at the point P on the hemisphere Ω^+.

In order to physically generate arbitrary hemispherical illumination patterns, we need to transform the desired hemispherical light field $L(\boldsymbol{\omega})$ to the projector image plane. To this end, we consider the back-projection Q of the point P, which is the orthographic projection of the intersection R of the parabola and the virtual ray FP. This projection is referred to as *parabolic projection* [HS99] and can be used to parameterize directions over the hemisphere in a plane. Geyer at al. [GD01] showed, that the parabolic projection is equivalent to the well-known *stereographic projection* [Nee97], which is additionally illustrate in Figure 2.1b.

To obtain a simple transformation rule for the parabolic projection, we identify points on the hemisphere Ω^+ using spherical coordinates, i.e., $P = (\theta, \phi)$ where $(\theta, \phi) \in \Omega^+$, and points in the projector image plane (x-y-plane) in polar coordinates, i.e., $Q = (\rho, \varphi)$ where $(\rho, \varphi) \in [0, 2f] \times [0, 2\pi)$. Since for the polar angle θ the following trigonometric relationship

$$\tan \theta = \frac{|FQ|}{|RQ|} = \frac{\rho}{f - \frac{\rho^2}{4f}}$$

is true, the transformation $\Phi \colon \Omega^+ \to [0, 2f] \times [0, 2\pi)$ from the illuminating hemisphere to the projector image plane can be expressed as

$$(\theta, \phi) \mapsto \left(2f \tan \left(\frac{\theta}{2} \right), \varphi \right) .$$

Note that due to the position of the camera, the polar angle θ in the presented device is limited to $\theta_{\min}$ to prevent a direct illumination of the camera. To sum up, we are able to produce arbitrary illumination patterns by emitting the parabolic projection of $L(\boldsymbol{\omega})$ to the projector image plane.

3   Photometric Description of Illumination Device

Besides the directional characteristics, the illumination device is able to control the spectrum of the illuminating light field by utilizing the color-forming mechanism

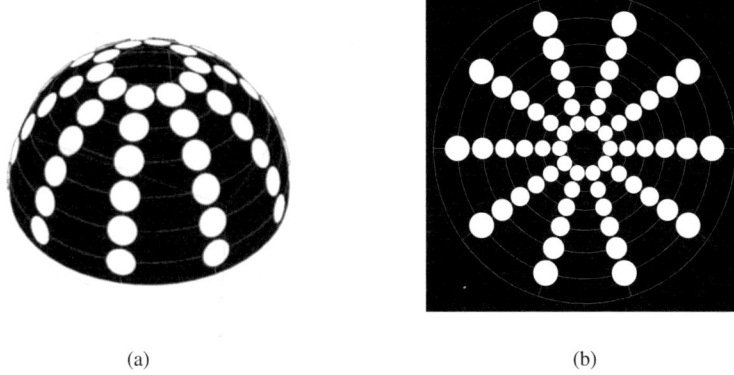

(a)   (b)

Figure 2.2: (a) Impulse-like illumination patterns on the hemisphere. (b) Parabolic projection of the hemispherical illumination pattern shown in (a). Since the parabolic projection is conformal, the shape of circles are conserved, however, their radii increases with increasing polar angle.

of the digital light projector. In our work, we use a LCD projector that employs three liquid-crystal display chips and dichroic mirrors to produce a 3-channel color images. Thus, the emitted radiance of the projector is composed of three spectrally distinct light sources, one for each color channel. The light's spectrum can be represented as

$$w(\lambda) = \sum_{k \in \{R,G,B\}} p_k w_k(\lambda), \tag{3.1}$$

where λ is the wavelength in the visible spectrum and $w_k(\lambda)$ denotes the spectral power distribution corresponding to color channel $k \in \{R, G, B\}$. The projector channels are weighted by the coefficients p_k, which represent the brightnesses of the individual color channels.

Since we use a color camera to image an illuminated object, the color channels of the camera and the projector interact with each other. This is illustrated by the following simple experiment: we place a white calibration panel at the focal point F of the parabolic mirror and sequentially project 256 (since we are using an 8-bit per channel projector) pure color images with increasing brightness for each projector color channel. For each projected brightness, we capture a high-dynamic range image containing relative radiance measurements and compute the channel-wise mean vector of the image. The results are illustrated in Figure 3.1, and obviously,

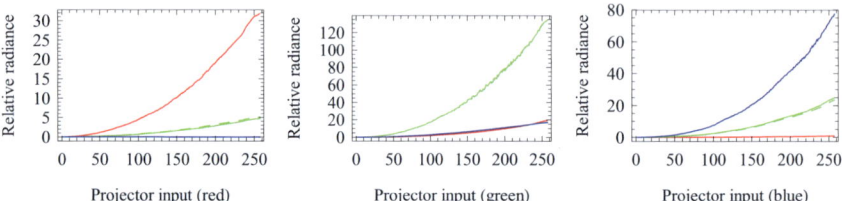

Figure 3.1: Camera response to increasing projector brightness. The brightness of each projector channel is increased separately, while the remaining channels stay turned off.

there is a significant amount of crosstalk between the color channels of the camera and the projector. Furthermore, it can be seen that the measured relative radiance values respond non-linearly to the projector inputs. Since we use a camera with a linear intensity response function, the non-linear response is due to the intensity transfer function of the projector. The intensity transfer function relates the pixel values (in digital numbers) in the projector input image to the brightnesses of the individual color channels.

Usually, this mapping is non-linear (but monotonic) and mimics the gamma function of a traditional cathode ray tube display. For the purpose of photometric characterization of the illumination device, it is desirable to obtain a linear relationship between projector input and camera response. We assume that the projector intensity transfer function is spatially invariant but different for each projector color channel. To linearize the illumination device, the intensity transfer function has to be acquired and its inverse must be applied to the projector input. In our experiments, we utilize a colorimeter[1] for projector profiling in order to create a profile with linear gamma function. The profile is then used to calibrate the projector by specifying a Look-Up Table (LUT) which is then loaded into the video card's memory.

To verify our approach, we sequentially project 256 pure color images with increasing brightness for each projector color channel and evaluate the corresponding camera images. The measured relative radiance values are shown in Figure 3.2. Now, with the projector calibration, an almost linear response behaviour of the projector-camera system can be observed.

As result of the projector calibration, we assume a linear intensity transfer and response function for the projector and the camera, respectively. This allows to

---

[1] Datacolor Spyder3Elite[TM]

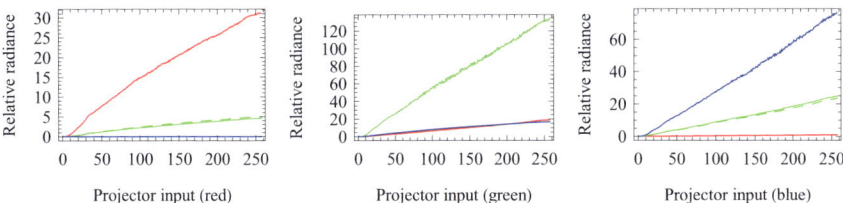

Figure 3.2: Camera response to increasing projector brightness, where the projector is calibrated to a linear gamma curve. The brightness of each projector channel is increased separately, while the remaining channels stay turned off.

apply the linear photometric model from [GPNB04] [NPGB03], which is

$$c_j = \int p_k w_k(\lambda) q_j(\lambda) s(\lambda) \, d\lambda. \tag{3.2}$$

Therein, p_k denotes the projector brightness for color channel $k \in \{R, G, B\}$; likewise c_j denotes the measured irradiance in color channel $j \in \{R, G, B\}$ due to the projector channel k. As in Equation (3.1), $w_k(\lambda)$ denotes the spectral power distribution of projector channel k and $q_j(\lambda)$ denotes the spectral quantum efficient function of camera channel j. The spectral reflectance of the calibration panel is $s(\lambda)$, for which we assume $s(\lambda) = 1$, since we are using an ideal white calibration panel. With this, the photometric model in (3.2) becomes

$$c_j = p_k \underbrace{\int w_k(\lambda) q_j(\lambda) \, d\lambda}_{=:V_{kj}}$$

and can be rewritten for multiple color channels simultaneously in vector-matrix form as

$$\mathbf{c} = \mathbf{V} \cdot \mathbf{p}, \tag{3.3}$$

with $\mathbf{c} = (c_R, c_G, c_B)^T$ and $\mathbf{p} = (p_R, p_G, p_B)^T$. The matrix $\mathbf{V} = (V_{kj})$ is referred to as the *color-mixing matrix* [NPGB03] and describes the crosstalk in the illumination device owing to broad and overlapping spectral distribution functions of the projector and camera color channels.

Due to the linearization of the projector-camera system, we assume that the captured pixel values (in digital numbers) in a given camera channel are linear in irradiance c_j and that the brightnesses p_k of the projector channels are linear in their input.

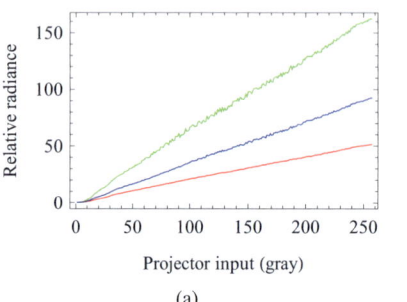
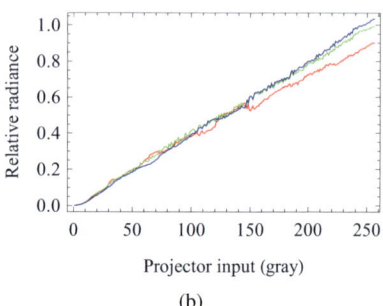

(a)	(b)

Figure 3.3: Camera response to achromatic projector brightnesses (i.e., $p_R = p_G = p_B$) without (a) and with color correction (b).

Therefore, we can produce corresponding pairs $\{\mathbf{p}_l, \mathbf{c}_l\}$, $l = 1, \ldots, n$ of projected brightness values and measured irradiance values by projecting different uniform color images and capturing the corresponding images. As before, $\mathbf{p}_l$ and $\mathbf{c}_l$ denote the channel-wise mean vectors of the images. In order to determine the color-mixing matrix $\mathbf{V}$ of the illumination device, we capture $n \geq 9$ image pairs and arrange them in the matrices $\mathbf{P} = [\mathbf{p}_1, \mathbf{p}_2, \ldots, \mathbf{p}_n]$ and $\mathbf{C} = [\mathbf{c}_1, \mathbf{c}_2, \ldots, \mathbf{c}_n]$. Then, if $\mathbf{P}^T\mathbf{P}$ is invertible, it follows from Equation (3.3) that we can compute a least squares estimate of the matrix $\mathbf{V}$ by

$$\hat{\mathbf{V}} = \mathbf{C} \cdot \mathbf{P}^+$$

where $\mathbf{P}^+ = (\mathbf{P}^T\mathbf{P})^{-1}\mathbf{P}$ is the Moore-Penrose pseudoinverse of $\mathbf{P}$. Note that the projected color images must not come from the gray axis only (i.e., $p_R = p_G = p_B$), otherwise $\mathbf{P}^T\mathbf{P}$ becomes singular and thus non-invertible.

The estimated color-mixing matrix $\hat{\mathbf{V}}$ describes the mutual crosstalk between the projector and camera channels and therefore delivers a photometric description of the illumination device. For instance, we can use $\hat{\mathbf{V}}$ to perform color correction to the captured camera images. The need for color correction becomes clear from the measurements illustrated in Figure 3.3a. Here, 256 achromatic brightnesses (i.e., uniform gray images with $p_R = p_G = p_B$) with brightness from 0 to 255 were projected and images of the white calibration panel were captured. As shown, the individual channel values differ in their values and thus, the calibration panel does not appear white in the camera's color space due to a shift toward green and blue. To compensate for this color cast and to make the calibration panel appear with neutral color, we define the color correction matrix

$$\mathbf{B} := \hat{\mathbf{V}}^{-1}$$

as the inverse of the color-mixing matrix. Then, the transformation

$$\mathbf{c}' = \mathbf{B} \cdot \mathbf{c}$$

applied to the camera output yields corrected channel values, so that the white calibration panel appears neutral under all achromatic projector brightnesses (i.e., $p_R = p_G = p_B$). This is illustrated in Figure 3.3, where the color correction has been applied to the captured camera channel values in Figure 3.3a. As it can be seen, for achromatic projector brightnesses, nearly equal camera channel values $c_R = c_G = c_B$ are produced and the calibration panel is captured with the desired neutral colors.

4   Summary and Outlook

We have presented a catadioptric illumination device that is able to illuminate small objects with arbitrary complex illumination patterns. In a geometric analysis, we showed that hemispherical illumination functions can be physically realized by utilizing a parabolic projection to obtain a planar representation of the hemispherical function. Furthermore, the photometric properties of the illumination device were evaluated and summarized in form of a color-mixing matrix, which describes the mutual crosstalk between projector and camera channels. The color-mixing matrix provides the basis for our further studies in which we will investigate spectrally-adapted hemispherical illumination patterns.

Bibliography

[GB11]   Robin Gruna and Jürgen Beyerer. Acquisition and evaluation of illumination series for unsupervised defect detection. In *Proc. IEEE Instrumentation and Measurement Technology Conference*, pages 192–197, Hangzhou, China, 2011.

[GD01]   C. Geyer and K. Daniilidis. Catadioptric projective geometry. *International Journal of Computer Vision*, 45(3):223–243, 2001.

[GPNB04] M.D. Grossberg, H. Peri, S.K. Nayar, and P.N. Belhumeur. Making one object look like another: Controlling appearance using a projector-camera system. In *Computer Vision and Pattern Recognition, 2004. CVPR 2004. Proceedings of the 2004 IEEE Computer Society Conference on*, volume 1, pages I–452. IEEE, 2004.

[HS99]   Wolfgang Heidrich and Hans-Peter Seidel. Realistic, hardware-accelerated shading and lighting. In *Proceedings of the 26th annual conference on Computer graphics and interactive techniques*, SIGGRAPH '99, pages 171–178, New York, NY, USA, 1999. ACM Press/Addison-Wesley Publishing Co.

[JSJ10]   Markus Jehle, Christoph Sommer, and Bernd Jähne. Learning of optimal illumination for material classification. In Michael Goesele, Stefan Roth, Arjan Kuijper, Bernt Schiele, and Konrad Schindler, editors, *Pattern Recognition*, volume 6376 of *Lecture Notes in Computer Science*, pages 563–572. Springer Berlin / Heidelberg, 2010.

[LPL07]   C. Lindner and F. Puente Leon. Model-Based segmentation of surfaces using illumination series. *Instrumentation and Measurement, IEEE Transactions on*, 56(4):1340–1346, 2007.

[Nee97]   T. Needham. *Visual complex analysis*. Oxford University Press, USA, 1997.

[NPGB03]   S.K. Nayar, H. Peri, M.D. Grossberg, and P.N. Belhumeur. A projection system with radiometric compensation for screen imperfections. In *ICCV Workshop on Projector-Camera Systems (PROCAMS)*, volume 3. Citeseer, 2003.

[WGSD09]   O. Wang, P. Gunawardane, S. Scher, and J. Davis. Material classification using BRDF slices. In *Computer Vision and Pattern Recognition, IEEE Computer Society Conference on*, volume 0, pages 2805–2811, Los Alamitos, CA, USA, 2009. IEEE Computer Society.

Integrated Multi-Sensor Fusion and SLAM for Mobile Robots

Thomas Emter

Vision and Fusion Laboratory
Institute for Anthropomatics
Karlsruhe Institute of Technology (KIT), Germany
thomas.emter@iosb.fraunhofer.de

Technical Report IES-2011-07

Abstract: To perform simultaneous localization and mapping (SLAM) mobile robots are equipped with several sensors. In order to precisely localize the robot while concurrently building a map of the environment, the information from all sensors has to be fused adequately. A flexible framework for integrated multi-sensor fusion and mapping, which is capable of combining different sensor configurations for diverse environments, is presented in this paper.

1 Introduction

because all sensor measurements are noisy, several sensors have to be used for self localization of a mobile robot. The fusion of measurements of motion and position sensors like odometry or GPS respectively can improve the self-localization of a mobile robot [EFK08].

In addition, sensors which observe the environment like a laser scanner or camera can be used for localization in a map. For navigation, a map is also advantageous as it provides the possibility of path planning beyond the actual sensor coverage. To build a precise and correct map, the robot has to simultaneously localize itself in the so far registered map which contains errors and has to update it continuously by current sensor data. As all data suffers from noise, the map becomes inconsistent unless the dependencies between the uncertainty in the pose, the uncertainty in the measurements and the errors in the map are taken into account. By observing and recognizing areas or features of the map several times, the uncertainties in the map are decreased and the map converges to a better solution. Several approaches of

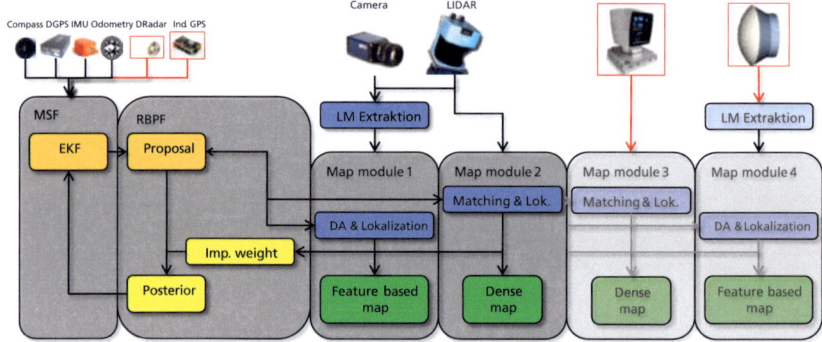

Figure 2.1: Integrated fusion framework.

probabilistic mapping exist to solve this so called simultaneous localization and mapping (SLAM) problem [DWB06a] and [DWB06b].

For the integration of multiple heterogeneous sensors, a probabilistic fusion framework has been developed combining methods of multi-sensor fusion to incorporate the motion, position, and attitude sensors with a SLAM algorithm capable of integrating several sensors, which observe the enviornment, and corresponding maps.

2 Integrated Multi-Sensor Fusion Framework

The fusion framework proposed in [Emt11] is shown in Figure 2.1. In the top left corner the motion, position, and attitude sensors are shown. They are fused in an Extended-Kalman Filter (EKF), which is explained in in more detail in [ESP10]. Its estimate serves as prior probability density for a SLAM algorithm as proposal distribution. As SLAM algorithm a Rao-Blackwellized particle filter (RBPF) based on [MTKW03] was chosen, due to its property of conditional independence between the landmarks, which enables a straightforward integration of a landmark model comprised of statistically independent attributes as presented in [EU10]. Furthermore, it allows to integrate and combine several maps like a dense map as presented in Section 3 as map modules. The combination of maps can be seen as map layers with different levels of abstraction of the same area, each one containing information provided by a certain sensor. The framework is designed for straightforward extensibility with additional position or motion sensors like an

IMU as well as other mapping sensors like a 3D laser scanner with according map modules all marked in red in Figure 2.1.

3 Combination of Landmark-based and Dense Maps

A feature map is built from specific features in the environment, called landmarks, which have to be extracted from the sensor data. In comparison dense maps like grid maps can be built directly from raw laser scanner data.

3.1 Feature-Based Mapping

Feature-based maps can be advantageous in cluttered environments, where spurious sensor measurements not originating from a feature can be omitted. As landmarks are most commonly described only by their position, the estimated position of the landmark depends on the pose uncertainty of the robot. In case of a high pose uncertainty of the robot, it can be difficult to distinguish landmarks being close together, as it may lead to an ambiguous data association between current observations and the landmarks in the map. The data association of landmarks can be improved, if the landmarks are additionally described by attributes being statistically independent of the position. Further details on the augmented landmark model and its integration in a particle filter SLAM algorithm can be found in [EU10].

3.1.1 Augmented Landmark Model

To achieve a robust data association in case of ambiguous situations, an augmented landmark model has been developed. This augmented landmark model consists not only of the position but also of additional geometric information and a visual signature. Both additional attributes are considered to be independent of the landmark's position.

Being developed for use in outdoor applications, the model describes vertical cylindrical objects like tree trunks, pillars or lamp posts. The common point landmark model (n, e), with north and east, is augmented with the horizontal dimension r, denoting the radius of the landmark, and a visual signature v, which consists of a normalized HSV-histogram, calculated from the image content inside a rectangular region derived from the position and radius of the landmark. The radius of a landmark is independent of the landmark's position and the visual signature is assumed to be invariant under changes in the direction of view, hence it does not depend on the position of observation.

3.1.2   Data Association

In order to associate an observation to an existing landmark in the map the likelihood is used as a statistical distance measure. The features of the described landmark model can be split into metric features $z_{m,k}$ and the visual signature $z_{v,k}$, which is statistically independent of the mobile robot's pose. Therefore, the overall likelihood for each particle $[l]$ can be divided into two parts

$$p\left(z_{ges,k}|s^{k-1,[l]}, z_{ges}^{k-1}, u^k, n^{k,[l]}\right) =$$

$$\underbrace{p\left(z_{m,k}|s^{k-1,[l]}, z_m^{k-1}, u^k, n^{k,[l]}\right)}_{p_m} \cdot \underbrace{p\left(z_{v,k}|z_v^{k-1}, n^{k,[l]}\right)}_{p_v}.$$

It is calculated by the multiplication of the likelihood of the metric features p_m and the likelihood of the visual signature p_v, whereas p_v is independent of the robot's localization.

The continuous metric features are assumed to be normally distributed, and the likelihood p_m can be computed as proposed in [MT07]. Whereas the visual signature is has a multi modal distribution defined by a 2D-histogram q calculated from the aforementioned HSV-histogram. The likelihood between a histogram $\hat{q}$ of an already known landmark in the map and the visual signature of a landmark q of the current observation can be calculated by

$$p_v = \exp\left\{-\lambda\, D\left(\hat{q}, q\right)\right\} \tag{3.1}$$

with $D\left(\hat{q}, q\right) = 1 - \sum_{b=1}^{B}\sqrt{\hat{q}\left(b\right) \cdot q\left(b\right)}$, where b denotes the histogram's bins. The distance D was derived from the Bhattacharyya-distance and was introduced by [PHVG02], who also proved that it conforms to a metric. As in [CRM00] the parameter λ was chosen to 20. Consequently, the likelihood of an observation can be calculated in a closed form .

Finally, the data association is performed with a maximum-likelihood estimator:

$$\hat{n}_k^{[l]} = \underset{n_k^{[l]}}{\arg\max}\; p_m \cdot p_v \tag{3.2}$$

For every particle, the likelihood between the current observation and each landmark is calculated. The landmark, which belongs to the maximum likelihood, is assigned with the current observation, while accounting for mutual exclusion. The estimation of the data association is stored in $\hat{n}$. Data associations obtained by the proposed scheme are more robust, as the likelihood calculation involves additional pose independent attributes and thus not only depends on the robot's pose uncertainty.

3.2 Grid Mapping

Grid mapping has the advantage that no assumption about the environment has to be made. In well-structured areas where plane or smooth objects like straight walls predominate, grid mapping leads to very accurate results. An occupancy grid map was used, where each cell contains the probability of occupancy, i.e. , the higher the probability the more likely the cell is occupied by an object. To build this map a ray cast of every beam is performed and in all cells it passes through, the probability is decreased except for the last cell. The probability in the last cell is increased as the beam is most likely reflected by an object.

The integration of grid mapping into particle filter SLAM is based on [GSB07]. In this approach the incorporation of the robots' localization into the proposal distribution is accomplished by scan matching. The scan matching process uses a hill climbing search per particle in order to find the maximum of the likelihood function of the current observation given the grid map.

To calculate this likelihood function, a scheme using a modified beam endpoint (BEP) model was used [TBF05]. For every beam endpoint the euclidic distance to the nearest occupied cell is determined and a likelihood over all beams of one scan is calculated. The modified BEP model covers for the fact that the laser beams are diverging with traveled distance. In addition, dividing the environment into cells introduces artifacts depending on the cell size, which is also accounted for. Assuming a uniform distribution, the variance σ^2 of the observation of a cell with a laser beam is calculated by

$$\sigma_j^2 = \left((r_j/d)^2 + (c)^2 \right)/12, \tag{3.3}$$

with r_j being the range of the jth beam and d being a factor accounting for the beam divergence. c denotes the cell size. The score ξ of the whole scan consisting of J beams is calculated by:

$$\xi = \prod_{j=1}^{J} \frac{1}{\sqrt{2\pi}\sigma_j} e^{-\frac{1}{2}\left(\frac{\Delta_j}{\sigma_j}\right)^2}, \tag{3.4}$$

with Δ_j being the distance of beam j to the nearest occupied cell. Apart from being used for localization, the likelihood function also allows for the calculation of the importance weights.

3.3 Combination of Feature-based and Dense Mapping

In unstructured outdoor environments with vegetation cover, laser beams are often reflected stochastically depending on the density of the foliage. For feature-based mapping, robust features are extracted and thus scattered or spurious measurements from jagged surfaces or foliage are omitted. On the other hand, models of objects in the environment have to be assumed, which can be absent in some areas. Areas lacking the expected features can lead to inaccuracies or even to failure of the mapping process as the robot has to travel blindly, i.e. , without the ability to localize itself in the map.

In mixed environments the mentioned disadvantages can be alleviated by a combination of the presented mapping strategies. In areas where no features can be observed the grid map supports the localization of the robot whereas in unstructured areas the extracted features increase the accuracy of the localization and the map respectively. As both mapping strategies are incorporated into a RBPF framework, the combination of both representations into a common coordinate system is straightforward: The map types can be assumed to be conditionally independent and both allow to calculate importance weights. Also, they both allow for the localization estimation of the robot for the refinement of the proposal as it is used in the FastSLAM 2.0 algorithm. For both mapping strategies the calculation of the importance weights results from the likelihoods used for localization.

3.4 Results of Feature-based Mapping

To validate the augmented landmark model, the recorded data has been processed with and without additional features. As proved in [MT07] the FastSLAM 2.0 algorithm has the property to be able converge with only one particle. The results of the course for one particle with the augmented landmark model is shown in Figure 3.1. The red line depicts the ground truth. The landmarks are shown with their number and their error ellipses for 3σ interval are drawn in blue. The position of the robot at the end of the course is depicted with a blue arrow. The arrow is located very close to the ground truth, and the map consists of 12 landmarks, which all have been recognized properly. This demonstrates that a robust data association greatly improves the mapping process. In case of using the standard point model for the landmarks without the additional information the the algorithm was not able to build a correct map with only one particle. As the main focus has been on robust features and several situations occurred where no features where observable, in only 20% of the time features could be extracted. For the result with one particle with the standard point model and further evaluations please see [EU10] and [Emt11].

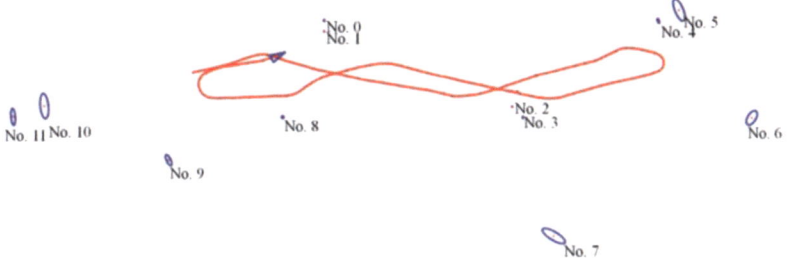

Figure 3.1: Map of one particle with additional features.

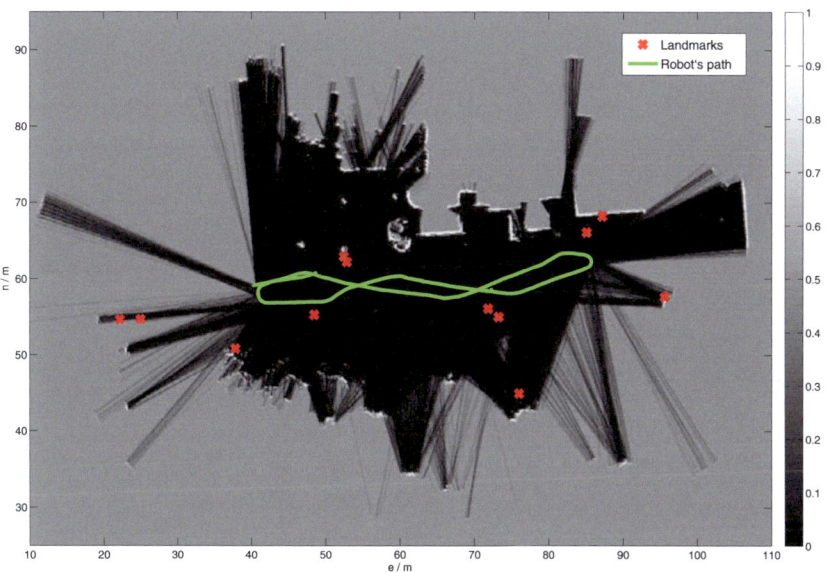

Figure 3.2: Map of one particle with combined mapping.

3.5 Results of Combined Mapping

In Figure 3.2 the result of the combined mapping is shown. The estimated path of the robot is shown in green and the landmarks as red crosses. The probability of occupancy of the cells is coded from free ($= 0$) in black to occupied ($= 1$) in white. The map is initialized with a probability of 0.5 (gray) in all cells, as no information is present at the beginning.

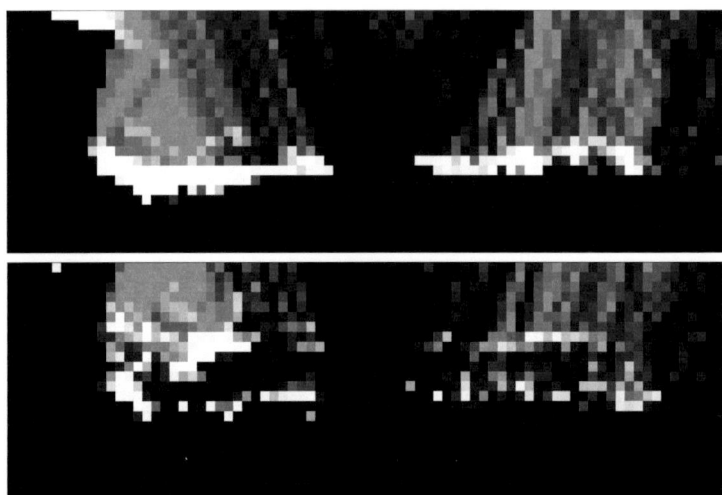

Figure 3.3: Map details of combined approach (top) and landmark only mapping (bottom).

In order to visually compare the combined mapping to the results of the landmark-only mapping described in Section 3.4 a grid map was recorded in parallel without using it for localization in the latter case. In Figure 3.3 a comparison of a detail of both maps is shown. The combined approach on the top shows a higher accuracy in the structure, whereas the landmark-only approach leads to doubling due to small estimation errors in the localization.

Figure 3.4 shows a comparison of the combined approach with grid mapping-only. The combined approach on the left shows a smoother structure, whereas the grid mapping approach leads to spurious outliers.

4   Combination of Multi-Sensor Fusion and SLAM

As mentioned in [MT07] the amount of particles needed for convergence is very hard to determine. It is known, that the larger a loop in the path, the more particles are needed. This emerges from the fact that while traveling along the loop, the mobile robot explores unknown terrain and its pose uncertainty grows. Due to particle resampling and the finite amount of particles this divergence can be coped with only to a certain extent, a fact which is also known as particle depletion.

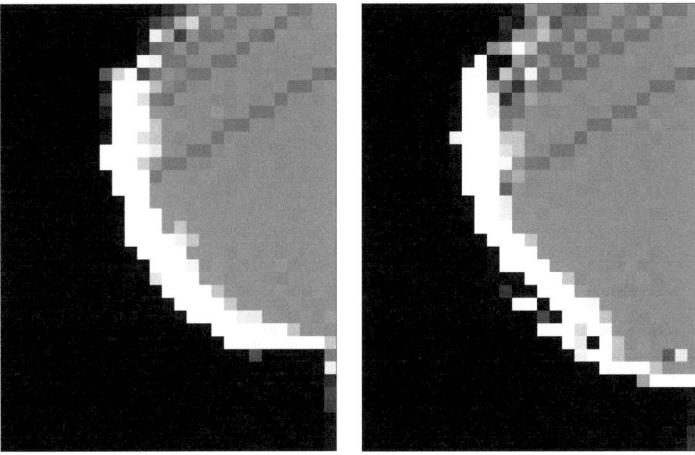

Figure 3.4: Map details of combined approach (left) and grid mapping (right).

A novel approach is proposed to reduce the particle depletion when traveling large loops in outdoor environment by means of combining particle filter SLAM with multi-sensor fusion. The basic idea is to limit the divergence with the aid of additional absolute sensors. The integration of these additional sensors can be accomplished with the fusion framework described in Section 2. Although the SLAM problem has been researched for many years, the combination with multi-sensor fusion has been neglected [Fre10].

The impact of additional sensors was evaluated comparing SLAM with odometry only to SLAM with fusion of odometry, GPS, and compass. In Figure 4.1 the paths of all particles can be seen for SLAM with odometry only in blue and SLAM with fusion of odometry, GPS, and compass in green. For better visualization, the particle resampling was deactivated. The same data set was used in both cases. It can be clearly seen, that the paths estimated with fusion of additional sensors do not diverge as much as the paths with odometry only. When closing the loop, less particles are to be deleted and therefore the particle depletion is reduced. In case of using an adaptive resampling strategy as described in [GSB07] the added absolute information leads to less frequent resampling and thus further reduces the particle depletion. Figure 4.2 shows an occupancy grid map generated by the combined fusion and SLAM algorithm.

As absolute position data is delivered by the GPS and an absolute heading by the compass, the resulting map can be joined with other georeferenced data, like a

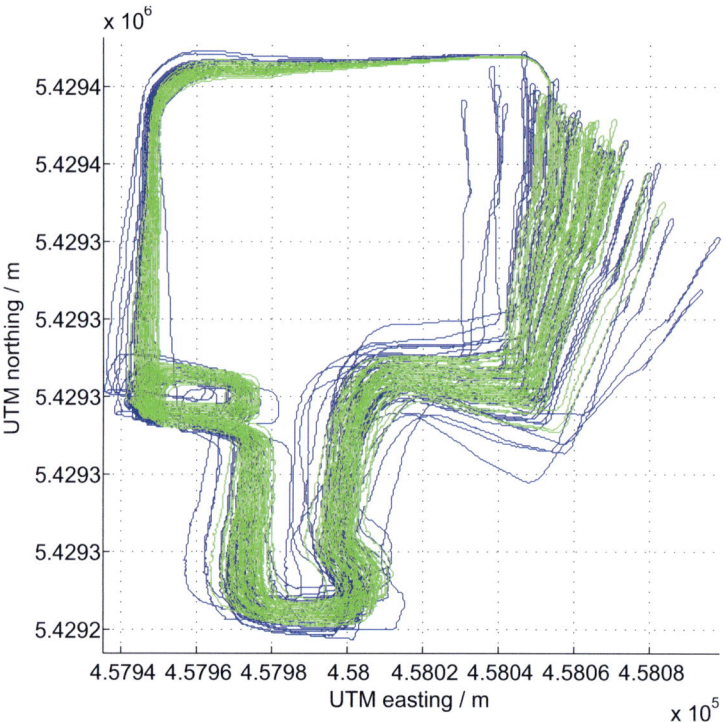

Figure 4.1: Paths of the particles of SLAM with odometry only (blue) and SLAM with fusion of odometry, GPS, and compass (green).

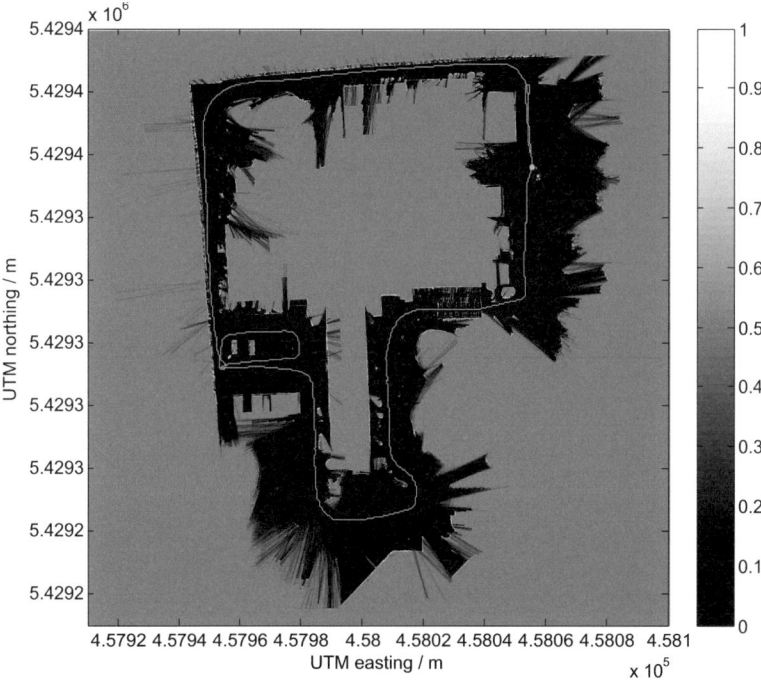

Figure 4.2: Map from fusion of odometry, GPS, and compass combined with SLAM.

satellite image, cf. Figure 4.3. Only the occupied cells (i.e. , the cells with a probability of occupancy greater than 0.5) are shown and depicted in red.

5   Modularity of the Framework

As the integrated fusion framework is designed for modularity, different configurations of sensors can be used. It is only required that a probabilistic model for the measurements of the sensor is provided. In case of sensors observing the environment an adequate map and a localization scheme are also needed.

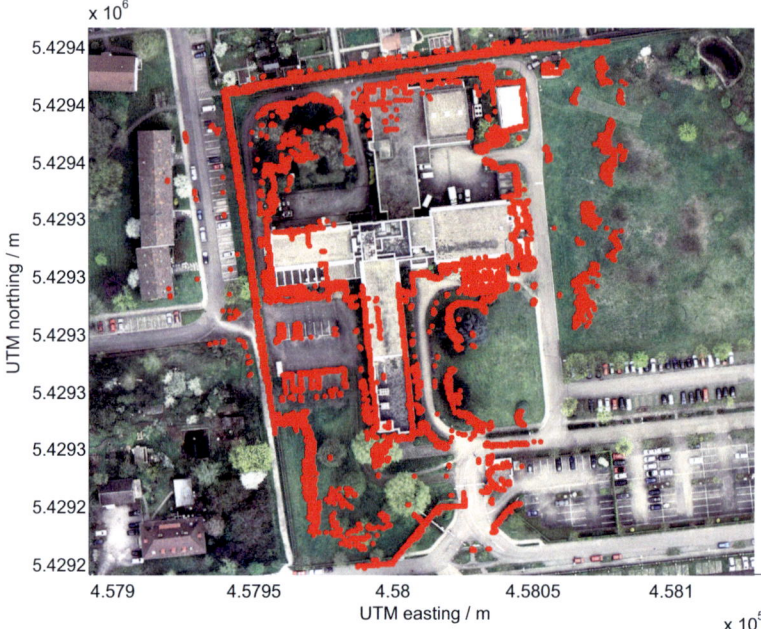

Figure 4.3: Occupied cells in red over georeferenced image.

5.1 SLAM with odometry and Kinect

The Kinect is a very affordable sensor from Microsoft™ for the XBOX 360 gaming console. It provides a 3D point cloud with color information with a rate of up to 30Hz. As the Kinect was designed for the gaming consumer market, it only covers a short range. Furthermore, it is quite susceptible to sunlight and thus only suitable for indoor applications. [Ste11]

As the sensor provides 3D data a colored 3D voxel map was chosen as environment model. The color information can be used as additional matching measure for scan matching. Especially in long corridors where lateral localization with only geometrical data possesses high uncertainty. Figure 5.1 shows a colored 3D grid map of the basement of our institute built with the fusion framework from odometry and Kinect data.

Figure 5.1: 3D voxel Map from SLAM with odometry and Kinect.

5.2 SLAM with IMU and Velodyne

The Velodyne HDL-64E 3D laser scanner has an output rate of 1.3 million points per second. It was combined in the fusion framework with motion estimation with sensor data from an IMU. Motion estimation with only data from an IMU is very challenging as it has a very short-time stability. Thanks to the high output rate of the Velodyne sensor and the SLAM algorithm a precise localization and mapping can be achieved [Rup11]. As efficient 3D model for the environment a multi-level surface (MLS) map was chosen. Compared to 2.5D maps which only store one elevation value per cell these MLS maps allow for modeling of underpasses as they allow to store multiple surfaces in each cell of a grid [TPB06]. The surface elements are built by clustering of the laser points which are located in the considered cell. Each surface element consists of a continuous height and depth bounding the corresponding cluster. On the other hand they allow for more efficient storage of 3D data compared to full 3D gird maps. In Figure 5.2 a multi-level surface 3D map built from IMU and Velodyne data can be seen.

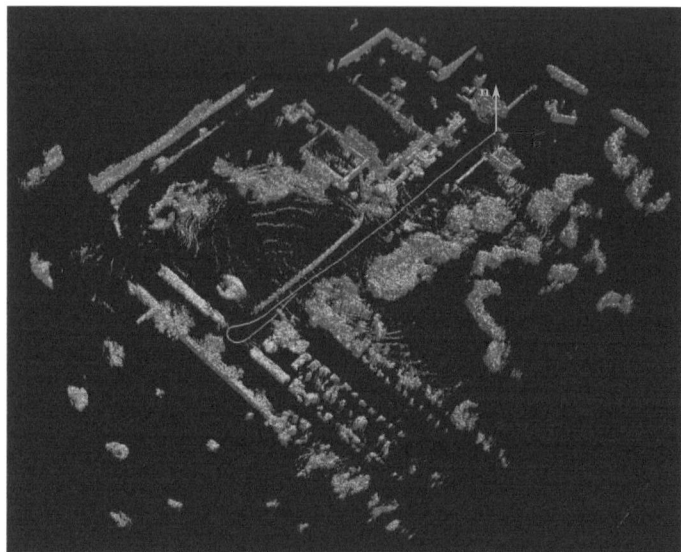

Figure 5.2: Map from SLAM with IMU and Velodyne 3D laser scanner.

6   Conclusion & Outlook

An integrated fusion framework has been presented which allows for incorporation of motion, position and attitude sensors combined with ambient sensors by means of multi-sensor fusion and SLAM. The SLAM algorithm of the fusion framework is based on FastSLAM 2.0 and is capable of combining multi-sensor fusion, feature-based mapping and dense mapping using different configurations of sensors.

The fusion of laser scanner data with images of a camera in the context of mapping and localization for a mobile robot was used to improve the resulting map. The presented strategy is twofold: regarding feature-based mapping, the fusion on sensor data level leads to a more robust data association and thus to a better map. Secondly, combining the extracted features with a grid map on the map level in the fusion framework additionally increases the accuracy of the mapping results.

The integrated fusion with absolute sensors like GPS and compass has been shown to further improve the localization and reduce the impact of the particle depletion caused by resampling. Furthermore the resulting map allows for georeferencing.

Bibliography

[CRM00]   Dorin Comaniciu, Visvanathan Ramesh, and Peter Meer. Real-time tracking of non-rigid objects using mean shift. In *Computer Vision and Pattern Recognition, 2000. Proceedings. IEEE Conference*, volume 2, pages 142–149 vol.2, 2000.

[DWB06a] Hugh Durrant-Whyte and Tim Bailey. Simultaneous localization and mapping: Part I. *IEEE Robotics & Automation Magazine*, 13, June 2006.

[DWB06b] Hugh Durrant-Whyte and Tim Bailey. Simultaneous localization and mapping: Part II. *IEEE Robotics & Automation Magazine*, 13, September 2006.

[EFK08]   Thomas Emter, Christian Frey, and Helge-Björn Kuntze. Multisensorielle Überwachung von Liegenschaften durch mobile Roboter - Multi-Sensor Surveillance of Real Estates Based on Mobile Robots. *Robotik 2008: Leistungsstand - Anwendungen - Visionen - Trends*, June 2008.

[Emt11]   Thomas Emter. Probabilistic Localization and Mapping for Mobile Robots. *Proceedings of the 2010 Joint Workshop of Fraunhofer IOSB and Institute for Anthropomatics, Vision and Fusion Laboratory*, 2011.

[ESP10]   Thomas Emter, Arda Saltoğlu, and Janko Petereit. Multi-Sensor Fusion for Localization of a Mobile Robot in Outdoor Environments. *In Proc. VDE-Verlag: ISR/Robotik 2010: Visions are Reality.*, June 2010.

[EU10]   Thomas Emter and Thomas Ulrich. Visuelle Information zur robusten Zuordnung von Landmarken fuer die Navigation mobiler Roboter. In *Forum Bildverarbeitung. Hrsg.: F. Puente León*, pages 95–106, 2010.

[Fre10]   U. Frese. Interview: Is SLAM solved? In *Künstliche Intelligenz*, volume 24, pages 255 – 257, September 2010.

[GSB07]   Giorgio Grisetti, Cyrill Stachniss, and Wolfram Burgard. Improved Techniques for Grid Mapping with Rao-Blackwellized Particle Filters. *IEEE Transactions on Robotics*, 23, February 2007.

[MT07]   Michael Montemerlo and Sebastian Thrun. *FastSLAM A Scalable Method for the Simultaneous Localization and Mapping Problem in Robotics*, volume 27 of *STAR - Springer Tracts in Advanced Robotics*. Springer Verlag, Berlin Heidelberg New York, 2007.

[MTKW03] Michael Montemerlo, Sebastian Thrun, Daphne Koller, and Ben Wegbreit. FastSLAM 2.0: An Improved Particle Filtering Algorithm for Simultaneous Localization and Mapping that Provably Converges. *Proceedings of the Sixteenth International Joint Conference on Artificial Intelligence (IJCAI)*, 2003.

[PHVG02] Patrick Pérez, Carine Hue, Jaco Vermaak, and Michel Gangnet. Color-Based Probabilistic Tracking. In *ECCV '02: Proceedings of the 7th European Conference on Computer Vision-Part I*, pages 661–675, London, UK, 2002. Springer-Verlag.

[Rup11]   Verena Rupp. Entwicklung eines SLAM-Algorithmus auf Basis von 3D-Laserscans. Master's thesis, Karlsruhe Institute of Technology (KIT), Institute of Photonics and Quantum Electronics (IPQ), 2011.

[Ste11]   Andreas Stein. Entwicklung eines probabilistischen 3D-SLAM-Verfahrens auf Basis des Kinect-Sensors. Master's thesis, Karlsruhe Institute of Technology (KIT), Institute of Photonics and Quantum Electronics (IPQ), 2011.

[TBF05]   Sebastian Thrun, Wolfram Burgard, and Dieter Fox. *Probabilistic Robotics*. The MIT
          Press, Cambridge, Massachusetts, 2005.

[TPB06]   R. Triebel, P. Pfaff, and W. Burgard. Multi-level surface maps for outdoor terrain mapping
          and loop closing. In *International Conference on Intelligent Robots and Systems, 2006*,
          pages 2276 –2282, 2006.

Towards new interaction techniques for augmented-reality applications using gaze analysis and gesture recognition

Jan Hendrik Hammer

Vision and Fusion Laboratory
Institute for Anthropomatics
Karlsruhe Institute of Technology (KIT), Germany
hammer@ies.uni-karlsruhe.de

Technical Report IES-2012-08

Abstract: Recent developments in the area of head-worn augmented-reality (AR) devices raise the demand for new intuitive interaction techniques. Such systems make it possible to perceive the environment of a user, track his gaze, display AR contents in his field of view - all in a non intrusive way. In the long run the goal is to infer the interest or intention of a user by analysing his gaze movements to be able to augment his reality with adapted, meaningful information. Furthermore there is the necessity to intuitively interact with AR contents and the system e.g. by using hand gestures. This article describes the roadmap for developing a multimodal analysis system consisting of two components: A gaze analysis module for computing visual attention and a hand gesture recognition from the user's point of view for intuitive interaction possibilities.

1 Introduction

Recently a novel head mounted device (HMD) using a bidirectional OLED microdisplay was presented by Richter et al. [RVH+11]. This HMD offers *optical see-through* reality, meaning that augmented-reality (AR) contents are visualised in the field of view while the environment is still perceived directly. This HMD equipped with a scene camera also offers the ability to observe hand movements. Other devices like the mobile research prototype used by Ajanki et al. in [ABJ+10] show the reality on near-to-eye displays where AR contents are projected into the shown frames that are captured by a scene camera. This type of augmenting the reality is called *virtual see-through* reality. Additionally both devices offer the ability to track the eye of the user wearing the HMD. By referencing the eye-movements to a 3D-model of the environment, the gaze is computed. Knowing that overall and visual attention often coincide, gaze analysis can reveal further insights into the user's world of thought. By inferring what is most relevant for the user, he can be provided with helpful AR contents corresponding to his interest. This adaptive way of visualising information enriches the user's life by guiding his experience of certain situations. E.g., a real-life situation of a museum visit with an adaptive AR HMD guiding and directing the user corresponding to his interest can be imagined.

Regarding this kind of mobile adaptive AR applications in terms of human-computer interaction, the interaction with the computer must be categorised into two types. First there is *implicit interaction* when the system observes the user freely viewing the environment or moving the hands when talking with other people. Second there exists *explicit interaction* of the user with the system, e.g., when selecting AR contents or pointing to some element of the real world by hand.

1.1 Structure

Since one of the main goals of adaptive mobile AR applications is interest detection and gaze analysis contributes to this challenge, section 2 covers what can be inferred from gaze, explaining how visual attention can be analysed by different metrics already used for other purposes. Section 3 deals with hand gesture recognition in mobile applications discussing the single steps from the raw images to the recognition of gesture.

2 Gaze analysis

To understand the visual perception of a scene, the two most important eye movement types have to be understood: Fixations and saccades. Fixations are the dwells during which the gaze almost remains still and saccades are the ballistic, rapid eye movements between fixations. Visual perception of the environment is only occurring during fixations [Tob10], when the field of view is imaged on the retina by the optical system of our eyes. Although the human field of view has a visual angle of around $190°$ in horizontal and $130°$ in vertical direction, the acuity declines by increasing distance to the intersection of the optical axis of the eye and the retina. The small area around this intersection point is called the *fovea centralis* with a visual angle of around $2°$ [Ray98]. By containing the highest density of cone cells that enable colour vision, the fovea offers the highest acuity. The fovea is surrounded by the parafovea to a visual angle of around $5°$ and the remaining region of the visual field called periphery with the lowest acuity. To perceive objects with greater visual angles than 2° in horizontal or vertical direction, the gaze must be shifted to compose the visual impression of such elements of different single retinal images. By tracking the gaze, visual attention can be computed but it has to be kept in mind that visual attention and overall attention do not have to coincide. Our mind's attention can be shifted without moving the eyes. We can observe something in the peripheral region of the visual field while focusing on something else. This is called covert attention. If our gaze follows attention shifts, we talk about overt attention. In contradiction to overt attention, we can even look at a scene and are blind for changes that should have been obvious. This phenomenon is called change blindness [SR05] and the lack of awareness can be explained by completely different expectations of possibly occurring changes.

In mobile AR applications the main contribution of eye-tracking to situation recognition is implicit interest detection and explicit interest indication. Before addressing these topics, the commonly used measures for gaze analysis are described.

2.1 Measures and metrics

To reveal information from eye tracking data, the commonly most important eye movement types for gaze analysis have to be extracted: Fixations and saccades. Detailed explanations of methods for computing fixations and saccades and their comparison concerning accuracy, execution speed, ease of implementation etc. can be found in [SG00] or in a more recent study focusing mainly on accuracy in [KJKG10]. As a conclusion from these studies the algorithms Velocity Threshold Identification (I-VT) and Kalman Filter Identification (I-KF) seem to be the methods of choice mainly due to their better accuracy. Since in mobile AR applications the distance from the head to the gaze point is not known before and objects to be looked at can have three dimensional extents, a computation as implemented in stationary applications, where the gaze points are usually located in one plane, is not possible and must be adjusted accordingly.

Based on saccades and fixations a variety of measures can be computed. The most important measures and metrics used by Goldberg and Kotval [GK99] and Goldberg and Helfman [GH10] are explained in the following section regarding their computation as well as their general interpretation.

2.1.1 Scanpath analysis

A scanpath is determined by an alternate sequence of fixations and saccades of a given temporal horizon. An example of a scanpath taken from Goldberg and

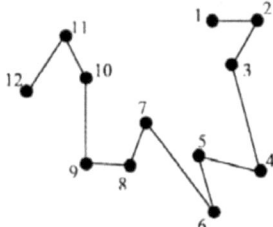

Figure 2.1: Visualisation of a scanpath taken from Goldberg and Kotval [GK99].

Kotval [GK99] can be seen in Figure 2.1. The total number of saccades or the sum of their amplitudes are measures for the scanpath length, which is an indicator for the extent of inspection. A long scanpath can be explained, e.g., by extensive search behaviour of a person. During fixations, people perceive the world. Statistics of fixation durations are a measure for the local extent of information processing or processing complexity. The total scanpath duration and the sum of fixation and saccade durations also reveal information about the processing complexity for the whole area attended. The ratio of fixation durations and saccade durations describes viewing behaviour in the following way: A very low value indicates extensive search behaviour, whereas a higher ratio reveals that more visual stimuli are processed and search or free viewing is reduced. Between consecutive saccades a relative angle can be computed. Summing up these relative angles results in the cumulative angle, a measure describing the directness of viewing. Based on the assumption that visual stimuli without any structure causes a gaze pattern with many changes in direction, a low value for the cumulative angle would suggest that the visual stimuli are arranged in a certain structure guiding the gaze.

2.1.2   Metrics using areas of interest

Since gaze analysis shall reveal information about the attractiveness or relevance of objects, areas containing these objects, so called areas of interest (AOIs), are defined which enable a linkage of fixations to the real world. There are two ways for their definition: One is placing a grid over the visual field, the other is adapting AOIs to the objects of interest that can have arbitrary spatial extents. The example of a 4×4 grid can be seen in the upper image of Figure 2.2. AOIs offer important additional metrics for gaze analysis. If we assume a grid of AOIs, the spatial density is the number of cells containing at least one fixation divided by the total number of cells of the grid. Larger values correspond to an evenly spread viewing behaviour and smaller values show less distribution of fixations, indicating that there is an underlying structure in the observed scene similar to the cumulative angle. The time to the first fixation of an AOI or the time after which each member of a particular set of AOIs has been fixated at least once reveals insight into the attractiveness of that AOI or set of AOIs. These times can also be ordered to see which AOIs or sets of AOIs attracted visual attention earlier than others. The number of post-target fixations on an AOI is the number of fixations following the first one. If an object has been captured and is not of relevance or interest, the post-target fixation value will be low, otherwise higher. The percentage of fixations within each AOI or the percentage of fixation durations on each AOI reveals an overview of the visual attention of a whole scene.

2.1.3 Analysing transition matrices

A further way of analysing gaze behaviour is the usage of transition matrices. Having defined a number of n AOIs, the transition matrix contains n^2 elements. For two AOIs i and j there is an element in the i-th column and j-th row in the matrix containing the number of transitions from i to j and another element in the j-th column and i-th row containing the transitions in the opposite direction. An example of such a transition matrix can be seen in Figure 2.2. The transition density is the number of non-zero matrix elements divided by the total number of matrix elements. Smaller values correspond to a more directed scanpath. Smaller transition densities involve smaller spatial densities. Further information of the relevance of an AOI can be inferred by analysing transition frequencies from a set of AOIs to a special AOI. The more transitions on a particular AOI occur, the more relevant this AOI is.

2.2 Implicit interest detection

Implicit interest detection describes the process of inferring the user's interest by analysing his gaze under free viewing conditions. This means from the user's point of view that he is not directly or explicitly interacting with the device.

By drawing conclusions for implicit interest detection using gaze analysis it is assumed that the user's overall and visual attention are interrelated and that overt attention is prevalent. Fortunately, the latter can be assumed, because covert attention has been found out to mainly assist active vision and being unusual to occur as a substitute process [Fin05]. On the other hand the former assumption does not have to be true and unveils the fact that overall attention and visual attention can be completely different. This attentional dissociation of mental operations and visual attention happens due to fatigue, boredom or when a person is in an aroused

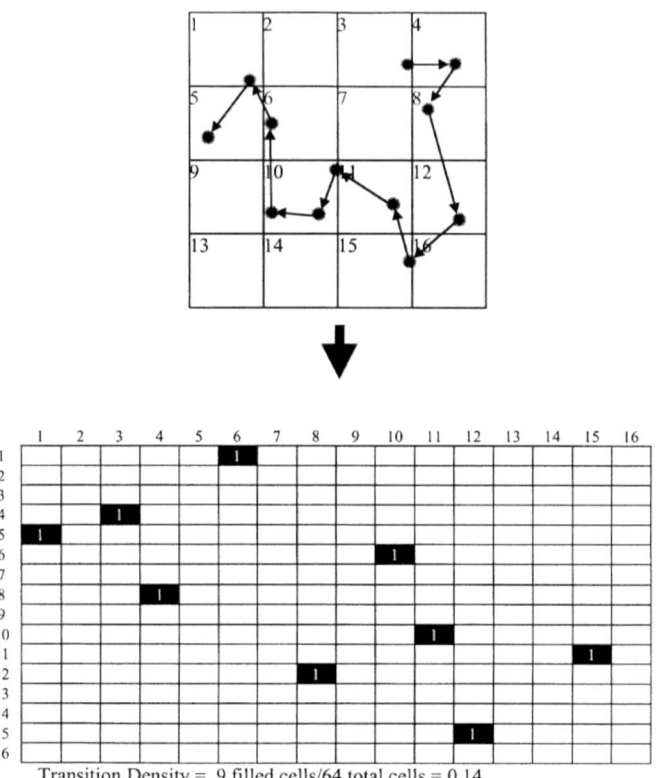

Transition Density = 9 filled cells/64 total cells = 0.14

Figure 2.2: Upper image: Definition of a grid of AOIs. Lower image: Transition matrix constructed of AOIs of upper image as found in [GK99] where also the pictures are taken from.

state [GH10]. Keeping this in mind, gaze analysis can only give information about the relevance of different objects in the visual field. Although something interesting will get more visual attention than something uninteresting, even the most relevant object - that with the most visual attention - does not have to be of interest. Accordingly the relevance can only be interpreted as a cue for interest, since relevance is not a sufficient criterion for interest.

2.2.1 Perceiving images and artworks

Below, a few studies are presented giving useful hints of how interest influences viewing behaviour. Regarding that mobile AR applications are very interesting particularly for museums, a few studies concerning gaze analysis and art under free viewing conditions are presented. These give interesting insights into value changes of eye measures.

Kaspar and Konig analysed in [KK11] how people with different interests looked at images of different categories. They found out that when a person was interested in an image focus of attention became more globally, fixation durations became shorter, saccade frequency increased, and the distribution of fixation became more extensive. Furthermore they observed a low inter-subject variance of fixation distribution when interest in images was high.

Buswell [Bus35] analysed the gaze of people freely viewing artworks. He concluded that eyes follow the direction of principal lines and that more processing of more visually complex areas produces longer fixation durations. The former conclusion is also supported by Engelbrecht et al. [EBKR10]. As described in section 2.1, measures for processing complexity and visual attention, which can be seen as necessary conditions for objects being of relevance, are the scanpath length, scanpath duration and statistics about fixation durations. To get a good overview of visual attention, the percentage of fixations within each AOI or the percentage of fixation durations on each AOI as well as the spatial density can be used. By analysing this overview of visually attended areas, it can be evaluated, if important parts of an artwork, necessary for its correct understanding, have been seen at all. Additionally, regions of general interest can be defined by areas most people attended to like, e.g., faces in artworks. The time to the first fixation of an AOI or the time after which each member of a set of AOIs has been fixated can reveal interesting insights into which part of artworks attract visual attention earlier than others. A further necessary condition for relevant objects is that their number of post-target fixations and the transition frequency from other AOIs to this object is relatively high compared to other objects.

Locher and Nodine [LN08] propose two phases to describe the process of people perceiving artworks: The first is for getting an overall impression of the composition of an image. Some kind of judgement of "its aesthetic quality" is also produced and it seems as if this judgement occurs during the first glance at an artwork. The overview gained by the first phase drives the second phase of going into more detail on relevant areas. Nodine et al. [NLK93] assume that this second phase consists of many survey fixations of 200-300 ms dwell time to locate relevant areas interspersed with examination fixations of around 400 ms to focus attention on those areas. Locher and Nodine also examined the gaze coverage of artworks after three and seven seconds as well as at the end of the experiment. They observed that after the first seven seconds almost no additional areas attracted visual attention. To detect the transition from the first phase of getting the gist of the artwork to the second phase of going into more detail, the ratio of fixation duration to saccade duration can be used. This ratio should be increasing over time, if the two-stage model of Locher and Nodine [LN08] represents the way a person perceives an artwork. The different temporal windows of the different phases, three, seven, and more than seven seconds can be used to determine the length of scanpaths to be analysed.

All these insights in how people look at artworks could be used in a mobile AR application as follows: The measures and metrics could for instance be analysed in real time, compared to thresholds or classified by trained machine learning algorithms. The next section describes first studies doing exactly this.

2.2.2 Detecting relevance

In this section a few studies are presented dealing about how relevance can be detected by gaze analysis using specific measures and metrics. The metrics are mostly joined together into a feature vector and classifiers are used to infer relevance values.

Klami et al. [KSdCK08] tried to detect relevance of images in a controlled scenario based solely on eye movements using simple features. The features they used were the total length of fixations, the number of fixations, the average length of fixations, the number of transitions between AOIs, the number of AOIs with at least one fixation and the number of fixations within each AOI. Their visual stimuli consisted of four images at a time, thus four AOIs at a time. To predict the relevance a linear discriminant analysis was realised.

Kandemir et al. [KSK10] conducted a feasibility study on inferring the relevance of objects in dynamic scenes from gaze. To decide about visualisations in their AR application they wanted to infer the degree of interest of the user for certain objects of a dynamic scene. Their definition of relevance is "the interest in seeing augmented information about an object in the scene at that particular time" [KSK10]. Features they used were the total and mean duration of fixations in sets of AOIs (objects and related AR contents), the mean distance of all fixations to the centre of the AOIs and the mean length of transitions into AOIs. For inferring relevance they used an ordinal logistic regression.

Ajanki et al. (2010) monitored the implicit interest of users in a mobile AR system to be able to decide what to display next. They estimated relevance of objects from gaze by proportion of the total time an object or its related AR contents have been under visual attention. Their application also used speech to infer relevance. To remark one aspect: Objects inferred to be relevant from speech were always assumed to be more relevant than objects inferred to be relevant from gaze.

2.3 Explicit interest indication

Explicit interest indication is another important aspect for mobile AR applications and comes into effect when digital contents are visualised in the field of view and the user has to choose or select contents. How can he select an AR content or slide through a menu? Hand gestures are designated for this task, but there has been a lot of research on the question how selection can be achieved with gaze only. Gaze is faster and less exhaustive than arm movements, but with recent approaches for gaze based selection less intuitive and more frustrating. Selection methods using only the eyes are very important in applications for severely disabled people who cannot move their arms or legs and gaze is the only modality that can be used for interaction. Moving the mouse cursor with the eye is intuitive, because location of the cursor and visual focus usually correspond. But replacing the selection by mouse click is difficult to realise and commonly tackled by defining *dwell times*. If the gaze rests on a selectable object for more than the dwell time, the selection is performed. Selection by dwell times results in the *Midas Touch* (Jacob, 1990) problem and just looking at something for a longer while and unintentionally issuing the selection command frustrates users. The problem of finding the perfect dwell time is that the user's intention of selecting or just looking cannot be inferred from gaze duration. People are even adapting by using avoidance strategies just to not initiate unwanted selections [ZGKV10] A recent approach of Zander et al. [ZGKV10] shows that by measuring brain activity using EEG and extracting certain learnt features, it is possible to recognise a binary command which can be used as selection command. This selection command can be initiated by imagining a special hand movement. This combination of gaze input with a brain-computer interface (BCI) was not significantly slower than solutions using dwell times for the selection command when performing some selection tasks. The accuracy of activating the selection command with this hybrid BCI approach was higher as with solely gaze based methods using short dwell times. The most important results of Zander et al. [ZGKV10] are a strong user preference of the hybrid BCI as well as less stated frustration when using brain activity for selection. This shows that combining gaze input methods and BCI can be a promising alternative for the future when hardware for measuring brain activity becomes less intrusive. As long as this is not the case dwell times seem to be the only way to initiate the selection command, since eye gestures as, e.g. ,glints are far away from being natural.

Therefore it is better to use another modality everybody uses: Hand gestures. Hand gestures are much more intuitive to be used for explicit interaction. A system for their recognition will be described in section 3.

3   Hand gesture recognition

Hand gesture recognition can be divided into two main steps: The first consist of localising the hands in each single frame and the tracking through a video sequence. The second step is the analysis of the tracking results to recognise gestures of a predefined vocabulary. The interpretation of a gesture depends on the application and the actual context, but this is not further addressed here.

In mobile applications the following challenges are prevalent: Lighting conditions may change constantly. Depending on the application direct sunlight can illuminate the scene resulting in the problem that an active illumination with near infrared cannot be used to simplify the hand segmentation. Therefore only algorithms should be chosen that process raw image data of optical camera sensors. Furthermore the field of view of the camera is not static. This implicates a highly dynamic background. Simple frame differencing with a pre-learnt background and a subsequent thresholding to get a binary image which is separating foreground and background is not possible. For that reason no assumptions about the background should flow into the localisation of hands. Recent procedures for hand gesture recognition in mobile application mainly use the following cues: Skin colour and motion information [WKSE11]. In the following sections first results of the development of a hand gesture recognition system for mobile applications are presented.

3.1   Hand segmentation using skin colour

When using skin colour for hand segmentation the probability of each pixel for being skin colour is computed. To accomplish this different possibilities exist. The colour space and the model for representing colour distributions must be chosen.

The choice of the colour space being best for skin colour segmentation has often been addressed ([KMB07], [PBC05]). Results revealed that three-dimensional colour spaces like HSV or RGB have advantages over those without luminance information and that there is no preference for a special three-dimensional colour space. RGB was chosen for the experiments conducted.

Histograms, Gaussian distributions or Gaussian Mixture Models (GMMs) can be utilised for modelling skin colour. Using a colour space with 256^3 Elements several subsequent colours have to be condensed into one class. Otherwise the memory size for saving the histogram becomes too large. Experiments have shown that 32 or 64 instead of 256 bins per dimension are a good choice. The memory costs - assuming 4 bytes of memory for each class - can thereby be reduced from 64 MBytes to 1 MByte when using 64 classes or 128 KBytes when using 32 classes. If there does not exist much training data, histograms mostly are sparsely populated. This problem can be reduced by smoothing the histogram resulting in lower false positive rates and higher true positive rates for certain thresholds when performance of skin colour detection is evaluated.

The advantage of Gaussian distributions over histograms is that they are parametrised by two values, the mean and the standard deviation and thus the memory costs are minimal. Their generalisation ability is better than those of histograms but therefor significantly more training data is needed. GMMs can adapt to certain colour distributions and parameters computed from large data sets are, e.g., revealed in [JR99].

Experiments have shown that the histogram approach enables better skin colour detection than with Gaussian distributions or GMMs. This may be explained by the low amount of training data used for the colour model. The resulting skin colour probability image is transformed to a binary by a threshold operation. After that contiguous regions of skin colour are searched. Results revealed that the segmentation is not exact enough to realise the extraction of a contour which could be post-processed to detect certain hand poses like, e.g., carried out by Bader et al. in [BRB09]. Since it is not possible to detect single fingers the overall shape could be considered here instead.

Another very important topic is the adaption of the skin colour model due to lighting changes as, e.g., accomplished by Spruyt et al. [SLG10]. Assuming that the hand segmentation works robustly the area of the hand can be used to update or replace the existing colour model. But since segmentation can be erroneous the danger of updating the colour model with wrong colours is omnipresent. Slightly wrong colour models reinforce further erroneous updates of the model, especially if only colour is used for hand segmentation. As can be seen this is a highly dynamic process that makes the development of a robust adaption strategy difficult.

3.2   Hand segmentation using motion information

Motion information is often gathered by simple frame differencing as in [SLG10]. High grey value changes above a certain threshold are considered as motion. It is obvious that this kind of motion information is not reliable because grey value differences can occur by just moving the head a little bit and thus moving the camera attached to the HMD without anything including the hand having changed their positions. The computation of dense optical flow yields much more precise motion information. For the present experiments the FlowLib [WPB10] was used in its standard configuration. There exist several methods for analysing such flow fields. Assuming that the background is the largest region of similar motion, a separation of foreground and background can be achieved by clustering the absolute values of the motion vectors. This results in a binary image indicating for each pixel if it belongs to the foreground motion or not whereby the hand is a foreground object. The FlowLib produces flow fields of high quality but the extraction of a contour for hand pose recognition unfortunately does not seem to be possible. Nevertheless motion information from optical flow seems promising as additional cue for a robust hand segmentation. One disadvantage is that the algorithms producing flow fields of high quality as the FlowLib in its standard configuration are not real-time capable. Accordingly there is need for fast reliable optical flow algorithms.

3.3   Multi cue hand segmentation

Many recent hand tracking algorithms are multi cue approaches where skin colour and motion information are combined in different ways ([KT04], [SWTO04], [SLG10]). Merging the binary images of both the colour segmentation and the motion segmentation process by a logical AND operation is a simple step. The result is a binary image where skin-coloured foreground objects are highlighted. Further experiments concerning the fusion of the previously described colour and motion segmentation have to be performed to evaluate the robustness of that approach.

3.4   Tracking and gesture recognition

Tracking the hand through consecutive frames can utilise the localisation results of the previous frame for the next one. Tracking algorithms like a particle filter predict the the current state by moving the previous state according to a motion model. After this transition the observations model is used to determine the weight of a state. This is done for all particles and only the best are considered for the next iteration. The difficulty lies in finding the appropriate state, motion and observation model regarding the available cues. Different possibilities are actually being evaluated.

The result of tracking is a trajectory describing hand positions that must be processed by a gesture recognition. Recent algorithms use hidden Markov models (HMM) or dynamic time warping (DTW) [WKSE11]. The latter is already under investigation but has to be further evaluated.

4 Conclusion

Eye-tracking and gaze analysis offer promising opportunities. They are already an indispensable tool for many applications. They serve as input modality replacing the mice and thus eable severly disabled people to control a computer, they are used for analysis of ads or user interfaces and serve for intention detection in vehicles. As mobile non-intrusive AR hardware with eye-tracking and scene capturing capabilites are on the horizon implicit relevance detection and explicit interest detection by gaze analysis become attractive contributors for inferring people's interest or intention. This paper summarises how gaze analysis is already used for these purposes. Similar approaches are going to be tested. Furthermore to enable intuitive explicit interaction with such mobile AR devices, mobile gesture recognition is the second topic of this paper. First developments have been presented and difficulties have been pointed out that are tackled in the near future not omitting the prevalent interplay of eyes and hands.

Bibliography

[ABJ⁺10]   A. Ajanki, M. Billinghurst, T. Jarvenpaa, M. Kandemir, S. Kaski, M. Koskela, M. Kurimo, J. Laaksonen, K. Puolamaki, T. Ruokolainen, and T. Tossavainen. Contextual information access with Augmented Reality. In *Machine Learning for Signal Processing (MLSP), 2010 IEEE International Workshop on*, pages 95 –100, 29 2010-Sept. 1 2010.

[BRB09]   Thomas Bader, Rene Räpple, and Jürgen Beyerer. Fast Invariant Contour-based Classification of Hand Symbols for HCI. In *Computer analysis of images and patterns: 13th international conference, CAIP 2009, Münster, Germany, September 2-4, 2009 ; proceedings*, Lecture notes in computer science; 5702, pages 689–696. Springer, Berlin [u.a.], 2009.

[Bus35]   G. T. Buswell. *How People Look at Pictures*. University of Chicago Press, Chicago, 1935.

[EBKR10]   M. Engelbrecht, J. Betz, C. Klein, and R. Rosenberg. Dem Auge auf der Spur: Eine historische und empirische Studie zur Blickbewegung beim Betrachten von Gemälden. *IMAGE 11 (January 2010)*, 2010.

[Fin05]   J. M. Findlay. Covert attention and saccadic eye movements. In L. Itti, G. Rees, and J. Tsotsos, editors, *Neurobiology of attention.*, pages 114–117. Elsevier Academic Press, London ; New York, March 2005.

[GH10]   Joseph H. Goldberg and Jonathan I. Helfman. Comparing Information Graphics: A Critical Look at Eye Tracking. In *Proceedings of the 2010 Workshop on BEyond time and errors: novel evaLuation methods for Information Visualization*, BELIV'10, pages 71–78, Atlanta, GA, USA, April 2010. ACM.

[GK99]   Joseph H. Goldberg and Xerxes P. Kotval. Computer interface evaluation using eye movements: methods and constructs. *International Journal of Industrial Ergonomics*, 24(6):631 – 645, 1999.

[JR99]   Michael J. Jones and James M. Rehg. Statistical Color Models with Application to Skin Detection. In *International Journal of Computer Vision*, pages 274–280, 1999.

[KJKG10]   Oleg V. Komogortsev, Sampath Jayarathna, Do Hyong Koh, and Sandeep Munikrishne Gowda. Qualitative and Quantitative Scoring and Evaluation of the Eye Movement Classification Algorithms. In *Proceedings of the 2010 Symposium on Eye-Tracking Research & Applications*, ETRA '10, pages 65–68, New York, NY, USA, 2010. ACM.

[KK11]   Kai Kaspar and Peter König. Overt Attention and Context Factors: The Impact of Repeated Presentations, Image Type, and Individual Motivation. *PLoS ONE*, 6(7):e21719, 07 2011.

[KMB07]   P. Kakumanu, S. Makrogiannis, and N. Bourbakis. A survey of skin-color modeling and detection methods. *Pattern Recognition*, 40(3):1106 – 1122, 2007.

[KSdCK08]   Arto Klami, Craig Saunders, Teófilo E. de Campos, and Samuel Kaski. Can Relevance of Images Be Inferred from Eye Movements? In *Proceedings of the 1st ACM international Conference on Multimedia Information Retrieval*, MIR '08, pages 134–140, New York, NY, USA, 2008. ACM.

[KSK10]   Melih Kandemir, Veli-Matti Saarinen, and Samuel Kaski. Inferring Object Relevance from Gaze in Dynamic Scenes. In *Proceedings of the 2010 Symposium on Eye-Tracking Research & Applications*, ETRA '10, pages 105–108, New York, NY, USA, 2010. ACM.

[KT04]   M. Kölsch and M. Turk. Fast 2D Hand Tracking with Flocks of Features and Multi-Cue Integration. In *Computer Vision and Pattern Recognition Workshop, 2004. CVPRW '04. Conference on*, page 158, June 2004.

[LN08]   P. Locher and C. Nodine. What Does Visual Exploration of an Artwork Contribute to a Viewer's Immediate Aesthetic Reaction to It? In *20th Congress of the International Association of Empirical Aesthetics*, Chicago, Illinois, USA, August 19-22, 2008.

[NLK93]   C F Nodine, P J Locher, and E A Krupinski. The Role of Formal Art Training on Perception and Aesthetic Judgment of Art Compositions. *Leonardo*, 26(3):219, 1993.

[PBC05]   S.L. Phung, Sr. Bouzerdoum, A., and Sr. Chai, D. Skin Segmentation Using Color Pixel Classification: Analysis and Comparison. *Pattern Analysis and Machine Intelligence, IEEE Transactions on*, 27(1):148 –154, January 2005.

[Ray98]   K. Rayner. Eye Movements in Reading and Information Processing: 20 Years of Research. *Psychological Bulletin*, 124(3):372–422, 1998.

[RVH+11]   B. Richter, U. Vogel, R. Herold, K. Fehse, S. Brenner, L. Kroker, and J. Baumgarten. Bidirectional OLED microdisplay: Combining display and image sensor functionality into a monolithic CMOS chip. In *Solid-State Circuits Conference Digest of Technical Papers (ISSCC), 2011 IEEE International*, pages 314 –316, feb. 2011.

[SG00]   Dario D. Salvucci and Joseph H. Goldberg. Identifying Fixations and Saccades in Eye-Tracking Protocols. In *ETRA '00: Proceedings of the 2000 Symposium on Eye-Tracking Research & Applications*, pages 71–78, New York, NY, USA, 2000. ACM.

[SLG10]   V. Spruyt, A. Ledda, and S. Geerts. Real-time Multi-colourspace Hand Segmentation. In *Image Processing (ICIP), 2010 17th IEEE International Conference on*, pages 3117 –3120, sept. 2010.

[SR05]   Daniel J. Simons and Ronald A. Rensink. Change blindness: Past, present, and future. 2005.

[SWTO04]   Caifeng Shan, Yucheng Wei, Tieniu Tan, and F. Ojardias. Real Time Hand Tracking by Combining Particle Filtering and Mean Shift. In *Automatic Face and Gesture Recognition, 2004. Proceedings. Sixth IEEE International Conference on*, pages 669 – 674, may 2004.

[Tob10]   Tobii Eye Tracking. An introduction to eye tracking and Tobii Eye Trackers, January 2010.

[WKSE11]   Juan Pablo Wachs, Mathias Kölsch, Helman Stern, and Yael Edan. Vision-Based Hand-Gesture Applications. *Commun. ACM*, 54:60–71, February 2011.

[WPB10]   Manuel Werlberger, Thomas Pock, and Horst Bischof. Motion Estimation with Non-Local Total Variation Regularization. In *IEEE Computer Society Conference on Computer Vision and Pattern Recognition (CVPR)*, San Francisco, CA, USA, June 2010.

[ZGKV10]   Thorsten O. Zander, Matti Gaertner, Christian Kothe, and Roman Vilimek. Combining Eye Gaze Input With a Brain-Computer Interface for Touchless Human-Computer Interaction. *International Journal of Human-Computer Interaction*, 27(1):38–51, 2010.

Multi-Label Graph Cuts including Prior Knowledge for Character Segmentation

Martin Grafmüller

Vision and Fusion Laboratory
Institute for Anthropomatics
Karlsruhe Institute of Technology (KIT), Germany
grafmueller@kit.edu

Technical Report IES-2011-09

Abstract: Recently, a character segmentation method based on graph cuts has been introduced. In this report, we extend this method to multi-label graph cuts. Instead of sequential segmentation of single characters from a text line, all characters are segmented at once. The method is especially suitable for applications where subsequent images contain the same (known) number of characters. This prior knowledge and the approximate positions of characters relative to the defined text region are included in the formulation of the energy functional. This approach provides significant segmentation quality improvement, in particular, when characters are touching, which may happen e.g. due to poor print quality or scratches on the material's surface. To illustrate the performance changes, we compare the results obtained with this and previously known methods, based on real data.

1 Introduction

To make Optical Character Recognition (OCR) more robust in industrial application, we introduce a reliable character segmentation method, which is based on multi-label graph cuts. The applications are reading product or serial numbers, to track the products over their whole life cycle, or to record automatically which parts are in which products. Up to now, the database check in has been mostly based on the entry of a human, which is very time consuming and error-prone.

The system is applied in pharmaceutical, electronic, food, or automotive industry, where the characters are printed, lasered, or engraved on different kinds of materials. This makes the recognition task very challenging and demands a very robust system with high performance. Most of the production cycles have strong real-time constraints, which require not only robust, but also very fast algorithms.

This kind of industrial applications have one main advantage. Except of the characters there is not much change in subsequent images. Thus, the line and character position remains almost the same within the text region. This knowledge can be used for character segmentation, especially if the characters are merged due to poor print quality or scratches on the material's surface. This does not only increase the segmentation performance, but also may increase classification performance, since there is at least a chance to classify the segmented characters correctly. This way, a more robust overall system will be achieved.

1.1   Contributions

Character recognition in industrial applications has one big advantage, namely that the text region position, the number of lines, and even the number of characters is mostly the same in subsequent images. For this reason we introduce a character segmentation procedure that especially exploits the knowledge of the number of characters and their approximate position to increase the overall performance of the system.

The method is based on the graph cuts approach for character segmentation, which was introduced in [GB11]. However, since the number of characters is known in advance, this method allows the segmentation of all characters simultaneously and has not to be applied iteratively as the method mentioned firstly. This is possible, since the binary label problem as in [GB11] is augmented to a multi-label problem, i.e. every character is assigned to one label. The problem is formulated based on an energy functional, which consists of two terms. One of them is related to the prior knowledge, which is given by an initial segmentation of the first image. It is a kind of teach in, where the user can do several settings. The second term is related to the intensity of the current image itself in order to achieve cuts in the light regions between the characters. Considering both, prior knowledge and information of the current image leads to a more robust segmentation and the performance of the entire recognition system can be significantly increased, as the experimental results show.

1.2   Structure

This technical report is about character segmentation using multi-label graph cuts considering prior knowledge given by the application. In Section 2, we briefly discuss related work that has been published and used. The problem is formulated in Section 3, where we discuss the approach and all necessary conditions that must be satisfied. In Section 4, we describe how multi-label graph cuts character segmentation can be applied and robustness to the given application is achieved. Some experimental results are given in Section 5, where this method is compared to some previously known methods on real data. Finally, the report is concluded in Section 6 and further ideas for future research are given.

2   Related Work

For character recognition not only a classifier with good performance is important, but also the character segmentation approach, since it is hardly possible to classify broken or merged characters correctly. This means that improving character segmentation may significantly improve character recognition. For character segmentation most approaches are based on projection profiles, connected component analysis, or hybrid forms of these methods. Some of the approaches even incorporate character recognition to improve the segmentation result. A summary of the most common methods can be found in [Lu95, CL96, SSR10]. One drawback of most of the commonly used methods is that they work on binary images, whereas binarization can even cause more touching or fragmented characters. Hence, we focus on a character segmentation approach that can be applied to gray scale images without binarization. Additionally, prior knowledge is used to make the segmentation more robust and reliable.

One method that is based on characters' pitch estimation was introduced in [TA86] about 25 years ago. Their approach is divided into two steps. They introduced a linear square error function to estimate the characters' pitch. Subsequently, the segmentation cuts are determined by applying dynamic programming, which is based on the optimization of a minimum variance criterion. However, they applied their character segmentation method to read mailing addresses. This is probably not the best application for this method to show off all its advantages, since in address reading they had to deal with variable character pitch as well. Unlike the method proposed in this report, they do not use the estimated pitch in subsequent images, they always make a new estimation of the pitch, since in address reading the pitch may change from image to image.

In [LSA94] a character segmentation approach was introduced that combines segmentation and recognition. Based on the ratio of the projection profile and its first derivative the method detects merged characters and selects possible segmentation points. The correct segmentation points are determined combining segmentation and classification recursively.

A similar method based on the ratio of projection profiles and the sum of vertical gradients, was introduced in [LeB97]. The method can be applied to gray scale images without binarization and according to [LeB97] it performs well on touching characters and under harsh conditions.

Dot-matrix character segmentation was the focus of [Yan00], where three methods for pitch estimation were investigated. The methods are based on autocorrelation, Fourier analysis, and peak valley analysis. The experiments showed that the peak valley analysis yields to the most promising results. However, the method fails if the lines are skewed or fonts are italic.

For character segmentation from license plate images a method was introduced in [ZZ03]. They combine projection profile analysis and Hough transform, which results according to the authors in a method that is robust to illumination changes. Furthermore, due to the Hough transform, there is no need for rotational correction.

A segmentation method for italic typewritten fonts was introduced in [LNCS04]. They use slant angle estimation and contour analysis to locate segmentation points of touching characters. To find the best segmentation path between certain segmentation points they use dynamic programming. The final decision whether a segmentation path is correct or not is based on a neural network.

Another approach for license plate character segmentation was proposed in [NYK+05]. The method adaptively detects fragmented, overlapped, or connected characters in binary images. According to the detection result the degradation is corrected with morphological operations. Character segmentation itself is based on the vertical histogram.

A character segmentation approach with the focus on smeared typewritten characters was introduced in [TCJY07]. In first instance connected component analysis is used to detect any smeared characters according to rules they defined. With a shortest path algorithm the best segmentation path is determined on the gray scale image. Due to their investigations, binarization has a big influence on the segmentation result. With respect to their method they recommend a binarization that rather yields to connected than to fragmented characters.

In [PYX08] another license plate character segmentation method was introduced. This is based on skew angle estimation in horizontal and vertical direction with a least-squares approach. To eliminate regions between the characters that are corrupted by noise, they apply an improved projection method.

A character segmentation method especially for dot-matrix fonts was introduced in [GB10]. It is based on projection profiles and an adaptive threshold estimation, which makes the method very robust to illumination changes and variations in font and size. This method was improved in [GB11] to be more reliable and robust to touching characters. The improvement is based on a graph cuts approach with two labels. This approach is applied in a more advanced way for multi-label graph cuts in this technical report.

3   Problem Formulation

This technical report focuses on character segmentation in image series. Classification of image series is very common in conventional industrial applications, e.g. bar code reading, inspection tasks, or OCR. The advantage in this kind of application is that there is not much variation between the images. At least the text region has always the same structure, i.e. the number of lines is always the same and every line always consists of the same number of characters. The only thing that definitely changes is the kind of characters. Moreover, the captured object can move a little or the illumination changes slightly, which is acceptable for these kind of industrial environments. However, sometimes it may happen that due to misprints or scratches on the object characters appear to be merged. This mainly causes difficulties in character segmentation, which in the worst cases leads to misclassification or rejection of the characters. To avoid this kind of segmentation errors, the intention is to use an initial segmentation result as basic concept for all the following segmentation tasks in this application. This initial segmentation result is obtained and checked by the user during the adjustment step of the camera, where also other camera settings are adjusted to the application. This ensures that the segmentation result is correct and reliable for the given OCR task. From the initial segmentation it is known how many characters are in each line and how many lines are in the image. More precisely, it is even known where approximately to cut between the characters. This knowledge can be exploited by the proposed multi-label graph cuts approach for the segmentation of merged characters. The initial character segmentation step and what kind of information of the initial segmentation result is considered, is discussed in detail in the next section.

3.1   Initial Character Segmentation

During the initial character segmentation step useful information of the OCR task is collected. The result is shown to the user who can check it and if necessary correct it manually. The information needed for multi-label graph cuts segmentation is the

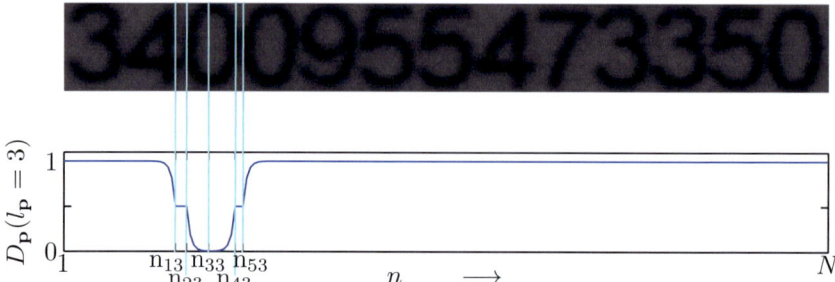

Figure 3.1: Line of characters and the corresponding position penalty $D_{\mathbf{p}}(l_{\mathbf{p}} = 3)$ for label $l_{\mathbf{p}} = 3$.

number of characters and the approximate position of the characters in a line. Both are given after initial segmentation, without any further user input.

An example of the initial segmentation result and some definitions for the introduction of multi-label graph cuts character segmentation can be found in Figure 3.1. In the plot below the character image, the position penalty for the third label—corresponding to the third character—is illustrated. The parameters n_{13} and n_{23} indicate the end and the beginning of the second and the third character, respectively. The middle of the third character is indicated by n_{33}. The end of the third character is given by n_{43} and the beginning of the fourth character by n_{53}. These are the five parameters that have to be determined in the initial segmentation process for every character in a line. The example in Figure 3.1 shows the idea of this approach and how the prior knowledge is considered. The definition of the energy functional and the two penalties are discussed in Section 4 in detail.

4 Multi-Label Graph Cuts Character Segmentation

For multi-label graph cuts character segmentation a line of characters is given. The characters are touching top and bottom, and on the left and right hand side of the image, i.e. the line is already segmented correctly. The image is a gray scale image

$$G(m, n) : \mathcal{P} := \{1, \dots, M\} \times \{1, \dots, N\} \;\rightarrow\; \{0, \dots, 255\}$$

with dark characters on a light background. The image height and width is indicated by M and N, respectively. For convenience, for the following derivation an ordered pair $\mathbf{p} := (m, n) \in \mathcal{P}$ of the pixel indices is defined.

This approach is based on the minimization of the energy functional

$$E(\mathbf{l}) := \sum_{\mathbf{p} \in \mathcal{P}} D_{\mathbf{p}}(l_{\mathbf{p}}) + \sum_{(\mathbf{p},\mathbf{q}) \in \mathcal{N}} V_{\mathbf{pq}}(l_{\mathbf{p}}, l_{\mathbf{q}}) \qquad (4.1)$$

in dependency of the label vector $\mathbf{l}$ with the elements $l_{\mathbf{p}} \in \mathcal{L}$. These elements indicate the labeling of pixel $\mathbf{p}$. Since the aim is to segment all characters from the line, the number of labels is given by the number of characters C, which leads to the label set $\mathcal{L} := \{1, \ldots, C\}$. The first term in equation (4.1) is called position penalty. It penalizes the cost of the labeling of pixel $\mathbf{p}$ in dependency on the position of the pixel in the image. The second term penalizes the labeling of pixel $\mathbf{p}$ if pixel $\mathbf{q}$ is labeled $l_{\mathbf{q}}$ with respect to the pixel's intensity. Hence, this term is called intensity penalty. The spatial coherence of this penalty is given by the neighborhood $\mathcal{N} \subseteq \mathcal{P} \times \mathcal{P}$. Here, only the eight nearest neighbors of pixel $\mathbf{p}$ are considered in $\mathcal{N}$.

4.1 Position Penalty

This penalty mainly influences where to cut the image to get every single character. Hence, the definition of the position penalty is based on the initial segmentation result obtained during the setup of the camera. To assign one label to each character region, the position penalty must be small in the corresponding region and larger in regions certainly belonging to different characters. In regions where it is uncertain if the region either belongs to the character in front or after the currently considered character, the penalties for the labels corresponding to these regions are equal. The labels are assigned to the characters in ascending order, so that the first character—most left character—in a line gets label $\lambda = 1$ and the last character   most right character— gets the label $\lambda = C$.

For the characters in between the first and the last character, which are corresponding to the labels $\lambda \in \mathcal{L} \setminus \{1, C\}$, the position penalty is

$$D_{\mathbf{p}}(l_{\mathbf{p}} = \lambda) := \begin{cases} 1 - 0.5 \cdot e^{-(n_{1\lambda} - n)} , & n \le n_{1\lambda} , \\ 0.5 , & n_{1\lambda} < n \le n_{2\lambda} , \\ 0.5 \cdot e^{-(n - n_{2\lambda})} , & n_{2\lambda} < n \le n_{3\lambda} , \\ 0.5 \cdot e^{-(n_{4\lambda} - n)} , & n_{3\lambda} < n \le n_{4\lambda} , \\ 0.5 , & n_{4\lambda} < n \le n_{5\lambda} , \\ 1 - 0.5 \cdot e^{-(n - n_{5\lambda})} , & n_{5\lambda} < n . \end{cases} \qquad (4.2)$$

The position penalty depends on label λ and the character position n, $n_{1\lambda}$ indicates the x-ordinate of the end of the character on the left hand side relative to the character corresponding to label λ. The values $n_{2\lambda}$, $n_{3\lambda}$, and $n_{4\lambda}$ indicate the beginning, the middle and the end of the character λ, respectively. The beginning of the subsequent character is indicated by $n_{5\lambda}$.

The exponential function in the position penalty can be interpreted as an exponential probability decay depending on the distance to the beginning or the end of a character, respectively. In the following, the example for label $\lambda = 3$ in Figure 3.1 is considered. If $n \leq n_{1\lambda}$ the position penalty increases with decreasing n, but this can be interpreted as an exponential probability decrease that these pixels belong to label $\lambda = 3$. In the range $n_{1\lambda} < n \leq n_{2\lambda}$ the penalty is constant, which means that the assignment of label $\lambda = 2$ or $\lambda = 3$ is equally likely. Similar to the first range, the exponential decrease in the range $n_{2\lambda} < n \leq n_{3\lambda}$ can be interpreted as an increasing probability for the values in this range to belong to label $\lambda = 3$. The same argumentation is valid for the remaining ranges and the corresponding labels. The exponential increase or decrease was chosen since usually there is not much tolerance for the cut position between two characters. Furthermore, many experiments have confirmed that this position penalty is appropriate.

If the current character is the first or the last one in the line, i.e. the labels are $\lambda \in \{1, C\}$, the position penalty is the same as given in equation (4.2) with the following exceptions

$$D_{\mathbf{p}}(l_{\mathbf{p}} = 1) := 0.5 \cdot e^{-(n_{4\lambda} - n)} , \qquad n \leq n_{3\lambda} ,$$

and

$$D_{\mathbf{p}}(l_{\mathbf{p}} = C) := 0.5 \cdot e^{-(n - n_{2\lambda})} , \qquad n_{3\lambda} < n .$$

This is done since no cut in front of the first and after the last character is needed.

All the factors $n_{i\lambda}$ are obtained in the initial segmentation step, which was discussed in Section 3.1. Hence, in every image that is segmented with multi-label graph cuts segmentation the knowledge of a correctly segmented image—the initial segmentation—has to be considered.

4.2   Intensity Penalty

Under ideal conditions the position penalty would be sufficient for segmenting the characters correctly from the images series. Unfortunately, in all applications one has to deal with noise, slight changes in illumination, blurring, misprints, or movement of the character region in the image, which may influence segmentation. Thus, the intensity penalty is introduced to take into account the pixel's neighborhood relations to achieve cuts between the characters in spite of noise.

Let the intensity penalty be

$$V_{\mathbf{pq}}(l_{\mathbf{p}}, l_{\mathbf{q}}) := f_{\mathrm{s}}(W(\mathbf{p}, \mathbf{q})) \cdot \delta(l_{\mathbf{p}} \neq l_{\mathbf{q}}), \quad (\mathbf{p}, \mathbf{q}) \in \mathcal{N},$$

with

$$\delta(l_{\mathbf{p}} \neq l_{\mathbf{q}}) := \begin{cases} 0, & l_{\mathbf{p}} = l_{\mathbf{q}}, \\ 1, & l_{\mathbf{p}} \neq l_{\mathbf{q}}, \end{cases}$$

which penalizes the labeling $l_{\mathbf{p}}$ if pixel $\mathbf{q}$ is labeled differently. The strength of the penalization is given by

$$W(\mathbf{p}, \mathbf{q}) := \begin{cases} (\bar{G}_{\mathbf{p}} + \bar{G}_{\mathbf{q}}), & (\mathbf{p}, \mathbf{q}) \in \mathcal{N}, \\ 0, & \text{otherwise}, \end{cases}$$

with the inverted gray values $\bar{G}_{\mathbf{p}} := 255 - G_{\mathbf{p}}$ of pixel $\mathbf{p}$ and $\bar{G}_{\mathbf{q}}$ of pixel $\mathbf{q}$. Since the aim is to force the cuts to be in the light background between the characters, the gray values are inverted with respect to the gray level interval. This is also the reason for using the sum of the neighboring pixels since this penalizes the intensity and not the smoothness like the difference would do. Moreover, the function $f_{\mathrm{s}}(\cdot)$ scales the penalty to the interval $[0, c_{\mathrm{s}}]$, where c_{s} is a parameter that weights the intensity penalty with respect to the position penalty.

4.3 Graph Representation

The energy functional (4.1) is minimized by minimum cuts that sever the graph $\mathcal{G}$ into C disjoint graphs. The graph $\mathcal{G} := (\mathcal{V}, \mathcal{E})$ is fully defined by the set $\mathcal{V}$ of vertices and the set $\mathcal{E}$ of edges. The set of vertices

$$\mathcal{V} := \{v_{\mathbf{p}} | \mathbf{p} \in \mathcal{P}\} \cup \{t_1, \dots, t_C\}$$

is the union of all vertices corresponding to one pixel of the image and the additionally introduced terminal vertices. The number of terminal vertices is given by the number of labels or characters. Thus, the number of vertices is

$$|\mathcal{V}| = |\mathcal{P}| + |\mathcal{L}| = M \cdot N + C.$$

Every vertex corresponding to one pixel is connected by an edge to its eight nearest neighbors. These edges are called n-links, which are denoted by $e_{\mathbf{pq}}$ if the edge connects vertices $\mathbf{p}$ and $\mathbf{q}$. Furthermore, each pixel is connected to every terminal node via an edge $e_{\mathbf{pt}}$, which are the t-links. The union of both results is the set of all edges

$$\mathcal{E} := \left\{ \bigcup_{(\mathbf{p},\mathbf{q}) \in \mathcal{N}} \{e_{\mathbf{pq}}\} \right\} \cup \left\{ \bigcup_{\mathbf{p} \in \mathcal{P}} \{e_{\mathbf{pt}_1}, \dots, e_{\mathbf{pt}_C}\} \right\} ,$$

of graph $\mathcal{G}$.

Since the graph $\mathcal{G}$ must be a representation of the functional (4.1), the question is how the edge weights have to be chosen. The position penalty is related to the edge weights

$$w_{\mathbf{pt}_\lambda} := D_{\mathbf{p}}(l_{\mathbf{p}} = \lambda) , \quad \mathbf{p} \in \mathcal{P} , \quad \lambda \in \mathcal{L} ,$$

which are dependent on the pixel's position $\mathbf{p}$ and the label λ, i.e. the edge weights of the edges that connect the vertices of the pixels with the terminal nodes. The edge weights between the neighboring pixels $\mathbf{p}$ and $\mathbf{q}$ are given by the intensity penalty, which is

$$w_{\mathbf{pq}} := V_{\mathbf{pq}}(l_{\mathbf{p}}, l_{\mathbf{q}}) , \quad (\mathbf{p}, \mathbf{q}) \in \mathcal{N} .$$

The cost of the cut

$$c_{\mathrm{cut}} := \sum_{i=1}^{C-1} \sum_{j=i+1}^{C} \left(\sum_{\substack{\mathbf{p} \in \mathcal{T}_i, \\ \mathbf{q} \in \mathcal{T}_j, \\ e_{\mathbf{pq}} \in \mathcal{E}}} w_{\mathbf{pq}} + \sum_{\substack{\mathbf{p} \in \mathcal{T}_i, \\ e_{\mathbf{pt}_j} \in \mathcal{E}}} w_{\mathbf{pt}_j} + \sum_{\substack{\mathbf{p} \in \mathcal{T}_j, \\ e_{\mathbf{pt}_i} \in \mathcal{E}}} w_{\mathbf{pt}_i} \right) ,$$

is the sum over all n-links and t-links that are cut. The set $\mathcal{T}_i$ indicates that vertex $\mathbf{p}$ belongs to label $i \in \mathcal{L}$.

4.4 Algorithm

According to Boykov [BVZ01] the α-expansion algorithm can be applied to this kind of energy functional, since $V_{\mathbf{pq}}(l_{\mathbf{p}}, l_{\mathbf{q}})$ is a metric. More precisely, the intensity penalty as formulated in Section 4.2 is consistent with the Potts model, which guarantees for the α-expansion algorithm that the minimum cuts are within a factor of two of the global optimum. In the article [BK04], Boykov and Kolmogorov have shown that their min-cut / max-flow algorithm applied during the α-expansion is much faster than other algorithms. Hence, we decided to use their algorithm to solve the min-cut problem as formulated in Section 4. For the experiments, we used their code, which was available on the website [CVR11].

5 Experiments

In this section the experimental results are discussed and the multi-label graph cuts approach is compared to an approach based on projection profiles [GB10] only and projection profiles combined with a graph cuts approach considering only two labels [GB11].

5.1 Experimental Setup

For the experiments 289 images were captured with an industrial camera. The camera was directly mounted after the printer, i.e. the setting is close to realistic conditions. In the text region there are four lines, which contain 42 characters in total. The first two lines contain numbers with thirteen and ten characters, respectively. The third line contains a date, which consists of month and year in the form *MM-YYYY*. In all of the first three lines there is no change of the content in subsequent images. The fourth line contains a number with twelve digits, which is incremented from image to image. The image for the initial segmentation is given in Figure 5.1, where the text region is framed by a blue rectangle. The selection of the text region was for all three methods the same, to avoid any differences in the experimental setup.

The first image was used for the initial segmentation in order to determine the position penalty for the multi-label graph cuts method. For the initial segmentation step the method proposed in [GB10] was used. This method was also used for line segmentation in all three methods that are compared in the next section. The experiments were performed on the remaining 288 images. For the evaluation two results were examined. The overall result, which is given with respect to the total number of characters (12096) and the result of the overall correctly segmented characters of line four (3456).

The design parameter of the proposed method was set to $c_s = 0.5$, which means that the position penalty and thus the prior knowledge has a higher influence on the energy functional than the knowledge given by the current image itself.

5.2 Results

Character segmentation from the test images chosen for the experiments is very hard, since the resolution is low and the characters are very close together—character distance mostly less than two pixels. However, the result with the proposed method looks promising. The result with respect to all characters is 99.62%, whereas the

Table 5.1: Segmentation results of the three methods compared.

	All characters	Characters of line 4
Multi-label GC	99.65%	98.78%
Projection profiles [GB10]	96.24%	89.38%
PP with GC [GB11]	97.04%	90.74%

segmentation result of the characters of line four is 98.78%. This shows that most of the segmentation errors occur in line four, which is mainly caused by the zeros. The reason is that they are very close together and in some cases the cost of the cut through the zeros is much cheaper than a cut between the zeros. The segmentation result of the projection profiles is a little inferior with 96.24% correctly segmented characters with respect to the total number of characters. However, if only the segmentation result of line four is considered the correctly segmented characters are close to 90%. The results of the graph cut approach with two labels show that this performs slightly better than using projection profiles only. However, with 97.04% correctly segmented characters there is a significant difference to the proposed method. If only the characters of line four are considered, the result be 90.74% correctly segmented characters. All results are summarized in Table 5.1, where the first row of the table contains the result of the proposed method, the second the result of the projection profiles only, and the third the result of the combination of projection profiles and the two label graph cut approach.

5.3   Discussion

The image series chosen for the experiments is hard to segment, since image quality and resolution is very low. The characters are very close together, which additionally makes segmentation very difficult. However, this is a very good set of images for comparison of robust segmentation algorithms on real data. The

Figure 5.1: Example of the text region chosen by the user.

experimental results show that the proposed multi-label graph cuts segmentation approach is superior to the others. The result did not show any merged character, but only fragmented ones. The most common error was cuts through zeros, which is only very hard to avoid. This is caused by the fact that the characters are very close together and most of the zeros are even touching. Thus, the cut is much cheaper through the zeros than through the region where two zeros are touching. However, the multi-label graph cuts approach significantly outperforms the other methods on real data, which is very promising and encouraging to make further investigations on this approach.

The multi-label graph cuts approach has only one free parameter, which allows a weighting of the intensity penalty with respect to the position penalty. This is not necessarily a disadvantage, since in some applications it may be definitely advantageous to have a parameter to control the segmentation result. Furthermore, the method is not very sensitive to the selection of the parameter and in most cases it can be easily seen whether the position or rather the intensity penalty is to be preferred during segmentation.

An improvement of the proposed multi-label graph cuts approach may be achieved, if not only the result of the initial segmentation is considered, but subsequent results as well. The prior knowledge in terms of the position penalty is more accurate and not only based on the initial segmentation result, i.e. the position penalty is more generalized.

It has been demonstrated that the multi-label graph cuts approach shows very promising results. However, more investigations have to be done on the mapping of the position penalty of the initial segmentation to the current image. This is due to the fact that some of the segmentation errors are caused by an inaccurate mapping. This is also very important in order to be robust to scaling and slight variations in characters' width.

6 Conclusion

In this technical report a new method for character segmentation has been proposed, which is based on multi-label graph cuts. The method allows to consider prior knowledge in terms of the approximate position of the characters and the number of characters in a line. The energy functional, which has to be minimized for segmentation, has been discussed in detail as well as the design of the graph based on the energy functional.

The experimental results have shown that multi-label graph cuts character segmentation is superior to other segmentation methods on image sequences as they occur in industrial applications.

Further investigations are performed to learn the position penalty not only from one image but during the application. This may further improve the segmentation result since the method is adaptive to changes over time.

Bibliography

[BK04]   Yuri Boykov and Vladimir Kolmogorov. An experimental comparison of min-cut/max-flow algorithms for energy minimization in vision. *IEEE Transactions on Pattern Analysis and Machine Intelligence*, 26(9):1124–1137, 2004.

[BVZ01]   Yuri Boykov, Olga Veksler, and Ramin Zabih. Fast Approximate Energy Minimization via Graph Cuts. *IEEE Trans. on Pattern Analysis and Machine Intelligence*, 23(11):1222–1239, November 2001.

[CL96]   Richard G. Casey and Eric Lecolinet. A Survey of Methods and Strategies in Character Segmentation. *IEEE Transactions on Pattern Analysis and Machine Intelligence*, 18:690–706, 1996.

[CVR11]   Computer Vision Research Group at the University of Western Ontario, November 2011. http://vision.csd.uwo.ca/code/.

[GB10]   Martin Grafmüller and Jürgen Beyerer. Segmentation of Printed Gray Scale Dot Matrix Characters. In Jorge Baralt, Nagib Callaos, Shigehiro Hashimoto, William Lesso, and Dale Zinn, editors, *Proceedings of the 14th World Multi-Conference on Systemics, Cybernetics and Informatics*, volume II, pages 87–91, June 2010.

[GB11]   Martin Grafmüller and Jürgen Beyerer. Robust High Performance Character Segmentation Based on Projections and Graph Cuts. In *Proceedings of the 13th IASTED International Conference on Signal and Image Processing*, December 2011.

[LeB97]   Frank LeBourgeois. Robust Multifont OCR System from Gray Level Images. In *Proc. 4th Int. Conf. on Document Analysis and Recognition*, volume 1, pages 1–5, 1997.

[LNCS04]   Yun Li, Satoshi Naoi, Mohamed Cheriet, and Ching Y. Suen. A segmentation method for touching italic characters. In *Proc. 17th Int. Conf. Pattern Recognition ICPR 2004*, volume 2, pages 594–597, 2004.

[LSA94]   Su Liang, M. Shridhar, and M. Ahmadi. Segmentation of touching characters in printed document recognition. *Pattern Recognition*, 27(6):825–840, 1994.

[Lu95]   Yi Lu. Machine printed character segmentation – An overview. *Pattern Recognition*, 28(1):67–80, 1995.

[NYK+05]   Shigueo Nomura, Keiji Yamanaka, Osamu Katai, Hiroshi Kawakami, and Takayuki Shiose. A novel adaptive morphological approach for degraded character image segmentation. *Pattern Recognition*, 38(11):1961–1975, 2005.

[PYX08]   Mei-Sen Pan, Jun-Biao Yan, and Zheng-Hong Xiao. Vehicle license plate character segmentation. *International Journal of Automation and Computing*, 5:425–432, 2008.

[SSR10]   Tanzila Saba, Ghazali Sulong, and Amjad Rehman. A Survey on Methods and Strategies on Touched Characters Segmentation. *International Journal of Research and Reviews in Computer Science*, 1(2), 2010.

[TA86]   Yositake Tsuji and Ko Asai. Adaptive Character Segmentation Method Based on Minimum Variance Criterion. *Systems and Computers in Japan*, 17(7):30–39, 1986.

[TCJY07]   Jia Tse, Dean Curtis, Christopher Jones, and Evangelos Yfantis. An OCR-independent character segmentation using shortest-path in grayscale document images. In *Proc. 6th Int. Conf. Machine Learning and Applications*, pages 142–147, December 2007.

[Yan00]   Berrin A. Yanikoglu. Pitch-based segmentation and recognition of dot-matrix text. *International Journal on Document Analysis and Recognition*, 3:34–39, 2000.

[ZZ03]   Yungang Zhang and Changshui Zhang. A New Algorithm for Character Segmentation of License Plate. In *Proceedings of the IEEE Intelligent Vehicles Symposium*, pages 106–109, 2003.

Towards Adaptive Open-World Modeling

Achim Kuwertz

Vision and Fusion Laboratory
Institute for Anthropomatics
Karlsruhe Institute of Technology (KIT), Germany
achim.kuwertz@kit.edu

Technical Report IES-2011-10

Abstract: In this technical report, extensions to the Object-Oriented World Model (OOWM) are proposed allowing for adaptive open-world modeling for artificial cognitive systems. In cognitive systems, a world model can serve as a central component for integrating, storing and disseminating information from an observed environment. Thus, a world model depicts an abstract, simplified representation of an observed real-world domain. For allowing high-level information processing on a semantic layer, representations of real-world entities, which are observed by sensors, can be semantically enriched by domain models. In general, a domain model contains only a fixed number of a priori defined concepts from a closed world. However, in many real-life applications, the considered environment is not closed. For coping with changing environments, a cognitive system must be equipped with an adaptive world model able to adjust to an observed open environment. Thus, this technical report discusses how the OOWM can be extended to facilitate semantically grounded open-world modeling.

1 Introduction

Information has become one of the most valuable assets in modern life. In fact, information is the building block from which knowledge is built, concerning almost any area of today's life like politics, business or even daily life. Information arises whenever data is interpreted in a meaningful way, be it the data of a radio signal in communications, scientific data observed in experiments or the data retrieved from online resources. With data nowadays being collected in growing quantities and the increasing presence of network enabled devices, information seems to be ubiquitously accessible. Thus, the unavailability of information in many cases no longer seem to pose a problem. Nevertheless, it still can be tedious to find, retrieve and integrate specific information from available sources in order to, e.g., establish a task-related situational overview or answer dedicated questions. In fact, the availability of a flood of information even worsens this problem. In this situation, modern technologies can be applied to guide and aid us in the task of processing and managing available information, supporting us just with relevant information or even information outlined on the right level of abstraction for our needs.

Another area of modern life where innovation and technological progress has led to the possibility of aiding and supporting humans by technical solutions is the field of assisted living and working. In this area, mechatronic systems autonomously manipulate their environment in order to fulfill supportive work or even specific tasks like heath care. In order to succeed at such tasks, autonomous technical systems must be able to sense, i.e., to acquire information about the environment they are operating in in order to determine the current environment state. Perception and adequate interpretation of a variable and possibly unknown environment are important prerequisites for a successful operation of these systems. Thus, autonomous systems also need the ability to acquire, process and integrate relevant information for establishing a task-related situational picture.

1.1 Artificial Cognitive Systems

In conclusion, one of the most relevant problems of today's profound decision taking no longer is the lack of information, but rather the tasks revolving around the separation of relevant from non-relevant information, the integration of retrieved information to form a consistent knowledge, the drawing of conclusions based on such knowledge and the presentation of desired derived information on the right level of abstraction. Hence, there is a need for technical systems being able to (semi-) autonomously fulfill these cognitive tasks. In this report, systems able to cope with such tasks will be subsumed under the notion of *artificial cognitive systems*.

In order to fulfill one of their central tasks, evaluating a sensed operational environment, artificial cognitive systems need to be equipped with several subsystems:

- a *sensing* input subsystem possibly consisting of multiple sensors of heterogeneous types and sensing modalities.

- an *information integration and storing* subsystem that consistently fuses all available sensor data and integrates it with a priori information into a comprehensive knowledge base.

- a *reasoning* subsystem able to process and answer information requests by interpreting acquired knowledge (e.g., extract current environment state).

- an output subsystem providing a channel for *relaying and displaying* the results of information requests on different levels of abstraction.

Furthermore, artificial cognitive systems can possess more functional subsystems like actuators for environment manipulation and locomotion, or subsystems for planning and scheduling such interaction. In addition to these functional aspects, artificial cognitive systems need to be provided with semantic information about their operational domain in order to evaluate their sensor observations in a meaningful manner. Such information can be given as an a priori *domain model*.

Areas of application for artificial cognitive systems include assisted living and working, disaster management, security and safety in public places, remote sensing for environment protection, maritime and land border surveillance as well as reconnaissance. In all these areas, data and information available from heterogeneous sources have to be integrated to support a situational awareness for decision making by establishing an overview of the current situation at hand.

1.2   Object-Oriented World Modeling

The task of integrating different information into a comprehensive semantical representation can be solved by a world modeling system as depicted in Fig. 1.1. The OOWM [GHB08, BKFB12], developed at Vision and Fusion Laboratory in collaboration with Fraunhofer IOSB, is an example of such a system. Its main purpose is to provide a consistent and integrated view on the current state of an observed environment. It thereby acts as an information hub for sensory and cognitive processes, allowing all subsystems to access the information required to perform their tasks. The OOWM possesses the following features ([GHB08, EGB08]):

- *object-oriented* information representation – observed real-world entities are represented as objects with attributes and relations.

- *semantic* background knowledge – observed entities are associated with semantic concept descriptions stored in a domain model.

- *Bayesian* information processing – information stored in the world model is treated as inherently uncertain and characterized by probability distributions interpreted as degrees of belief, which allows for integrating new information in a uniform way by applying fusion methods. [HGPLB10].

Figure 1.1: World modeling: a given domain, the world of interest, is observed by heterogeneous sensor systems. Sensor data and extracted information are passed on to a world modeling system in order to be integrated, stored and serve as a basis for evaluating the current state of the world of interest.

- *dynamic* environment description – stored information is not static but can both be dynamically updated by new observations and age in time.

- level-of-detail *abstraction* – information provided to subsystems can be represented on a task-relevant hierarchical level of abstraction [HGPLB10].

1.3   Adaptive World Modeling

The ability of a world model to represent and semantically evaluate the current state of an observed domain strongly depends on the presence of a semantic domain model. In general, domain models are created both manually by human experts and prior to the operations of a cognitive system. Therefore, the semantic expressiveness of a world model is limited by the set of a priori modeled concepts. As a consequence, only a closed world segment can be represented. To integrate unforeseen events and entities, the world model has to be able to dynamically adjust its prior knowledge to the current state of the observed domain. This ability to adjust and extend existing knowledge is at the heart of *adaptive world modeling*.

A main part of adaptive open-world modeling is concerned with extending knowledge by learning new concept definitions. Concept learning for artificial cognitive systems comprises of several different subtasks. These tasks include deciding when and which concept should be learned at all, acquiring a perceptual representation and a symbolic name for a learned concept as well as defining its meaning by learning unobservable semantic attributes. In order to enable concept learning for world models, this technical report proposes to extent the OOWM. For this purpose, a formal non-shallow knowledge representation will be introduced and an interoperable top-level ontology for OOWM knowledge will be defined.

This technical report is structured as follows. Sec. 2 gives a brief overview of the object-oriented world modeling system and its notions. Sec. 3 proposes extensions to the object-oriented world model for allowing adaptive world modeling. Sec. 4 then takes a closer look at semantics, meaning and symbol grounding for different artificial cognitive systems. In Sec. 5, various concept learning approaches relevant for grounding adaptive world modeling are examined. The report concludes with an outlook on planned future work.

2   Notions of Object-Oriented World Modeling

The term *world modeling* refers to generating an abstract representation of a real-world domain, as depicted in 1.1. The resulting model contains simplified, but formal representations of real-world entities. In world modeling different approaches for taking into account time-dependent features can lead to different types of models. On the one hand, static models describe the static, non time-dependent properties of a modeled domain, e.g. facts, structures or statements that hold true regardless of the point of time they are considered. Such models are often called domain models. On the other hand, in contrast to static modeling a dynamic model tries to capture the current state of an observed domain. Based on sensor measurements of time-dependent properties, dynamic world models focus on providing a snapshot of features like inherent states, positions or constellations of entities. In order to represent a domain in a comprehensive way, both state information and static knowledge are necessary. Thus, the object-oriented world model presented in the following employs a domain model and a dynamic model in combination.

2.1   System Overview and Notions

Within object-oriented world modeling, the relevant part of the real world is called the *world of interest* [FHB10]. The world of interest is a domain-specific or task-specific view on a spatio-temporal segment of the real world. Conceptually, the world of interest consists of various different *entities* like objects, persons or abstracta. This view of the world of interest, taking into account not only physical objects but also abstract concepts, constitutes a human-related perspective to artificial cognition. This ensures a compatible, consistent view and a mutual

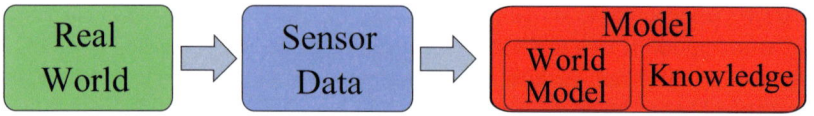

Figure 2.1: High-level overview and notions of object-oriented world modeling.

comprehension for human-related artificial cognitive systems and their human operators.

For acquiring dynamic information, observable *attributes* of individual entities like their extent, color or position are monitored by sensors. The sensor data, representing a view or projection of the world of interest to sensing modalities, serves as input for the OOWM. The OOWM consists of two modeling subsystems [BKFB12]: the dynamic *World Model* representing the current state of an observed world of interest, and the *Knowledge* subsystem representing domain knowledge. An overview of object-oriented world modeling is depicted in Figure 2.1.

2.1.1 Knowledge

The *Knowledge* subsystem provides a static model of the world of interest. As an important part, the semantics of the considered domain have to be captured within the model. In object-oriented world modeling, the semantics of entities are formally represented by *entity concepts*, which describe the observable and unobservable attributes of an entity and its defining relations. Attributes comprise time-varying state attributes (e.g., a position) and immutable property attributes (e.g., a color). Relations can either describe necessary relationships, which have to hold any time and for all instances of a concept, or possible relationships which, e.g., can hold only for certain instances or distinct periods of time. Entity concepts can be modeled prior to system operations by domain experts. Thus, they serve as a priori information. Yet, OOWM knowledge does not just consist of prior knowledge, as it is designed to support adaptive open-world modeling and can be extended by newly learned concept definitions.

Using a semantic domain model enables an artificial cognitive system to share a meaningful set of symbols with its environment. Based on prior knowledge it is not only possible to classify a real-world entity given observations of its features, but also to derive unobservable features or to interpret symbolic information requests, e.g. being phrased in natural language.

2.1.2   World Model

The *World Model* in the OOWM is responsible for processing and storing the dynamic environment data given by sensor observations. Sensor observations are associated with a *representative* of the real-world entity they originate from and are stored as a container set of attribute values [KBS+10], as exemplary illustrated in Fig. 2.2. Observed attribute values are represented by probability distributions characterizing the measurement value as well as its uncertainty as a Degree-of-Belief (*DoB*). For integrating heterogeneous sensor observations, techniques for data and information fusion are employed, supported by techniques for information management (like an aging mechanism, consistency checks, etc.) [BKFB12]. Using a set-based entity representation allows to represent unknown entities as well, as long as the observed attributes are known. Furthermore, blank objects allow to represent just the presence or rather existence of something. If relations between different objects are observed, the current state of a world of interest is represented as a semantic network in the World Model. In addition, past environment states are represented in a history of recent state information. The World Model thus is time-dependent and dynamic.

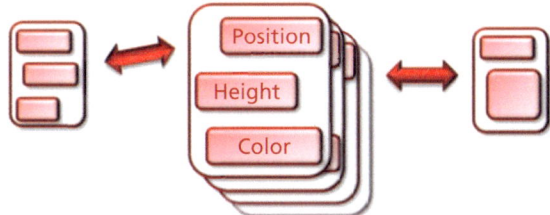

Figure 2.2: The World Model as a semantic network with history and past states.

2.2   Areas of Application

The OOWM is designed to be an information integration and storage facility of general purpose being applicable, as a part of a cognitive system, in various areas of application. Up to now, the OOWM has been successfully applied in several domains including assisted living [KBS+10], indoor security [EGB08], real estate surveillance or maritime border surveillance [FB10]. In many cases though, only a shallow model was employed to represent semantic domain knowledge. In order to allow for a semantic open-world modeling, a formal structure for representing non-shallow domain knowledge must be defined. This extension to object-oriented world modeling is introduced in the following section.

3   Extending the Object-Oriented World Model

In adaptive world modeling knowledge can be modified by acquiring new concept definitions during the time of system operations. As stated in [KHB10], the task of dynamic concept acquisition constitutes an extension to the classical concept learning problem [Mit97]. Classical concept learning is aimed at learning concepts, represented as boolean functions over sets of attributes, from given labeled training data in a supervised manner. As a kind of inductive learning problem, concept learning requires a formal structure in which concepts can be represented, i.e., a concept space. The process of learning new concepts can be regarded as a search within this space for the most suited representation of a considered concept given a set of training data [Mit97]. The structure for concept representation constitutes the inductive bias necessary for learning and generalization.

3.1   A Meta-Model for Entity Concepts

In object-oriented world modeling, up to now no explicit structure for entity concepts exists. To allow for sophisticated concept learning in adaptive world modeling, a meta-model formally defining the space of entity concepts will be introduced in the following. Extending our ideas presented in [BKFB12], a formal structure for the most basic entity concepts in OOWM knowledge will be defined. In summary, entity concepts are governed by intra- and inter-class relationships. Intra-class relationships are modeled by attributes (e.g., the height of an entity), which are instances of attribute concepts (e.g., a height attribute being a non-negative real-valued variable of a certain length unit). Inter-class relationships are modeled by relations (e.g., one entity being part of another), which are instances of relation concepts. Relation concepts again are characterized by attributes. Fig. 3.1 shows an overview of the meta-model for entity concepts in OOWM knowledge described subsequently.

3.1.1   Individual Concepts

The essential entity concepts in object-oriented world modeling are *individual concepts*, which model the common features of entities like things, persons, roles, functions, qualities, etc. Individual concepts are defined by

- a unique name,

- a parent individual concept (given as a reference),

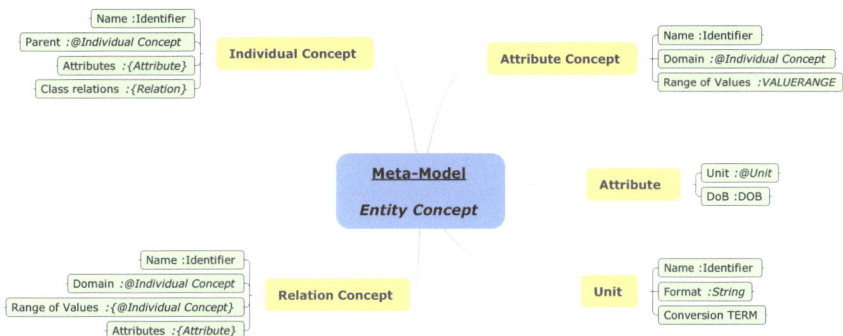

Figure 3.1: Meta-model structure for entity concepts in OOWM knowledge. The displayed concept definitions specify the syntax for individual concepts, relation concepts, attribute concepts, attributes and units.

- a set of attributes, and

- a set of class relations.

Attributes and class relations (i.e., relations necessarily holding for all instances of a concept) serve to semantically define specific features of individual concepts. The reference to a parent concept allows to establish a concept hierarchy.

3.1.2   Attribute Concepts

For characterizing an individual entity, attributes describing the entity features are instantiated from *attribute concepts*. An attribute concept is specified by

- a unique name,

- an attribute domain (given as a reference to an individual concept), and

- a range of values defining admissible attribute values.

By defining a range of values, the type of an attribute concept is determined as well (e.g., nominal vs. cardinal attributes). This allows the use of specialized fusion and learning methods adjusted to attributes for this concept. The reference to an individual concept serves as semantic definition for this attribute.

3.1.3   Attributes and Units

When instantiating an *attribute* from a given attribute concept (e.g., a height), an attribute additionally needs to define

- its unit (given as a reference to a unit concept), and
- a DoB probability distribution (characterizing the expected attribute values).

Not specifying units within attribute concepts, but later within attributes allows for multiply instantiating a single attribute concept with attributes of different units. Following the presented structure, the height of a cup can for example be described as being given in cm and being equally distributed from 9 to 10 (cm). In order to enable this structure, *unit concepts* are defined as consisting of

- a unique name,
- a syntax string, and
- a conversion term (allowing to convert related units, e.g. cm to m).

The syntax string of a unit defines the format of values given in this unit. Representing the data format of values then allows to define a conversion term, which can be used for automatic conversion of given values to a standard unit.

3.1.4   Relation Concepts

An individual concept is not only characterized by its attributes (defining intra-class relationships), but also by relationships to other entity concepts. As mentioned earlier, there are two types of relations within world modeling: class relations holding for all instances of an entity concept and thus being part of its definition, and instance relations that can hold just for individual instances (e.g., being situated near to something). In general, a *relation concept* consists of

- a unique name,
- a domain for which this relation can be applied (given as a reference to an individual concept),
- a range of values for this relation (given as set of references to individual concepts), and
- a set of attributes.

When specifying an individual concept as domain or as part of the range of values for a relation concept, relation instances can be applied to instances of the given individual concept as well as all its children in the concept taxonomy.

3.2   Top-Level Knowledge Ontology

Semantic concept learning, besides a syntactic metastructure for OOWM knowledge, also requires an initial semantic structure for organizing its entity concepts. When knowledge is represented by ontologies, abstract high-level ontologies called upper ontologies or top-level ontologies can be employed to introduce a semantic structure. A *top-level ontology* thereby defines high-level entity concepts, i.e., entity concepts that occur independent of and across many application domains, in an abstract and extendable way. Examples of top-level ontologies include, e.g., DOLCE [GGM+02] or WordNet [MBF+90]. An important purpose of top-level ontologies is to enable semantic interoperability between different application-specific domain ontologies. Thus, a top-level ontology structure seems to be good anchor for a semantic and interoperable extension of OOWM knowledge as required for adaptive open-world modeling.

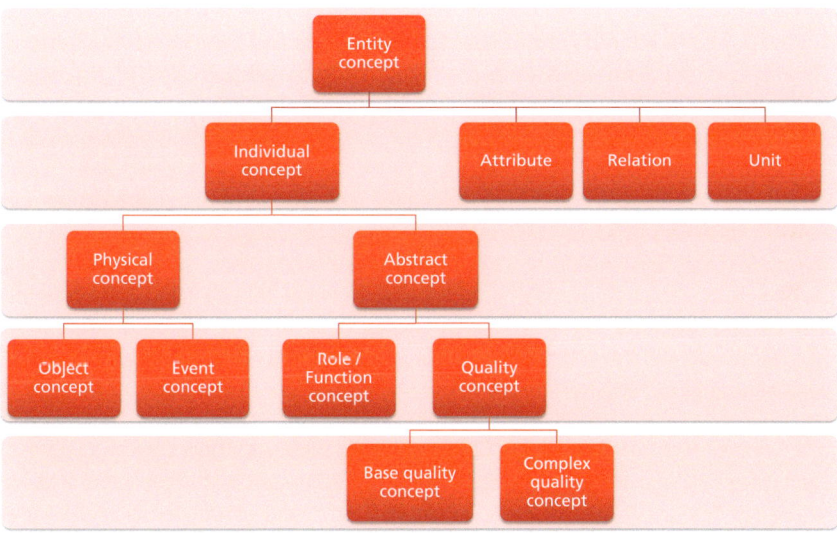

Figure 3.2: Top-level ontology for structuring entity concepts in knowledge.

As a semantic structure for OOWM knowledge, the approach depicted in Fig. 3.2 was chosen. This approach is in some parts based on the principles used for designing the DOLCE ontology [GGM+02]. As can be seen in Fig 3.2, entity concepts are semantically subdivided into four *basic concept categories*, namely individual concepts, attribute concepts, relation concepts and unit concepts, reflecting the structure used within the meta-model. At the moment, only a conception for further partitioning individual concepts has been elaborated. Individual concepts are semantically subdivided into concepts for physically existing entities and concepts for abstract entities. *Physical concepts* are further subdivided into object concepts for physical entities existing in space and event concepts for physical entities existing in time. Object concepts thereby include concepts for persons and things. *Abstract concepts* are divided into role-function concepts on the one hand, describing the roles a person can embody as well as the functions a thing can fulfill. On the other hand, quality concepts describe the features that real-world entities can possess. In future work, the structure of the remaining basic concepts as well as more level-of-detail for the presented concepts has to be elaborated.

3.3   Towards Adaptive Object-Oriented World Modeling

Figure 3.3 gives an overview of system components and their interactions relevant for adaptive object-oriented world modeling. As in the present OOWM, information within knowledge is used to classify real-world entities based on sensor observations of their attribute values [BKFB12]. When classified, additional information, for example on unobservable attributes, can be derived from knowledge. During operations, the system is likely to encounter real-world entities that have not been a priori modeled in knowledge and thus cannot be uniquely mapped to an entity concept. Being represented as set of observed attribute values, such entities can then be passed to a concept learning subcomponent responsible for adaptively extending knowledge. Besides being driven by sensor observations, concept learning can also be necessary if the world model is queried for instances of concepts not yet represented in knowledge.

The concept learning component is bound by the meta-model structure in respect of how information is learned and stored in knowledge and by the top-level ontology in respect of what information can be learned. The meta-model describes the syntax of concept definitions and thus formalizes what a system itself "knows" about the information stored in knowledge. This means that all features described by the metal-model can be interpreted in a meaningful way by the system. The top-level ontology provides a semantic foundation for concept learning by abstractly defining the basic partition of concept space as well as defining the semantics of measured and learned attributes. For managing the information modeled in meta-model and top-level ontology or represented in knowledge, a model editor component seems to be a valuable supplement. This editor in addition could serve as a tool to display and manually verify newly learned concept definitions.

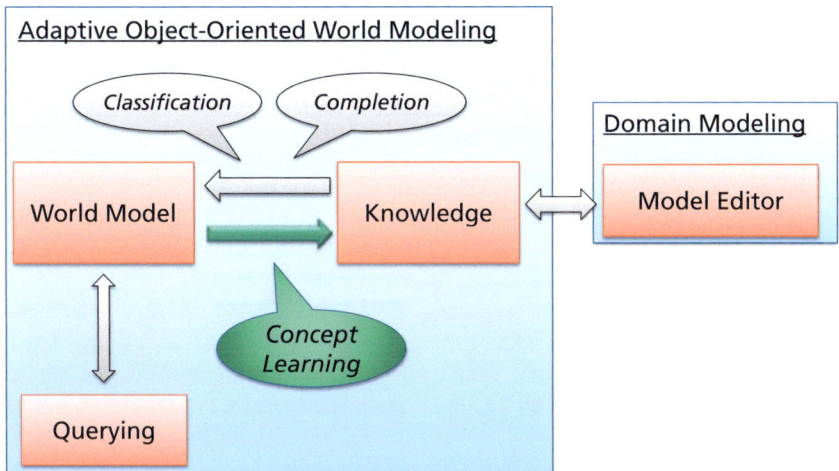

Figure 3.3: Overview of adaptive object-oriented world modeling. In addition to the interaction of world model and knowledge for classifying observed entities and completing the information represented for this entities, dynamic information from world model is used as input for extending knowledge by concept learning.

3.4   Concept Learning Example

The conceptions of adaptive world modeling shall be illustrated by a brief high-level example. Suppose a number of entity concepts is given, formally describing tangible real-world objects as defined in the meta-model. In fact, a more specific structure defining a kind of prototype concept for tangible objects could be imagined (for example, a common parent node in concept taxonomy). The attributes of this prototype concept (e.g., its extent, shape, mass, position, color, etc.) then have to be semantically defined within an extended top-level ontology, for example by defining related attribute concepts and synonymic symbolic names, and within an extended meta-model by defining the data type properties for each attribute.

Now, suppose a yet unmodeled entity is observed and several of its attributes get measured. First, each sensor measurement has to be associated with an attribute concept. This for example is possible, if all sensors formally describe their sensing modalities a priori as attribute concepts. Then, one can try to learn the distribution of values for each attribute of the unmodeled concept. Knowing the data type of attributes, different methods for learning this distribution can be employed, for example to learn nominally, ordinally and cardinally scaled attributes and represent them as Gaussian mixture models. Having an initial estimate of the distribution of each attribute, one then can try to separate attributes relevant for concept definition from non-relevant attributes, e.g. by evaluating the entropy of each attribute distribution: The lesser an entropy, the more relevant an attribute is since it then seems to be a good indicator for separating concept instances from non-instances based on observed values.

If not enough measurement data is given for an observable attribute, or when trying to learn unobservable attributes, more data can be acquired by specific requests, e.g., to a human operator or by searching information on the World Wide Web. Acquiring information in such ways on the one hand requires a symbolic name or description for the concept to be learned. On the other hand, semantic information on relevant attributes is necessary to find data which can serve as training data for learning attribute distributions. Which attributes have to be learned could thereby, for example, be determined by a high-level service in order to performing its tasks.

4 Meaning and Semantics in World Modeling

An important aspect of world modeling for artificial cognitive systems is to represent an observed environment in a meaningful way. A cognitive system shall not only store its observations according to world modeling data structures, but should also be able to understand its environment and perhaps interact with it in a useful manner. Ideally, an artificial cognitive system should be able to autonomously explore its environment and "get a feeling" for the entities it encounters. Getting a feeling for entities means to establish in internal representation, a model, of the perceptual and action-related features which real-world objects do possess. Furthermore, a cognitive system should be able to learn abstract concepts from textual descriptions, e.g. explanations given by humans. Moreover, again ideally, a cognitive system should end up with the same idea of its environment as a human would have. Thus, artificial cognitive systems require human-related world modeling subsystems, that is a world model at least capable of establishing an environment representation being compatible to a human's conception.

4.1 Semantics in World Modeling

The term meaning can be interpreted in a lot of different ways according to in which scientific discipline or even philosophical movement it is used. One way to interpret meaning is to say that it subsumes all information related to finding a *referent*, i.e., a real-world entity, for a given symbol, e.g., a word. Within world modeling, this kind of meaning is relevant for identifying entities in the real world which are instances of a concept given by a symbolic description, for example by natural language. Thus, following the referent interpretation, the meaning of a concept is basically given by its observable attributes and its defining relations deducible from this attributes.

Yet, this interpretation disregards the remaining attributes which, for example, describe unobservable features. When looking for a cup, we not necessarily use the feature of a cup being a vessel to carry liquids for discriminating real-world objects. Nevertheless, being a vessel for liquids is part of the semantics of a concept for cups. Thus, another way to interpret the meaning of a concept is to subsume all its features, attributes and relations, especially features that describe functions or roles. In some way, these features can be seen as higher-lever semantics.

For artificial cognitive systems, meaning can be defined within the knowledge of a world modeling subsystem. Concepts contained in knowledge characterize the mapping from real-world entities to representatives in the world model in a homomorphic way [Syd82]. The main purpose of this mapping for cognitive systems is to share a meaningful set of symbols with their environment: on the one hand this mapping allows for classifying and identifying observed entities based on their attribute values, thus fulfilling the referent interpretation of meaning. On the other hand concepts allow to interoperably exchange meaningful information, e.g., when receiving requests from humans. Based on the mapping of representatives to concepts, human requests and sensor data can be interrelated and, furthermore, represented entities can be enhanced with unobservable semantic features.

4.2   Symbol Grounding

After having seen that meaning in world modeling is useful for identifying and classifying real-world entities as well as processing symbolic requests, the next step is to take a look at how meaning can be acquired by cognitive systems. This is closely related to the symbol grounding problem in cognition as stated in [Har90]. The question at hand in symbol grounding is how a "semantic interpretation" of symbols, e.g., attribute and relation concepts in the case of world modeling, can "be made intrinsic to the system rather than just" existing as "meanings in our heads" [Har90]. Recognizing and addressing this problem can be seen as a first step to bridging the semantic gap. If one, for example, formally models a given set of facts within an ontology, one can reach semantic interoperability in a sense that different humans can interpret the symbols contained in the ontology in a consistent way. Yet, one does not necessarily enable a system employing this ontology to semantically understand its symbols. This difference can be made clear by imagining an ontology in which the symbolic concept names have been exchanged for numbered variables.

Since this is the perspective a system has onto an ontology, the question arises if this ontology still does define meaning?

To solve this problem, different solutions are imaginable. For example, it is possible to try to formalize a set of facts or a whole domain in such a rigid way (e.g., by using a formal language) that, from a human perspective, by exchanging symbolic names no information would be lost. But this approach seems to be rather complex and time-consuming. Another solution is to ground the occurring symbols as proposed in [Har90]. Basically, a bottom-up grounding of semantic concepts within non-symbolic representations is proposed, where concepts are being hierarchically constructed from grounded symbols. The basic non-symbolic representations are given by sensor observations of entity features. How this approach, envisioned as a psychological model of human cognition, could be transferred to world modeling in artificial cognitive systems shall be examined in the following section.

4.3 Symbol Grounding for Artificial Cognitive Systems

The notion of artificial cognitive systems presented in this report subsumes autonomous systems and information systems. Prior to considering a symbol ground for these systems, their similarities and differences shall be pointed out.

4.3.1 Types of Cognitive Systems

A *cognitive autonomous system* is a system which is able to autonomously, i.e., without human interaction, make decisions, based on observations of its environment on the one hand and internally stored knowledge on the other hand, and then, as implied by these decisions, accordingly interact with its environment. Thus, an autonomous system can be characterized by its subsystems fulfilling the tasks of

- environment perception,
- data and information processing,
- decision making (goal-directed), and
- environment interaction (e.g., manipulation, mobility, etc.).

The two tasks of actively perceiving and interacting with its environment are fundamental for autonomy: on the one hand, a autonomous system has to be able to interpret signals from its environment in order to capture the current state of the environment and react to state changes. On the other hand, autonomous systems are constructed to serve a specific purpose and therefore need ways to interact with their observed environment. To relate perceived environment observations to interactions, the cognitive tasks of information processing and decision making are necessary. Examples of autonomous systems situated in different environments range from humanoid robots (perceiving and manipulating their environments in a human-like sense) over autonomous service robots (e.g., for performing some specialized tasks like room cleaning) over feedback control systems to software agents (perceiving and interacting for example within a simulated or abstracted environment as avatars, like trading agents for stock exchange). Some types of autonomous systems are designed to perform more complex tasks in an open environment, like interacting with humans. These systems have to be equipped with sophisticated cognitive processing abilities, able to understand a part of their observed environment in a way compatible to human comprehension.

Apart from systems able to interact with their environment in a physical (relevant or simulated) way, there are artificial cognitive systems primarily concerned with processing, managing and displaying high-level information. These *cognitive information systems* like autonomous systems consist of subsystems responsible for the cognitive tasks of

- information processing and
- decision making.

Yet unlike autonomous systems, cognitive information systems do not directly interact with an observed environment but communicate their processing results, like conclusion or alerts, to a human operator. Also these systems do not directly observe an environment but are presented with preprocessed data and information as input. Examples of such systems include information management systems, decision support system and situation awareness support systems.

4.3.2   Grounding Attribute Concepts

Since in world modeling sensor observations serve as input for attribute values, concept grounding has to start with attribute concepts. Attribute concepts in world modeling can be divided into sensomotoric and semantic attributes. *Sensomotoric* attributes, being either perceptual attributes or effector attributes, are especially relevant for cognitive autonomous systems as these systems directly observe and interact with their environment. Perceptual attributes (e.g., the height, color or speed of an entity) are grounded within the sensor components providing value information for these attributes to the world model. Effector attributes (like weight, shape, etc.) are grounded within the actuators used to manipulated real-world entities based on the represented values for these attributes [Ken98a]. As can be seen, there is no sharp boundary between perceptual and effector attributes, and which attribute is grounded by which sensomotoric component of an autonomous system in general depends upon the task currently to be executed. By relying on this sensomotoric grounding, cognitive autonomous systems are in principle able to autonomously acquire symbolic descriptions of concepts for observable entities grounded in sensor projections of the real-world. They are further able to ground action-related attributes of physical concepts in their interaction and manipulation of the respective real-world objects.

Furthermore, there are attributes in knowledge that can neither be associated with a sensor or an actuator component. Examples are attributes concerning roles and functions of entities and information like if and how an entity can be moved or where it is usually resting. These attributes constitute *semantic* attributes as they either result from acquired knowledge or long-term experience. Semantic attributes are unobservable and include physical properties, behavior and capabilities of real-world entities. They are the kind of attributes usually dealt with in cognitive information systems. As they originally may have been, at least partially, provided by a sensor system, they get preprocessed prior to being input to the information system. Thus these attributes cannot be grounded in sensor projections. Yet these semantic attributes also play an important role in world modeling for autonomous systems. Here they describe higher-level information like objection functions, e.g. a cup serving as a drinking vessel. In order to ground semantic attributes, symbolic descriptions can be used, e.g. given as text. In that way, semantic attributes can either be related to attributes and entity concepts grounded in sensor projections, as necessary for autonomous systems, or they can be defined in the context of semantic networks, as might be sufficient for cognitive information system that do not directly interact with their environment.

5   Types of Concept Learning

In order to enable adaptive open-world modeling for cognitive systems, techniques have to be employed for extending the existing knowledge of a world model with new entity concepts. This acquisition of concepts is often denoted as concept learning. The term concept learning is widely used in different scientific disciplines. These disciplines for example include cognitive sciences, where human concept learning is modeled, and computer sciences, where the term describes computational concept learning, e.g., as part of machine learning. In computational concept learning, there again are several different terms used to describe methods for learning new concepts, such as

- dynamic category building (e.g. [BB09]),
- concept acquisition (e.g. [Ken98b]),
- autonomous concept generation (e.g. [Ken98a]), or
- category learning (e.g. [DLST09], [TA08]),

which all focus on different aspects of concept learning. Furthermore, there is classical concept learning as e.g. stated in [Mit97]. Besides using various terms to denote concept learning, there are several subtypes of concept learning concerned with learning different kinds of models from observed data. These models differ in respect of what attributes are to be learned for representing an entity, and thus operate on different levels of semantics. The subtypes of concept learning include

- visual concept learning,
- symbolic concept learning,
- object learning, or
- ontology learning.

For adaptive open-world modeling, several of these concept learning subtypes have to be combined to learn about perceptual as well as symbolic and semantic features of observed entities. In this section, a short overview of some of these concept learning subtypes shall be given.

5.1 Visual Concept Detection and Learning

Visual concept learning or visual categorization has been a topic of research for decades [DLST09]. In visual concept learning, one tries to learn, detect, recognize and classify objects in video and image data by relying object shapes or even classifying whole situations depicted in imagery. The goal is to recognize already learned concepts in new imagery data and continuously update their representations. In this kind of learning, concept models emphasize syntax, not semantics, but the methods are for example applicable for automating image exploitation.

5.1.1 Cross-Modal Visual Concept Learning Based on Collateral Data

In [SLS05b] video data is tagged with concepts contained or depicted in single frames - for the purpose of semantic information retrieval and indexing. Concepts, hereby understood as keyword tags modeling image features, are detected within video data by classifiers trained in a supervised manner. For training, the approach proposed in [SLS05b] does not require tedious manual tagging of extensive training samples. Instead, an automatic labeling algorithm is employed, based on recognizing speech from correlated audio data, e.g. contained on the sound track of a video. This multimodal approach thus allows for learning visual concepts by abstracting their defining features from relevant image samples indicated by collateral audio data. Furthermore, the learned concepts are coincidently labeled with semantically interpretable names. In [SLS05a], the authors pick up on this fact and try to retrieve visual concepts solemnly based on accompanying speech information. The speech can be analyzed for keywords being related to a concept in terms of keyword expansion based on ontologies like WordNet.

5.1.2 Web-Based Visual Concept Learning

The World Wide Web (WWW) can be seen as another data source of collateral information for image data. This fact is for example exploited in [UBB10], where weakly labeled web videos are used in an unsupervised training for video indexing. A weakly label video thereby denotes a web video, for example retrieved from a video platform like YouTube, which has been manually tagged by a human user. Classifiers resulting from training with these videos shall then be able to detect objects, locations and even activities in videos.

In a similar fashion, as [UBB10] states, it is possible to use Google Search to find image examples for text-based concept descriptions. Google Search thereby uses the correlation between the textual descriptions of or located near by pictures in websites. Based on Google labels, there exists methods to create more robust labeling, e.g., by clustering the results and using the most promising cluster for concept detecting. Also, a manually chosen subset of Google Search results or a subset provided by text and meta-data analysis could be used as training data for training more robust concept classifiers.

5.1.3 Statistical Data-Driven Visual Concept Learning

Another approach to visual concept learning is taken by [DLST09]. In this approach, a special focus is laid on concept representation in order to achieve a high generalization performance for the learned models. Visual concept models thereby are composed of different shape primitives modeling the contours of objects. They are built in a *hierarchical* data-driven manner by an unsupervised *statistical* bottom-up learning algorithm. Combining statistical learning and a hierarchical representation allows for selecting only relevant shape primitives, based on given image data, on a lower level, which then serve as building parts for objects contours on a higher level.

On the highest level, a few hand-picked training examples are used for learning the specific category models, which then can be assigned a label (e.g., "cups"). The presented approach reaches a promising generalization performance for correctly classifying object shapes in previously unseen images.

5.2 Ontology Learning

Since visual concept learning focuses on the perceptual attributes of entity concepts, ontology learning seems to be a suitable supplement for adding semantics to perceptual concepts. Therefore, in future work methods for ontology learning, perhaps based on acquiring symbolic knowledge from online resources like the WWW or existing ontologies, have to examined in more detail.

6 Conclusion

This technical report proposes a conception to adaptive open-world modeling for artificial cognitive systems. Several important aspects concerning semantic modeling and concept learning have been discussed, including the structure of concept representation, semantic grounding of knowledge and different existing approaches to concept learning. All these aspects thereby play an important role when designing an adaptive system for open-world modeling.

Future work should further examine many of these areas and elaborate them in more detail. In total, adaptive world modeling in general and concept learning for world models in particular can be regarded as an information management problem. Future work to this problem includes determining when concept learning should be initiated, i.e., which observed concepts should be learned in order to be of use for a world modeling system. Based on this, frameworks have to be developed, on the one hand able to perform inductive probabilistic concept learning grounded in attribute observations and, on the other hand, enabling semantic attribute learning based on symbolic descriptions for supplementing perceptually acquired entity concepts. Finally, procedures for managing ontological concept taxonomies and integrating newly learned entity concepts into such a taxonomy are required.

Bibliography

[BB09]   Joscha Bach and Joscha Bach. The MicroPsi architecture. In *Principles of Synthetic Intelligence PSI: An Architecture of Motivated Cognition*, volume 1, pages 233–265. Oxford University Press, Oxford, England, 1 edition, November 2009.

[BKFB12]   Andrey Belkin, Achim Kuwertz, Yvonne Fischer, and Jürgen Beyerer. World Modeling
           for Autonomous Systems. In *Information System (to appear)*, number 1. InTech, 2012.

[DLST09]   Sven J. Dickinson, Ales Leonardis, Bernt Schiele, and Michael J. Tarr. Learning Hier-
           archical Compositional Representations of Object Structure. In *Object Categorization*.
           Cambridge University Press, 2009.

[EGB08]   Thomas Emter, Ioana Gheta, and Jürgen Beyerer. Object Oriented Environment Model
           for Video Surveillance Systems. pages 315–320, 2008.

[FB10]   Yvonne Fischer and Alexander Bauer. Object-Oriented Sensor Data Fusion for Wide
           Maritime Surveillance. In *Proceedings of 2nd NURC International WaterSide Security
           Conference*, Marina di Carrara, Italien, November 2010.

[FHB10]   Yvonne Fischer, Marco Huber, and Jürgen Beyerer. World modeling for advanced
           surveillance systems. Technical Report IES-2010-02, Vision and Fusion Laboratory,
           Institute for Anthropomatics, KIT, 2010.

[GGM+02]   Aldo Gangemi, Nicola Guarino, Claudio Masolo, Alessandro Oltramari, and Luc Schnei-
           der. Sweetening ontologies with dolce. In *Proceedings of the 13th International Con-
           ference on Knowledge Engineering and Knowledge Management. Ontologies and the
           Semantic Web*, EKAW '02, pages 166–181, London, UK, 2002. Springer-Verlag.

[GHB08]   Ioana Gheta, Michael Heizmann, and Jürgen Beyerer. Object Oriented Environment
           Model for Autonomous Systems. In Henrik Boström, Ronnie Johansson, and Joeri van
           Laere, editors, *Proceedings of the second Skövde Workshop on Information Fusion Topics*,
           pages 9–12. Skövde Studies in Informatics, November 2008.

[Har90]   Stevan Harnad. The Symbol Grounding Problem. *Physica D: Nonlinear Phenomena*,
           42(42):335–346, June 1990.

[HGPLB10] Michael Heizmann, Ioana Gheta, Fernando Puente Leon, and Jürgen Beyerer. Information
           fusion for environment exploration. In *Reports on industrial information technology*,
           volume 12, pages 147–166. KIT Scientific Publishing, Karlsruhe, 2010.

[KBS+10]   Benjamin Kühn, Andrey Belkin, Alexej Swerdlow, Timo Machmer, Jürgen Beyerer, Jürgen
           Beyerer, and Kristian Kroschel. Knowledge-Driven Opto-Acoustic scene analysis based
           on an object- oriented world modeling approach for humanoid robots. In *Robotics (ISR),
           2010 41st International Symposium on and 2010 6th German Conference on Robotics
           (ROBOTIK)*, pages 1–8. VDE, June 2010.

[Ken98a]   Catriona M. Kennedy. A Conceptual Foundation for Autonomous Learning in Unforeseen
           Situations. In *Intelligent Control (ISIC), 1998. Held jointly with IEEE International
           Symposium on Computational Intelligence in Robotics and Automation (CIRA), Intelligent
           Systems and Semiotics (ISAS), Proceedings*, pages 483–488. IEEE, September 1998.

[Ken98b]   Catriona M. Kennedy. Anomaly driven concept acquisition. 1998.

[KHB10]   Achim Kuwertz, Marco Huber, and Jürgen Beyerer. On Adaptive Open-World Modeling
           Based on Information Fusion and Inductive Inference. Technical Report IES-2010-16,
           Vision and Fusion Laboratory, Institute for Anthropomatics, KIT, 2010.

[MBF+90]   George A Miller, Richard Beckwith, Christiane Fellbaum, Derek Gross, and Kather-
           ine Miller. WordNet: an on-line lexical database. *INTERNATIONAL JOURNAL OF
           LEXICOGRAPHY*, 3:235—244, 1990.

[Mit97]   Tom M. Mitchell. *Machine Learning*. McGraw-Hill Education (ISE Editions), 1st edition,
           October 1997.

[SLS05a]   Xiaodan Song, Ching-Yung Lin, and Ming-Ting Sun. Autonomous Learning of Visual Concept Models. In *IEEE International Symposium on Circuits and Systems, 2005. ISCAS 2005*, pages 4598–4601 Vol. 5. IEEE, May 2005.

[SLS05b]   Xiaodan Song, Ching-Yung Lin, and Ming-Ting Sun. Speech-Based Visual Concept Learning Using Wordnet. In *IEEE International Conference on Multimedia and Expo, 2005. ICME 2005*, pages 1138–1141. IEEE, July 2005.

[Syd82]   P. H. Sydenham. *Handbook of Measurement Science: Theoretical fundamentals*, volume 1. Wiley, 1982.

[TA08]   S. Todorovic and N. Ahuja. Unsupervised Category Modeling, Recognition, and Segmentation in Images. *IEEE Transactions on Pattern Analysis and Machine Intelligence*, 30(12), December 2008.

[UBB10]   Adrian Ulges, Damian Borth, and Thomas Breuel. *Visual Concept Learning from Weakly Labeled Web Videos*, chapter 8, Video Search and Mining. Springer, 2010.

Optical Preprocessing in Spectroscopy

Miro Taphanel

Vision and Fusion Laboratory
Institute for Anthropomatics
Karlsruhe Institute of Technology (KIT), Germany
miro.taphanel@ies.uni-karlsruhe.de

Technical Report IES-2011-11

Abstract: This technical report reviews the state of the art in optical prepro-
cessing for spectroscopic applications. In particular, unconventional spectral
techniques are reviewed that do not use a spectrometer, or make no use of it
in the classical manner. In a theoretical part of this technical report, a vector
space representation is derived to describe spectral processing and necessary
assumptions are outlined. Based on this mathematical concept, optimal optical
filters for spectroscopic applications can be designed. The second part of the
technical report is about the optical hardware of these unconventional spectral
technics.

1 Introduction

The near-infrared NIR spectral range $800 - 2500$nm is very interesting for technical
applications. In contrast to the visible range, a transmission or reflectance spectrum
is related to stretch-and-bend vibrations of covalent bonds in molecules. In detail,
NIR reports on 1st, 2nd and 3rd vibrational overtones, combinations, and echoes of
those that occur in the mid-IR [GL10]. These mechanisms cause broaden, often
overlapping, peaks. On the other hand, the mid-IR range has higher technology
cost.

In addition to the classical spectroscopy, a lot of efforts were done to develop
unconventional methods, which do not use a spectrometer, or not in the classical way
[Bia86b, BBWB08a, MSK$^+$02a, PSB99, DUDL07, FH95a, FH95b, MSL$^+$01a,
HM04a, NAD$^+$98a, CUL05a, SGB11]. The reasons for these developments are
higher signal-to-noise ratio [BBWB08a], easier instrumentation [Bia86b] and faster
data acquisition [MSK$^+$02a]. Every time, when an application is limited by noise,
costs, or speed, these technics can be an option.

Over the years a lot of keywords were used for merchandising purposes. This is an overview for the most important acronyms:

- OSP Optical Signal Processing [Bia86b]

- OC Optical Computing [ML05]

- OR Optical Regression [PSB99]

- MOE Multivariate Optical Element [MSK$^+$02a]

- MFC Molecular Factor Computing [DUDL07]

- CP Computational Photography [HKW]

- MOC Multivariate Optical Computation [BBWB08a]

- ISP Integrated Sensing and Processing [ML05]

- HICI Hyperspectral Integrated Computational Imaging [CUL05a]

- PAT Process Analytical Technology [DUDL07] (general topic)

2 Vector Space Representation for Continuous Light Spectra

The natural character of light spectra is continuous. The natural character of measured light spectrum is discrete. In between there is a sampling process, which is referred to as measurement process. The reduction of continuous spectra into discrete values allows to arrange these as a vector. The vector $\mathbf{t} = (t_1, t_2, \cdots, t_n)^\top$ describes a transmission spectrum sampled at n discrete wavelengths.

In the following, it is discussed how this vector representation can be used to describe an optical filtering process and a filtering process in combination with an additional camera sensor. A filter $\mathbf{f} = (f_1, \cdots, f_n)^\top$, regardless of its optical realization, describes a wavelength dependent percental transmission $f_i \in [0, 1]$. This transmission describes the percental throughput of intensity, when light passes this element. The spectrum of the light intensity $\mathbf{I}^0 = (I_1^0, \cdots, I_n^0)^\top$ is modulated according an element-wise multiplication:

$$\mathbf{I}^1 = \mathbf{f} \circ \mathbf{I}^0 = (f_1 I_1^0, \cdots, f_n I_n^0)^\top,$$

when passing the filter $\mathbf{f}$. In the case of an additional photon sensitive sensor, which is typically sensitive for multiple wavelengths. The sensor signal s becomes:

$$s = \alpha \mathbf{f}^\top \mathbf{I}^0 \sim \mathbf{f}^\top \mathbf{I}^0, \tag{2.1}$$

and can be described as vector dot product. The factor α is necessary for physical unit consistency, because the unit of s is not specified here. In literature, s is often defined as gray value. In this case α is a factor that maps light intensity to grey value. The target of most of the unconventional spectroscopic technics is to connect the sensor signal s with a quantity of interest. So far no assumptions were necessary.

2.1   Vector Space Representation and Concentration Changes

Spectroscopy is well suited to measure concentrations of molecules in mixtures. In this article, the convention is used to name a specimen *analyt* if concentrations are of interest and *material* if the chemical composition is static. Furthermore, unimportant analyts are named as *interferents*. The following section discusses the problem of changing concentrations in spectroscopy [Mor77c] and the use of a vector representation. The impact of concentration changes to the analyt spectrum can be modeled by the Beer-Lambert law:

$$t_A(\lambda) = \frac{I^1(\lambda)}{I^0(\lambda)} = e^{-\epsilon_A(\lambda)c_A l}. \tag{2.2}$$

The continuous transmission spectrum $t_A(\lambda)$ is defined as the ratio of the output intensity $I_1(\lambda)$ behind the analyt A and input intensity $I_0(\lambda)$, respectively. The transmission $t_A(\lambda)$ is an exponential function of the absorption coefficient $\epsilon_A(\lambda)$, the concentration c_A, and the path length l of the light travelling through the volume. In general, there is no limitation to transmission spectra $t_A(\lambda)$, however, the path length l of a reflectance spectrum $r_A(\lambda)$ is unknown and must be determined empirically. In vector space representation, equation (2.2) can be rewritten as:

$$\mathbf{t}_A = \frac{\mathbf{I}^1}{\mathbf{I}^0} = e^{-\epsilon_A c_A l},$$

where $\mathbf{t}_A$ and ϵ_A are vectors. According to the Beer-Lambert law, there is no linear relationship between a transmission spectrum $t_A(\lambda)$ and a concentration c_A. To use this law in a linear vector space it needs to be linearized. For example, if the signal s of equation (2.1) shall be proportional to a concentration c and the task is to determine an adequate filter vector $\mathbf{f}$, this undertaking will fail due to the nonlinearity of the Beer-Lambert law. However, under the assumption of small concentrations $c \approx 0$ the Beer-Lambert law can be suitable linearized using a Taylor approximation of degree 1:

$$t_A(-\epsilon_A(\lambda)c_A l) = e^{-\epsilon_A(\lambda)c_A l}$$

$$\approx e^{-\epsilon_A(\lambda)c_A l}|_{c_A=0} + (c_A - 0)^1 \frac{\partial e^{-\epsilon_A(\lambda)c_A l}}{\partial c_A}|_{c_A=0}$$

$$= 1 - \epsilon_A(\lambda)c_A l$$

In this form the transmission spectrum $t_A(\lambda)$ scales linear with changes in concentration c_A. Hence, it is possible to use equation (2.1) to find a linear relationship of signal s_A and a concentration c_A. This is an approximation and will fail when concentrations become to high.

Normally, applications do not just deal with one analyt, but a mixture of them. The Beer-Lambert (2.2) law can be extended for this case. If a second absorber B is introduced, the overall transmission is the entry-wise product of the transmission $\mathbf{t}_A$ and $\mathbf{t}_B$.

$$\mathbf{t} = \mathbf{t}_A \circ \mathbf{t}_B = e^{-\epsilon_A c_A l} \circ e^{-\epsilon_B c_B l} = e^{-\epsilon_A c_A l - \epsilon_B c_B l}$$

For small concentrations this can be approximated to:

$$\mathbf{t} = \mathbf{1} - \epsilon_A c_A l - \epsilon_B c_B l.$$

and an useful extension is to use the difference from a reference level:

$$\boldsymbol{x} = \mathbf{1} - \boldsymbol{t} = \epsilon_A c_A l + \epsilon_B c_B l \qquad (2.3)$$

In this form $\boldsymbol{x}$ is the absorbance vector as the result of the vector addition of the absorbance components $\epsilon_A c_A l$ and $\epsilon_B c_B l$.

The assumption of small concentrations is quite strict. The same formula (2.3) can be derived by the use of negative log transmissions:

$$\boldsymbol{x} = -\ln(\mathbf{t}) = \epsilon_A c_A l + \epsilon_B c_B l$$

Although this is exactly the same result as (2.3), it is not an approximation anymore. The negative logarithm transformation converts the exponential Beer-Lambert law into a linear form. However, in practice every channel of a spectrometer must be transformed according to the negative logarithm separately. Furthermore, you one to ensure that the spectral width of the bandpass filters is small enough, so only slightly changes of $\epsilon(\lambda)$ can be guaranteed. In this case $\epsilon(\lambda)$ can be approximated by a single constant $\bar{\epsilon}(\lambda_k)$ for the spectral interval of the bandpass filter [Mor77c].

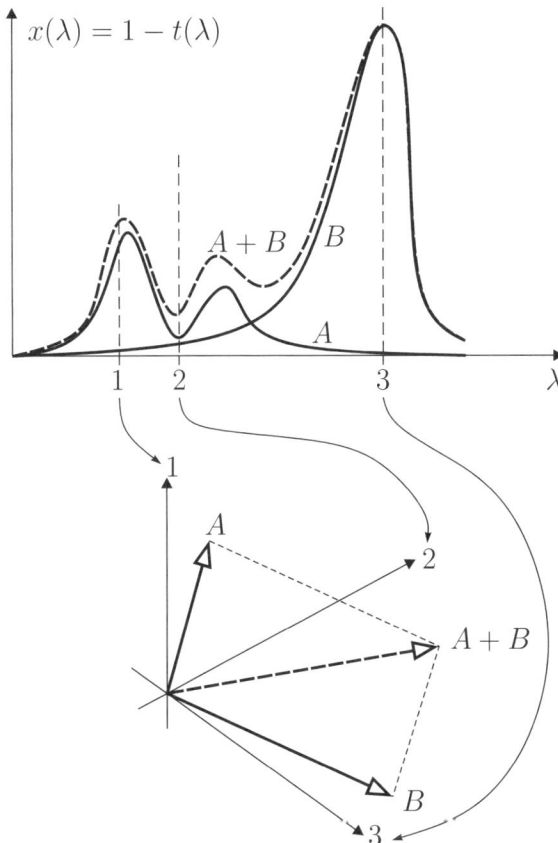

Figure 2.1: Vector space representation of sampled light spetra of analyt A and B. Each sampling wavelength defines one dimension of the vector space. Extracted from [Mor77c]

In summary, with an approximation for low concentrations it is possible to derive a linear relationship of the concentration c and the absorbance spectrum $\mathbf{x}$. Arbitrary concentrations can be handled by a linear model, if each channel is transformed according to the negative logarithm. The mixture of two absorbance spectra can be modeled by an addition of the absorbance vectors. These two properties proportionality and additivity satisfy the requirements of a linear vector space.

2.2   Vector Space Representation and Constant Concentrations

Applications using materials with a static chemical composition are quite common. For Example in remote sensing one task is to perform a spectral unmixing while the potential components are known. The problem in remote sensing is that each pixel of a hyperspectral imaging system images more than a single material. With the linear mixture model[KM02]:

$$\mathbf{r} = a\mathbf{r}_A + b\mathbf{r}_B + \cdots + \mathbf{n}$$

a measured reflectance spectrum $\mathbf{r}$ can be explained by a linear combination of known spectra $\{\mathbf{r}_A, \mathbf{r}_B, \cdots\}$, with linear coefficients $\{a, b, \cdots\}$ and a noise vector $\mathbf{n}$. The linear modell can be imagined as checkerboard distribution of multiple pure materials. In contrast to applications where the concentration of analyts can change, the chemical composition is fixed. For this reason the spectra of the known materials can be treated as ground truth, also called *endmembers*. The reflectance vector $\mathbf{r}$ is a linear combination of other vectors $\{\mathbf{r}_A, \mathbf{r}_B, \cdots\}$. The two properties proportionality and additivity are satisfied and the requirements for a linear vector space are fulfilled. With the vector dot product [Mor77c] it is possible, e.g., to design a filter $\mathbf{f}$, so that the signal $s_A = \mathbf{f}^\top \mathbf{r}$ is proportional to a, describing the spatial proportion of material A.

3   Optimal Filter Design Rules

The linear vector space theory is used in this section to derive optimal filter designs. The way how spectra can be represented in a linear vector space dependents on the application. If concentrations are of interest an analyt vector represents an absorbance vector $\mathbf{x}_A = -\ln(\mathbf{t}_A)$ or the approximation $\mathbf{x}_A = \epsilon_A c_A l$ of analyt A. If reflectance spectra are treated as ground truth, the target vector $\mathbf{r}_A$ describes a reflectance vector.

In this section it is not necessary to distinguish between different applications any longer, because an uniform vector space representation is possible. In certain circumstances, a filter vector $\mathbf{f}$, however, cannot be directly interpreted as a filter transmission characteristic. Fore example if the vector $\mathbf{x}_A = -\ln(\mathbf{t}_A)$ is used instead of the transmission vector $\mathbf{t}_A$, the resulting optimal filter vector $\mathbf{f}$ should be transformed inversely $\mathbf{f}' = e^{-\mathbf{f}}$, to receive the transmission characteristic for the optical filter.

The task of optimal filter design is to find a filter $\mathbf{f}$, so that a concentration or proportion of a target vector $\mathbf{a}$ can be determined. The relationship between a

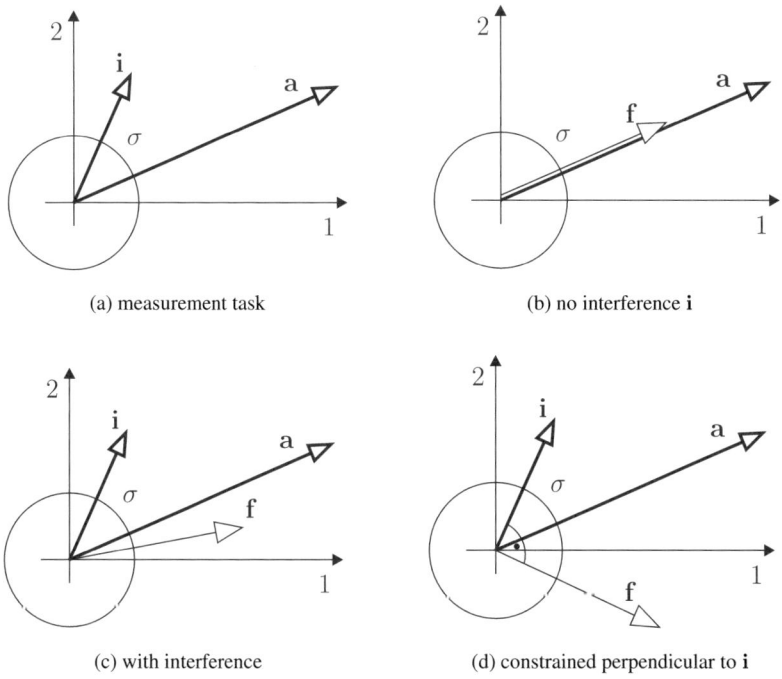

Figure 3.1: Optimal filter vectors **f** for different optimum criteria. A measurement vector $\mathbf{m} = \mathbf{a} + \mathbf{i} + \mathbf{n}$ is composed of a target vector **a**, an interference vector **i** and a noise vector **n** depicted as the standard deviation σ. Vectors shown in a two dimensional vector space, with each dimension corresponding to a sample wavelength. Extracted from [Mor77c].

concentration and a target vector can be defined by the vector dot product.

$$s \sim \mathbf{f}^\top \mathbf{m},$$

in which $\mathbf{m} = \mathbf{a} + \mathbf{i}^1 + \mathbf{i}^2 + \cdots + \mathbf{n}$ is the vector addition of the target vector $\mathbf{a}$, the other interference vectors $\{\mathbf{i}^1, \mathbf{i}^2, \mathbf{i}^3, \cdots\}$, and a system noise vector $\mathbf{n}$. The filter $\mathbf{f}$ is designed in such a way, that the signal s is proportional to a concentration or a proportion respectively. The system noise vector $\mathbf{n}$ is a random variable which describes the sum of all involved noise sources, with $E\{\mathbf{n}\} = \mathbf{0}$ and $\text{Cov}\{\mathbf{n}\} = \sigma^2 \mathbf{I}$.

The optimal criteria can be defined heuristically, with or without constrains, and by a signal-to-noise ratio. In the following, different optimal filter vectors are designed using these optimal criteria. The first case is an optimal filter for a single target $\mathbf{a}$. The measurement vector is defined as $\mathbf{m} := \mathbf{a} + \mathbf{n}$ (depicted in Fig. 3.1b). Using the signal-to-noise ratio [Mor77c],

$$
\begin{aligned}
\text{SNR} &= \frac{E\{\mathbf{f}^\top \mathbf{m}\}}{(\text{Var}\{\mathbf{f}^\top \mathbf{m}\})^{\frac{1}{2}}} \\
&= \frac{\mathbf{f}^\top \mathbf{a}}{\mathbf{f}^\top (\text{Cov}\{\mathbf{n}\}\mathbf{f})^{\frac{1}{2}}},
\end{aligned}
\tag{3.1}
$$

as optimum criterion, an optimal filter $\mathbf{f}$ is found if both vectors $\mathbf{f} = \mathbf{a}$ point in the same direction, while the noise vector $\mathbf{n}$ is uniform and uncorrelated. The author[Mor77c] calls this filter the *matched filter*, because $\mathbf{f} = \mathbf{a}$.

If, in addition, an interferent vector $\mathbf{i}$ with random length disturbs the target vector, the optimal filter vector tends away from this interferent (depicted in Fig. 3.1c). The optimal filter vector then again can be derived by solving the SNR (3.1) for this case. According to [Mor77c] the solution is

$$\mathbf{f} = (\sigma^2 \mathbf{I} + \sigma_\mathbf{i}^2 \mathbf{i}\mathbf{i}^\top)^{-1} \mathbf{a},$$

with the assumption of white noise and $\mathbf{I}$ as identity matrix.

To describe the distribution of the concentration of a known interferent $\mathbf{i}$ as white noise can be problematic. An option to get rid of this problem is to design the filter vector perpendicularly to the interferents. This is depicted in 3.1d for a single interferent. In this case, a change of the interferent analyt has no effect to the resulting signal s. If the filter vector $\mathbf{f}$ should be perpendicular to multiple interferents and the number of interferents is less than the dimension of the vector space, the target vector $\mathbf{a}$ can be projected onto the subspace of these interferents. Then, $\mathbf{f}$ is optained by the difference of $\mathbf{a}$ and the projection of $\mathbf{a}$ onto this subspace

[Mor77c]. In detail

$$\mathbf{f} = (\mathbf{I} - \boldsymbol{\Phi}(\boldsymbol{\Phi}^\top \boldsymbol{\Phi})^{-1} \boldsymbol{\Phi}^\top)\mathbf{a} \text{ and}$$
$$\boldsymbol{\Phi} = [\mathbf{i}^1, \mathbf{i}^2, \cdots],$$

with the matrix $\boldsymbol{\Phi}$ that organizes the interferents vectors colom wise. Another way how to obtain a filter vector that is orthogonal to the interferents was introduced by [Bia86b]. By the Gram−Schmidt process a new orthogonal basis can be constructed with one direction orthogonal to all interferents. Again, the interferents vectors are arranged colom wise, but this time the target vector $\mathbf{a}$ is added at last

$$\mathbf{M} = [\mathbf{i}^1, \mathbf{i}^2, \cdots, \mathbf{i}^p, \mathbf{a}]$$
$$\mathbf{M} = \mathbf{QR} \text{ (QR-factorization)}$$
$$\mathbf{f} = \mathbf{q}_l, \text{ with } \mathbf{Q} = [q_1, \cdots, q_l].$$

This matrix $\mathbf{M}$ can be decomposed into an orthogonal matrix $\mathbf{Q}$ and an upper triangular matrix $\mathbf{R}$ using the Gram-Schmidt process. The optimal filter is then the last colom vector $\mathbf{q}_n$ of the matrix $\mathbf{Q}$.

Beside these analytical motivated methods, also heuristically methods are very common. In Section 2.1 it was already discussed, that changes in concentration cause nonlinear changes in the spectrum due to the Beer-Lambert law. In the majority of articles [BBWB08a][MSK$^+$02a][HM04a][NAD$^+$98a][DUDL07][PSB99], a linear regression approach is chosen, that do not pay attention to this problem. Often linear regression is combined with a principle component analysis. The linear regression model [HM04a]

$$s = \mathbf{f}^\top \mathbf{a} = \sum_{j=1}^{l} f_j a_j$$

can be reduced to a vector dot product with regression coefficients f_j equal to the filter vector entries. l is the maximal number of wavelengths and equivalent to the dimensionality of the vector space.

4   Filter Technology

This section gives an overview of different possibilities how optical filters can be realized. Only filter design methods are of interest, that allow to produce custom filter transmission characteristics. In general, a filter can be placed before or behind the analyt, filtering the illumination part or the image formation part, respectively. If the illumination part is filtered, the filter need not fulfill image formation quality and this enables some methods that are prohibited in the image formation part. Optical filter technologies:

- Partial glass filter according to Dresler[Ric81]. Multiple standard glas filter are spatial assembled side by side and in series. The single glass filter fragments are chosen in such a way, that the resulting filter approximates the target filter characteristics. This filter is placed in the plane of the aperture.

- Chromatic light dispersion with filter mask [Bia86b]. This kind of filter works only in the illumination part. Polychromatic light is split up and projected onto a mask. The intransparent part of the mask absorbs wavelength dependent light proportions. After remixing the illumination, the light features the target spectrum. State of the art are programmable filter mask for prototyping issues.

- Narrowband laser line illumination [Mor77c]. Laser lines are monochromatic and can replace single channels of spectrometers.

- Liquid analyt mixture [DUDL07]. A cuvette is filled by multiple analyts of known spectral characteristics. The mixture can approximate a target filter characteristic.

- Interference filters [LM08]. A sequence of thin films is applied onto a substrate. In theory arbitrary target filter characteristics can be design.

- Nano structured plasmons filters [KTE$^+$99]. Structured metal films with holes and other geometries in nano scale show are wavelength dependent transparency. The transmission characteristic can be influenced by the dimensions and the layout of the metal structure.

- Material as Screen for intermediate images [SGB11]. Similar to an analyt mixture that is used as transmission filter, intransparent materials can be used in reflectance mode as filter. Either as reflectance mirror in the illumination part, or as screen for intermediate images in the image formation part.

- Spectrometer with weighted integration time for each channel [BBWB08a]. This is a virtual filter and a spectrometer is still required. According to the target filter design the integration time is weighted for each channel.

These methods suffer from the problem of negative coefficients of the target filter design. This problem can only be solved by the use of two filters, one for the positive coefficients and one for the negatives. An elegant solution was proposed by [MSK$^+$02a] who used an interference filter as beam splitter. The transmission characteristic of this interference filter approximates the positive target filter coefficients and the reflected the negative ones.

5 Conclusion

Unconventional spectroscopic technics can be described in an uniform way, using a vector space representation. Instead of a spectrometer, only one or a few sensors are used, together with complex filter transmission characteristics. According to the application an optimal criteria can be formulated to determine the corresponding optimal filter. On the hardware side, a lot of technics were developed to realize arbitrary filter transmission characteristics.

Bibliography

[BBWB08a] Marc K Boysworth, Soame Banerji, Denise M Wilson, and Karl S Booksh. Generalization of multivariate optical computations as a method for improving the speed and precision of spectroscopic analyses. *Journal of Chemometrics*, 22(6):355–365, June 2008.

[Bia86b] Stephen E. Bialkowski. Species discrimination and quantitative estimation using incoherent linear optical signal processing of emission signals. *Analytical Chemistry*, 58(12):2561–2563, October 1986.

[CUL05a] Lisa A Cassis, Aaron Urbas, and Robert A Lodder. Hyperspectral integrated computational imaging. *Analytical and Bioanalytical Chemistry*, 382(4):868–872, February 2005.

[DUDL07] Bin Dai, Aaron Urbas, Craig C. Douglas, and Robert A. Lodder. Molecular factor computing for predictive spectroscopy. *Pharmaceutical Research*, 24(8):1441–1449, March 2007.

[FH95a] Andrew Fong and Gary M. Hieftje. Simple Near-Infrared spectrometric Sorption-Based vapor sensor. *Applied Spectroscopy*, 49(9):1261–1267, 1995.

[FH95b] Andrew Fong and Gary S. Hieftje. Near-IR multiplex bandpass spectrometer utilizing liquid molecular filters. *Applied Spectroscopy*, 49(4):493–498, April 1995.

[GL10] Bosco Gerra L. James l. waters symposium 2009 on near-infrared spectroscopy. *TrAC Trends in Analytical Chemistry*, 29(3):197–208, March 2010.

[HKW] Ralf Habel, Michael Kudenov, and Michael Wimmer. Practical spectral photography. *Eurographics 2012*, May.

[HM04a] Frederick G. Haibach and Michael L. Myrick. Precision in multivariate optical computing. *Applied Optics*, 43(10):2130–2140, April 2004.

[KM02]   N. Keshava and J.F. Mustard. Spectral unmixing. *Signal Processing Magazine, IEEE*, 19(1):44–57, 2002.

[KTE⁺99]   Tae Jin Kim, Tineke Thio, T. W. Ebbesen, D. E. Grupp, and H. J. Lezec. Control of optical transmission through metals perforated with subwavelength hole arrays. *Optics Letters*, 24(4):256–258, February 1999.

[LM08]   Stéphane Larouche and Ludvik Martinu. OpenFilters: open-source software for the design, optimization, and synthesis of optical filters. *Applied Optics*, 47(13):C219–C230, May 2008.

[ML05]   Joseph Medendorp and Robert A Lodder. Applications of integrated sensing and processing in spectroscopic imaging and sensing. *Journal of Chemometrics*, 19(10):533–542, October 2005.

[Mor77c]   D.R. Morgan. Spectral absorption pattern detection and estimation. i. analytical techniques. *Applied Spectroscopy*, 31(5):404–415, 1977.

[MSK⁺02a] M. L. Myrick, O. Soyemi, J. Karunamuni, D. Eastwood, H. Li, L. Zhang, A. E. Greer, and P. Gemperline. A single-element all-optical approach to chemometric prediction. *Vibrational Spectroscopy*, 28(1):73–81, February 2002.

[MSL⁺01a] M. L. Myrick, O. Soyemi, H. Li, L. Zhang, and D. Eastwood. Spectral tolerance determination for multivariate optical element design. *Fresenius' Journal of Analytical Chemistry*, 369(3-4):351–355, February 2001.

[NAD⁺98a] Matthew P. Nelson, Jeffrey F. Aust, J. A. Dobrowolski, P. G. Verly, and M. L. Myrick. Multivariate optical computation for predictive spectroscopy. *Analytical Chemistry*, 70(1):73–82, January 1998.

[PSB99]   Anna M. C. Prakash, Christopher M. Stellman, and Karl S. Booksh. Optical regression: a method for improving quantitative precision of multivariate prediction with single channel spectrometers. *Chemometrics and Intelligent Laboratory Systems*, 46(2):265–274, March 1999.

[Ric81]   Manfred Richter. *Einführung in die Farbmetrik*. de Gruyter, Berlin u.a., 1981.

[SGB11]   Miro Sauerland, Robin Gruna, and Jürgen Beyerer. Materialidentifikation mittels optisch realisierter kreuzkorrelation der reflektanzspektren. In *XXV. Messtechnisches Symposium des Arbeitskreises der Hochschullehrer für Messtechnik e.V. 22.-24. September 2011 in Karlsruhe*, volume 1, pages 91–102, Achen, September 2011. Shaker.

Dynamic World Modeling with Prior Knowledge Matching for Autonomous Systems

Andrey Belkin

Vision and Fusion Laboratory
Institute for Anthropomatics
Karlsruhe Institute of Technology (KIT), Germany
belkin@ies.uni-karlsruhe.de

Technical Report IES-2011-12

Abstract: Modern autonomous systems are challenged by complex time-critical tasks. In order to perform reactive and pro-active activities, these systems have to employ a robust and efficient memory component, particularly a high-level memory structure. This structure represents a world modeling, containing all known information about the surrounding environment. The world modeling includes dynamic models, describing the current state of the environment and its past states, and prior knowledge, containing predefined expert knowledge about possible classes, entities and relations in the surrounding world. Moreover, such high-level memory structure has to deal with multimodal information flow, gathering and fusing incoming sensor information into existing description, analyze the models in order to determine its quality, the missing information, and possible conclusions, and provide all information to other sub-systems of the autonomous system.

The main topic of this analysis is a matching of dynamic models to prior knowledge concepts. This connection allows for recognition of known entities either by classifying it by predefined class concepts or finding a complete description among known entities. In both cases, the modeling entity obtains semantic meaning and missing information from the prior knowledge side. The connection is performed by depth search in the prior knowledge graph with subsequent comparing of all concepts to the entity by structural (e.g. Tanimoto metric) and attribute values (e.g. relative entropy calculation) analysis.

1 Introduction

Since the creation of machines there was the idea of a creation of autonomous intelligent systems. These systems have to be seamlessly integrated into social life, able to function stand-alone and cooperative to human or other machines. A formal definition of autonomous intelligent systems was given in *IBM Autonomic Computing Initiative* [IBM01], [KC03] as follows:

- *Self-Configuration* – self-configuration or reconfiguration under internal and external changes;

- *Self-Optimization* – optimization of its functioning;

- *Self-Healing* – faults discover and correction;

- *Self-Protection* – self-identification and protection;

- *Self-Awareness* – knowledge of own components, current status, ultimate capacity and connections to other systems;

- *Environment-Awareness* – perception and comprehension of the surrounding environment and context.

The functioning of autonomous systems implies handling of *reactive* and *proactive* activities. The reactive behavior is required for immediate reactions on changes, such as balancing or grasping. The proactive analysis is vital for planning and sophisticated decision making, e.g. assisting people in a household. Such activities demand a constant *situation awareness* – perception of changes in the surrounding environment, comprehension of their meaning and projection of their status in the future as defined in [End95].

The situation awareness involves complex information acquisition, processing and management and discussed in details in [BKFB12]. An example of such information workflow is presented in Fig. 1.1. The workflow starts by a sensor sub-system that acquires data from the surrounding environment, called *world of interest* (WoI). This data is processed and fused into *dynamic models* within the world modeling sub-system. The world modeling contains information about the environment and the autonomous system itself and serves as a global information hub for all other sub-systems. The dynamic models contain an actual description of the WoI, expressing each real-world entity with a virtual *representative*. Since such descriptions are created from sensory information, they lack semantic meaning and expected properties. Each representative can be matched any time to *prior knowledge concepts* that contain expert knowledge about possible classes and individual items. Further, cognition and planning modules fetch the content of the dynamic models, assess the situation at hand and possible future states, and plan further actions. Then these actions are performed by actuators that interact with the world of interest.

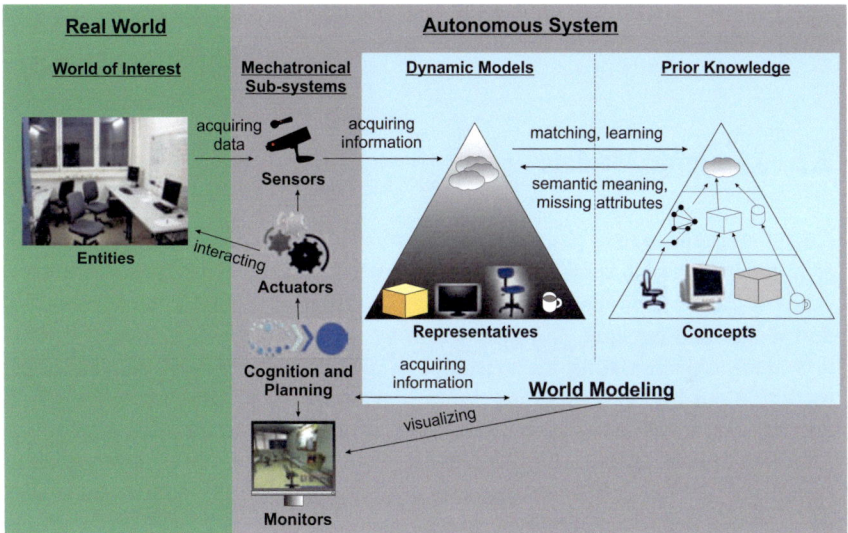

Figure 1.1: Information workflow of autonomous systems.

Since world modeling serves as a sophisticated memory structure to the autonomous system, it has often the following key points [BKFB12]:

- Slim *symbolic description* of the environment;

- *Gathering depot* for all available information;

- *Interpretable* for humans and machines;

- *Object-oriented*;

- Unified *probabilistic uncertainty handling*;

- *Information hub* for all sub-systems;

- Handling of *unknown objects*;

- Extensible concepts under the *Open World* assumption.

2   World Modeling

The world modeling system consists of two parts: dynamic models and prior knowledge. The dynamic models describe the surrounding environment of the autonomous system. The prior knowledge specifies possible classes and entities of the environment.

2.1   Dynamic Models

An autonomous system perceives the surrounding environment with sensors. The acquired information is fused into dynamic models that describe the actual and past states of the environment. This description consists of representatives, describing real things and persons, and their relations. At the beginning, a representative is a blank object, stating the existence of something. As soon as a new information about the corresponding entity is acquired (e.g. position or color), the description (attributes as probability distributions) is fused into this blank object [Bel09], [Bel10], [BGB⁺10a], [BKFB12]. By this principle, all representatives are structured in a pyramid hierarchy of abstraction levels with blank objects at the top and completely described representatives at the bottom [GHB08]. Qualitative and quantitative analysis of the dynamic models is given in [BB12] considering situation analysis.

2.2   Prior Knowledge

Prior knowledge specifies class and entities concepts of the surrounding world in form of an ontology [Bel09]. It can be predefined with expert knowledge offline and, possibly, extended during the operational functioning. Each concept represents attributes and relations in form of prior probability distributions. These distributions can be flat over the allowed attribute definition set or contain a statistical information about a typical attribute distribution. For example, it can contain typical size distribution for tea cups based on a statistical analysis over all cups in a household.

The exact structure of the ontology can be sophisticated. The concepts are connected to each other with multiple relations, forming a complex graph as in Fig. 2.1. Several subgraphs are forming trees of semantically consistent hierarchies (for example, "is a" relationship tree). These kind of hierarchies are similar to abstraction levels in dynamic models and represent clustering of more abstract concepts (with probability assignment) into particular concepts (e.g. "furniture" → "table", "chair"). In order to maintain total probability of 1, each abstraction level is supplemented by a "dummy" concept that includes "everything, except already listed" (e.g. "furniture" → "table", "chair", "dummy (everything, except table and chair)").

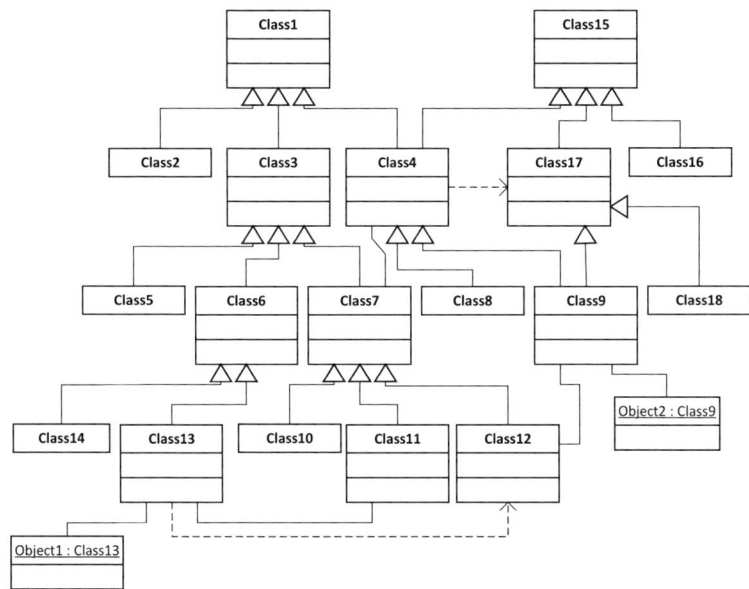

Figure 2.1: A prior knowledge graph of concepts with dummy classes depicted as simple boxes and ordinary classes as threefold boxes.

2.3   Matching

Representatives from the dynamic models can be any time matched to prior knowledge in order to get semantic meaning and missing attributes. Since matching of one representative to a complex prior knowledge graph is computationally hard, only one generalization hierarchy is considered. For example, only a "is a" relationship tree is chosen from the complete graph as shown in Fig. 2.2. Next, the chosen tree is processed with a depth search, finding concepts similar to the representative under consideration with some similarity score higher than a threshold (Fig. 2.3). At the end, all concepts similar to the representative are marked and the representative is assigned to concepts by means of probability distribution, based on the similarity score, as shown in Fig. 2.4.

The similarity comparison of the representative and prior knowledge concepts is performed by structural and probability distributions analysis. The structural analysis finds out the intersection between representative's attributes set and concept's attribute set, i.e. how many attributes are observed by the real world entity out of all possible attributes defined in prior knowledge. The probability distribution analysis

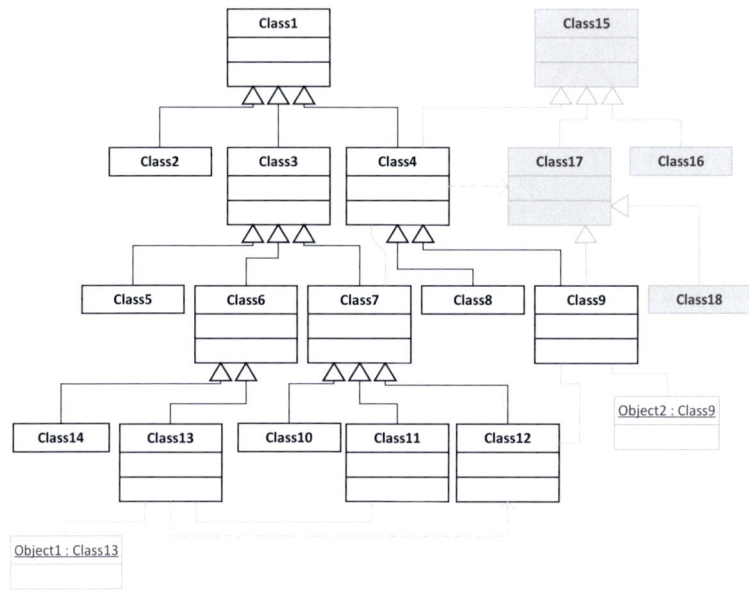

Figure 2.2: The selected "is a" relationship tree (white) and excluded sub-graphs (gray).

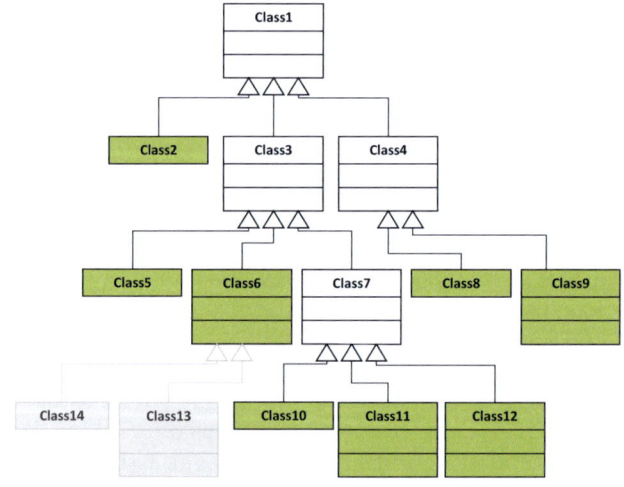

Figure 2.3: A result of the depth search for finding concepts similar to a given representative (green).

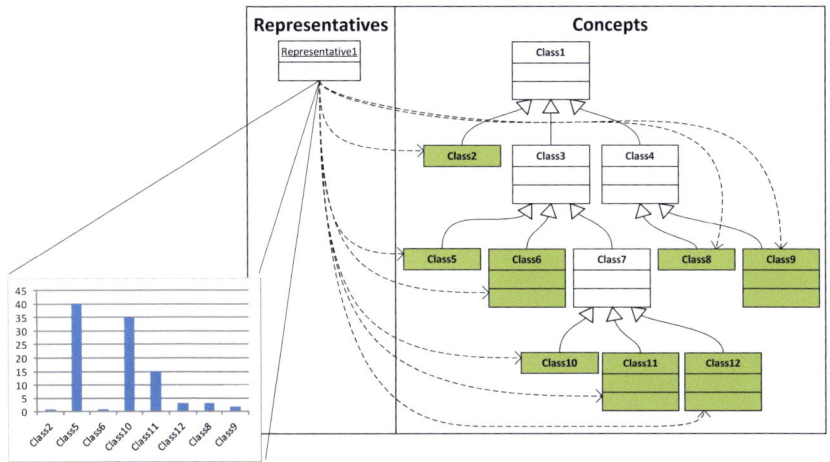

Figure 2.4: An assignment of concepts to a given representative.

compares each attribute's value in form of Degree-of-Belief to a prior probability distribution. The final concepts-matching DoB distribution is written as $P(c|r)$, where r denotes the representative under consideration and $c \in C_r$ – concepts from the set of found by depth search tree nodes. Each matching can be expressed by some metric $d(r, c)$ that quantifies the similarity of r and c. A normalization of the metric d can be done by some functional f, projecting all metric values onto the range of $[0; 1]$. So, the matching DoB distribution is formalized as follows:

$$P(c|r) := f(d(r, c)),$$
$$f(d(r, c)) : [0; \infty) \to [0; 1],$$
$$\sum_{c \in C_r} f(d(r, c)) = 1,$$
$$d(r, c) = \underbrace{d(A^r, A^c)}_{\text{structural similarity}} + \lambda \cdot \underbrace{d_{A^r \cap A^c}}_{\text{value (DoB) similarity}},$$

where A^r and A^c are representative and concept attributes and λ is a weighting factor.

The structural similarity component of the metric d can be calculated by Tanimoto-metric or other Jaccard distance modification, or Sørensen index:

$$d_{Tanimoto}(A^r, A^c) = \frac{N_{A^r} + N_{A^c} - 2N_{A^r \cap A^c}}{N_{A^r} + N_{A^c} - N_{A^r \cap A^c}},$$

$$d_{Jaccard}(A^r, A^c) = \frac{N_{A^r \cup A^c} - N_{A^r \cap A^c}}{N_{A^r \cup A^c}},$$

$$d_{Sorenson} = \frac{2N_{A^r \cap A^c}}{N_{A^r} + N_{A^c}},$$

where N_{A^r} and N_{A^c} are numbers of corresponding attribute sets and $N_{A^r \cap A^c}$ is the number of elements of the intersection of two corresponding sets.

The value similarity $d_{A^r \cap A^c}$ can be represented by the following sum:

$$d_{A^r \cap A^c} = \sum_{A \in A^r \cap A^c} g_A \cdot d_{DoB}(A),$$

where g_A is a weighting factor for the attribute A and $d_{DoB}(A)$ is a metric for the difference between $P(A^r)$ and $P(A^c)$ DoBs of the attribute A with a value a.

The metric $d_{DoB}(A)$ is usually calculated by relative entropy equation:

$$d_{DoB}(A) = d_{RE}(P, Q) = \sum_a P(a) \log \frac{P(a)}{Q(a)},$$

$$d_{DoB}(A) = d_{RE}(P, Q) = \int_{-\infty}^{\infty} p(a) \log \frac{p(a)}{q(a)} da,$$

where P and p denotes posterior and Q and q prior Degree-of-Belief distribution. Alternatively, the value similarity can be calculated with a normalized Wasserstein metric L^2:

$$d_{DoB}(A) = d_{L^2}(p_1, p_2) = \int \left((\acute{p}_1(a) - \acute{p}_2(a)) \right)^2 da,$$

$$\acute{p}_i = \frac{p_i(a)}{\sqrt{\int p_i(a)^2 da}}.$$

In the case of "hard" decision for the matching (i.e. only one best assignment has to be given), the Maximum A Posteriori (MAP) classification or costs-function employment (statistical decision theory) has to be performed. In MAP classification, the $P(c|r)$ is interpreted as a posterior DoB for the matching and is performed as follows:

$$\hat{c}_{MAP} := \arg \max_{\gamma \in C_r} P(\gamma|r) = \arg \min_{\gamma \in C_r} d(r|\gamma).$$

The costs-function employment implies a search of the optimum decision with some function $l(\hat{c}, c)$ that describes costs of the $\hat{c}$ decision when the true concept c

is:

$$\hat{c}_l := \arg\min_{\gamma \in C_r} \sum_{\gamma \in C_r} l(\gamma, c) P(c|r).$$

3 Conclusion

The analysis presented in this paper is dedicated to the connection of dynamic models to prior knowledge information. This connection allows for recognition of known entity either by classifying it by predefined class concepts or finding a complete description among known entities. In both cases, the modeling entity obtains semantic meaning and missing information from the prior knowledge side. The connection is performed by depth search in the prior knowledge graph with subsequent comparing of all concepts to the entity by structural (e.g. Tanimoto metric) and attribute values (e.g. relative entropy calculation) analysis. The proposed connection was implemented and tested within the DFG SFB 588 research project for humanoid robots [DFG12].

Bibliography

[BB12]   Andrey Belkin and Jürgen Beyerer. Information entropy and structural metrics based estimation of situations as a basis for situation awareness and decision support". In *Proceedings of the IEEE Conference on Cognitive Methods in Situation Awareness and Decision Support*, 2012.

[Bel09]   Andrey Belkin. Object-oriented world modelling for autonomous systems. Technical report, Institute for Anthropomatics, Vision and Fusion Laboratory, Karlsruhe Institute for Technology, 2009.

[Bel10]   Andrey Belkin. Information management in world modeling. Technical report, Vision and Fusion Laboratory, Institute for Anthropomatics, Karlsruhe Institute of Technology (KIT), 2010.

[BGB+10a]   Marcus Baum, Ioana Gheţa, Andrey Belkin, Jürgen Beyerer, and Uwe D. Hanebeck. Data association in a world model for autonomous systems. In *Proceedings of the IEEE 2010 International Conference on Multisensor Fusion and Integration for Intelligent Systems*, 2010.

[BKFB12]   Andrey Belkin, Achim Kuwertz, Yvonne Fischer, and Jürgen Beyerer. *Information System*, chapter World Modeling for Autonomous Systems. InTech – Open Access Publisher, 2012.

[DFG12]   DFG SFB 588. Humanoid robots – learning and cooperating multimodal robots, 2001-2012.

[End95]   M. R. Endsley. Towards a theory of situation awareness in dynamic systems. *Human Factors*, 37(11):32–64, 1995.

[GHB08]   Ioana Gheţa, Michael Heizmann, and Jürgen Beyerer. Object oriented environment model
          for autonomous systems. In Henrik Boström, Ronnie Johansson, and Joeri van Laere,
          editors, *Proceedings of the second Skövde Workshop on Information Fusion Topics*, pages
          9–12. Skövde Studies in Informatics, November 2008.

[IBM01]   IBM. Autonomic computing: Ibm's perspective on the state of information technology.
          Manifesto, October 2001.

[KC03]   Jeffrey O. Kephart and David M. Chess. The vision of autonomic computing. *Computer*,
          36(1):41–50, January 2003.

Visual inspection in the far infrared spectrum

Sebastian Höfer

Vision and Fusion Laboratory
Institute for Anthropomatics
Karlsruhe Institute of Technology (KIT), Germany
sebastian.hoefer@kit.edu

Technical Report IES-2011-13

Abstract: Most applications for thermal infrared imaging in non-destructive-testing can be narrowed down to the measurement of the surface temperature or the thermal response of the object under test. Apart from these obvious applications for thermal imaging, the differing optical properties can be utilized for special optical inspection tasks. This technical report will give a brief overview of the differences in technology for capturing and displaying images in the far-infrared spectrum. While the camera technology for this spectrum is well matured, infrared display technology for civil uses is practically non available.

1 Introduction

Since the first infrared imaging technology emerged in the early 1930s, this field was subject to a steady progress of development. While the driving force behind infrared imaging technology was - and still is - the use in military applications, the field of civil applications likewise took advantage of its advancement in the last decades. Apart from its obvious uses in surveillance at night, the uses comprise mainly diagnostic or measurement functions. Thanks to imaging infrared sensors, the capability to take remote temperature measurements and correlate them with exact positions, is a substantial advantage in medical and engineering tasks. Especially when troubleshooting faults a broad range of possible defects are accompanied by a change in temperature. For example mechanical faults through increased friction, electrical faults through resistance or faulty building-isolation visible through unwanted temperature exchange. All these applications have in common, that they passively observe temperature changes.

More sophisticated applications induce such temperature change on purpose and instead of simply measuring the temperature, the thermal behavior over time is evaluated. Namely impulse- and lock-in-thermography belong to this category [Mal01]. For these techniques a single heat-impulse or a periodic heat signature is brought into the surface under test, mostly by use of flashlight. The incident light gets absorbed and dissipates into the material. This can be used to obtain information about the materials structure beneath the surface. Defects, like entrapped air beneath a coating exhibit a differing thermal conductivity coefficient compared to the surrounding material, which in turn manifests itself as a slower (or faster - depending on material and defect) cooling of the surface, so that these defects can be detected and located with an thermal imaging camera.

All these application have in common, that they only base on a temperature measurement of an object. However, other properties of the far infrared spectrum go unregarded or are even regarded as disturbing factor. On the other hand does this change of optical properties enable the use of visual inspection techniques, which are otherwise not applicable in the visible spectrum. A whole new field of possible applications becomes apparent, where visual inspection in the visible spectrum fails due to unfit optical properties of a material, like reflectivity, transmittance and absorptance. Since these properties are mostly dependent on the wavelength, the shift to the thermal infrared spectrum can potentially avoid these unfitting properties. In this technical report we will focus on deflectometry as in the visible spectrum established technique and go into details about the necessary adaptions of camera an display equipment for enabling the use in the thermal infrared spectrum.

2   Applications in visual inspection

Deflectometry describes the inspection of a specular surface in regard to its geometry [Wer11]. By observing the reflection of an known code-pattern on the surface under test, its geometry can be derived by evaluating the distortions induced by its shape. This method is obviously dependent on the specularity of the surface. It is suitable for the inspection of e.g. lacquered surfaces, mirrors and polished metals, but will fail on surfaces which exhibit no reflection, either because of its material or its surface roughness.

Preceding publications have shown that a longer wavelength has a beneficial effect for deflectometry on various surfaces [HK05, SKKW10a, SKKW10b]. This applies in particular to metal surfaces, which become completely reflective with increasing wavelength. That implies equally a loss of the emissivity, which is why metal surfaces are unsuitable for the inspection with thermography. But then, this change

(a) (b)

Figure 2.1: Images of a glass lens in the visible light spectrum between 400-700nm (a) and in the thermal infrared spectrum between 8-14μm (b). In the visible spectrum the stripe pattern in the background is seen multiple times because of internal reflections, while the thermal spectrum show only the reflection on the surface.

of properties is just desirable for methods which are dependent on the specularity of a surface, like deflectometry. Besides the aforementioned change in optical properties, another peculiarity takes effect simultaneously. The impact of the surface roughness on its specularity is - as a rule of thumb - expressed with the Rayleigh-criterion [HK05]. Herein the relationship between the RMS roughness of the surface σ, the wavelength of the reflected light λ and its angle of incidence θ is expressed as:

$$\lambda < 8\sigma \cos{(\theta)}.$$

This means for a surface to exhibit a specular reflection the wavelength has to be at least eight times higher than the RMS roughness. With the use of a thermal camera for the LWIR spectrum (see App.A), which operates between 8 and 14 μm, surfaces with a roughness up to 1 μm still have a specular appearance.

Another interesting field of application for deflectometry in the thermal infrared spectrum are transparent materials, like glass or plastics. In the visible spectrum internal reflections and light passing through the material interfere with the reflection on the surface, while the differing optical properties in the far infrared spectrum suppress these disturbing factors. This allows for a reliable surface inspection of transparent objects like lenses, windows or glassware [HRWB11].

Although the use of thermal infrared radiation for deflectometry sound promising in theory, the practical realization proves difficult. While there is already matured camera technology available, the required display technology for thermal infrared spectrum is unavailable. In the following section we will go into the possible available solutions and their realization for deflectometric measurement in the thermal infrared spectrum.

3   Thermal infrared displays

Until now the need for thermal image displays has only arisen in military applications. Back in the 1970s the demand for thermal infrared display technology originated in weapon testing [WIS05]. The military needed a simulation environment for heat seeking missiles and as a result miscellaneous display technologies were developed. Initial candidate technologies included liquid crystal light valves, resistor arrays, digital mirror devices, infrared CRT, scanned laser devices and later, laser diode arrays. Every technology exhibits its limitations and today are resistive emitter arrays the prevailing technology [BSJ06]. Such resistive arrays consist of a matrix of resistors in the size of a microchip. In principle is it the same fundamental technology as in thermal microbolometer cameras (A), with the difference that the resistors produce the heat instead of sensing it. But even if this technology would be available for civil uses, it would not be applicable for the use in deflectometry. In their intended application these thermal screens are directly coupled with the hardware under test through special optics. There is no actual screen with the thermal image, which would be necessary for a deflectometric measurement setup.

3.1   Resistor Array Screen

An obvious approach for realizing a thermal screen for deflectometry in the infrared spectrum is to build a screen from an array of resistive elements in the necessary size. This can be realized on a standard circuit board with resistors in surface-mount technology. Every resistor represents a single pixel on the screen. The single resistors allow for a precise control of their temperature by regulating the current flowing through them. Tiling these arrays allows for an modular construction of even bigger screens.

While it is easy to produce heat with resistors it remains the problem of cooling them down. If a pixel is supposed to display cold after being hot, one has to wait until the heat dissipates or radiates off. This means the time for changing the displayed image is limited by this process. Another problem is the containment of the heat to the resistors. Through heat transfer the supporting material and surrounding resistors will also heat up, so that the thermal image gets blurry. So the

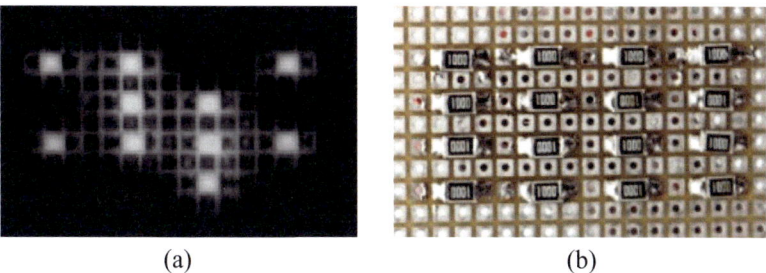

(a)   (b)

Figure 3.1: Prototype of a resistor array build from SMT components viewed in the visible (b) and thermal infrared spectrum (a).

challenge in such a construction is the thermal management by choosing the right materials and an elaborate assembly.

3.2 Infrared Laser Projection

With the availability of image projectors in the visible light spectrum there is always an easy way for realizing big image displays on arbitrary surfaces. But like regular displays there is no such technology for the thermal infrared spectrum - at least not for civil uses - available. One approach to realize an projector for the thermal infrared is the use of a powerful laser combined with a scanning unit (see Fig. 3.2). Industrial carbon dioxide lasers for example produce a beam with a wavelength of 10,6 μm. This leaves two possible ways for producing thermal images [BIIW09].

On one hand could the image be written directly with the laser. The wavelength of the laser is covered by the spectral sensitivity range of thermal cameras for the LWIR-spectrum. Therefore the camera can see the scattered light from the laser beam directly. So provided the laser scanner is fast enough or the camera does the image integration during the whole image buildup, a image projector for thermal infrared radiation can be realized.

Another possibility is to produce the image with the laser indirectly by using it to heat up a projection screen. Like with the previous method the laser writes the image onto a screen. The difference is, that the laser light gets absorbed by the screen material and the image to display is created by the emitted thermal radiation. The Problem herein is that because of thermal diffusion the written lines immediately start to blur, so that when the last lines are written the first lines are already blurred out. This process has to be considered in the image buildup process.

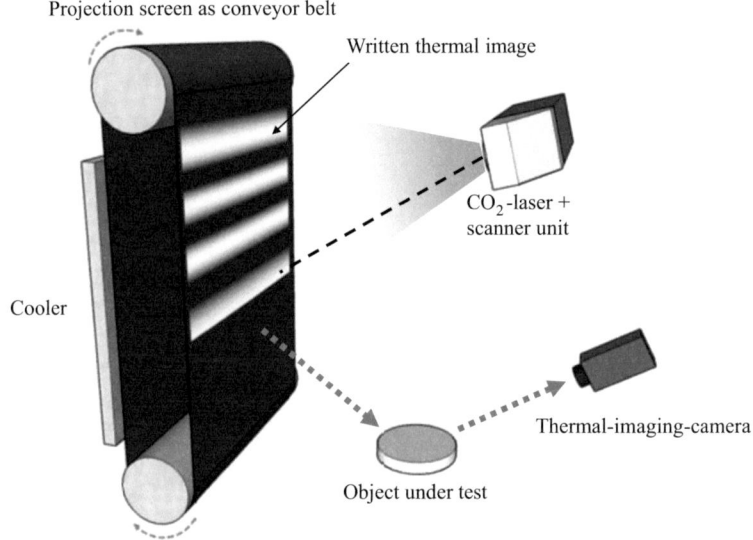

Figure 3.2: Thermal image creation by absorption of laser-light. The laser writes the image onto the projection screen, which is realized as conveyor belt. A written image can so cool down on the back surface, while the next image gets written onto the front.

Like with the resistor arrays, here again the problem of cooling the image down has to be addressed. One solution is to build the projection screen like a conveyor belt so that after a image is written, it can be rotated to the back of the screen to cool down. Meanwhile the next image can be written to the front of the screen. Another advantage is that a linear displacement of the image is easily realized by moving the conveyor belt. In this way the translation of phase shift patterns can be simulated, while the thermal pattern is for a short time persistent on the projection surface.

4   Summary

We have presented the possible advantages of conducting deflectometric measurement in the thermal infrared spectrum to make additional materials and surfaces accessible for deflectometric surface inspection. A survey of existing infrared display technologies showed that currently there are no adequate solutions for a deflectometric measurement setup. Furthermore, two possible solutions for creating the necessary infrared display where presented. Future work will evaluate the practical feasibility of this display setups and assess their usability for thermal infrared deflectometry.

Appendix

A Thermal infrared radiation

The term infrared radiation used in this technical report refers to thermal radiation. It is not to be confused with infrared radiation near the visible spectrum, as it is used for example in tv-remotes. This infrared radiation with comparatively short wavelength (SWIR) is particularly interesting in material classification task, especially because it can still be detected with conventional image sensors on silicon basis. In this report we will focus on infrared radiation with a wavelength one magnitude higher than the visible spectrum. While the same physical laws as in the visible spectrum still apply, the differing optical material properties in this spectrum often lead to a unexpected behavior in visual inspection tasks.

These differing properties cause some constraints when using this spectrum, which will here only be summarized. First of all do many materials exhibit totally different wavelength dependent characteristics like transparency, reflectivity and absorption. The most prominent example would be glass, which looses it's transparency with increasing wavelength. Therefore is conventional glass unusable for optics in the thermal infrared spectrum. Instead special lenses made of germanium or zinc-selenide have to be used.

Another essential constraint is the transmittance of the atmosphere itself. Absorption at the molecules of the air lead to specific gaps in the transmission spectrum of the atmosphere, with the result that only a few spectral ranges are practicable for the use in remote temperature measurement. Apart from the atmospheric window that includes the visible spectrum (SWIR) there are only two usable ranges between $3 - 5\mu m$ (MWIR) and $8 - 14\mu m$ (LWIR) (see Fig. A.1).

Moreover the comparatively long wavelength of thermal radiation requires a different sensor technology as the photon energy is to low to overcome the bandgap E_G [Bud10]. For silicon with $E_G = 1,1$ eV the maximum wavelength arises from

$$\lambda_C = \frac{hc}{E_G} = \frac{6,626 \cdot 10^{-34} \text{ W s}^2 \cdot 2,998 \cdot 10^8 \text{ m/s}}{1,12 \text{ eV}} = 1,11 \ \mu m.$$

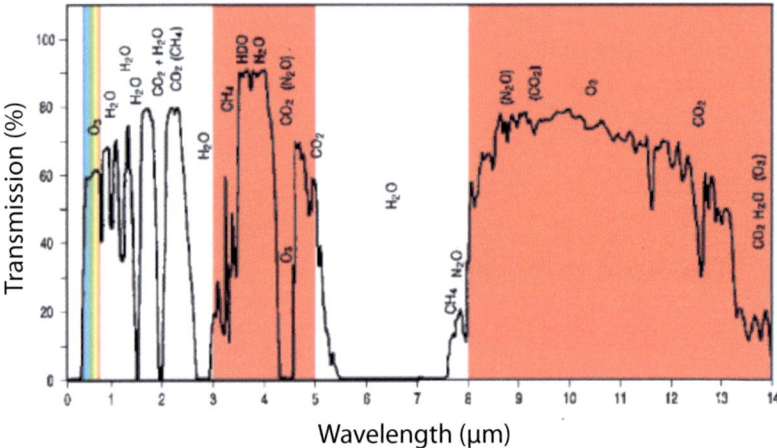

Wavelength (µm)

Figure A.1: Atmospheric transmission spectrum at room temperature. Every molecule in the composition of the air shows up as a specific absorption line in the spectrum. This constrains remote temperature sensing and especially imaging primarily to two transmission windows between $3 - 5\mu m$ and $8 - 14\mu m$.

Thus for the production of photon detecting sensors in the infrared spectrum one has to fall back on other semiconductor materials with a lower bandgap. Alternative sensor technology is based on microbolometers, where every pixel consists of a temperature sensing element (bolometer). The incident electromagnetic radiation gets absorbed whereby the element warms up, what in turn can be detected as a change in the bolometers resistance. Due to the small thermal mass of these elements on the sensor chip, even image acquisition with video frame rates can be archived.

Bibliography

[BHW09]   J. Beyerer, M. Heizmann, and S. Werling. Konzept zur Erzeugung eines räumlich und/oder zeitlich veränderbaren thermischen Strahlungsmusters. *European Patent EP 10191409.1*, 11 2009.

[BSJ06]   Paul Bryant, Steve Solomon, and Jay James. Bolometers running backward: the synergy between uncooled ir sensors & dynamic ir scene projectors. volume 6207, page 62070J. SPIE, 2006.

[Bud10]   Gerald Budzier, Helmut ; Gerlach. *Thermische Infrarotsensoren : Grundlagen für Anwender*. Wiley-VCH, Weinheim, 2010.

[HK05]   Jan Horbach and Sören Kammel. Deflectometric inspection of diffuse surfaces in the far–
            infrared spectrum. In J. R. Price and F. Meriaudeau, editors, *Machine Vision Applications
            in Industrial Inspection XIII*, volume 5679 of *Society of Photo-Optical Instrumentation
            Engineers (SPIE) Conference Series*, pages 108–117, 2005.

[HRWB11]   Sebastian Höfer, Masoud Roschani, Stefan Werling, and Jürgen Beyerer. Verfahren und
            Vorrichtung zur Inspektion von Glasoberflächen. In *XXV. Messtechnisches Symposium des
            Arbeitskreises der Hochschullehrer für Messtechnik e.V.*, pages 127–138. Shaker, 2011.

[Mal01]   Xavier P. Maldague. *Theory and practice of infrared technology for nondestructive testing.*
            Wiley series in microwave and optical engineeringA Wiley-Interscience publication. Wiley,
            New York, 2001.

[SKKW10a]   Zoltan Sarosi, Wolfgang Knapp, Andreas Kunz, and Konrad Wegener. Detection of
            surface defects on sheet metal parts by using one-shot deflectometry in the infrared range.
            In *Infrared Camera Applications Conference 2010*, pages 243–254, Las Vegas, USA,
            2010.

[SKKW10b]   Zoltan Sarosi, Wolfgang Knapp, Andreas Kunz, and Konrad Wegener. Evaluation of re-
            flectivity of metal parts by a thermo-camera. In *Infrared Camera Applications Conference
            2010*, pages 475–486, Las Vegas, USA, 2010.

[Wer11]   Stefan Bruno Werling. *Deflektometrie zur automatischen Sichtprüfung und Rekonstruktion
            spiegelnder Oberflächen.* PhD thesis, 2011.

[WIS05]   Owen M. Williams, George C. Goldsmith II, and Robert G. Stockbridge. History of
            resistor array infrared projectors: hindsight is always 100 percent operability. volume
            5785, pages 208–224. SPIE, 2005.

Towards Automated Planning of Deflectometric Inspection

Masoud Roschani

Vision and Fusion Laboratory
Institute for Anthropomatics
Karlsruhe Institute of Technology (KIT), Germany
roschani@ies.uni-karlsruhe.de

Technical Report IES-2011-14

Abstract: During a deflectometric inspection, the size of an object or the complexity of its shape may prevent one from capturing the whole surface with a single measurement or with uniform resolution. To solve this problem, we propose a probabilistic planning approach. It determines sequentially optimal sensor configurations in order to minimize some metric of uncertainties given the realistic constraints on e.g. time. In this report we formulate the problem as a Partially Observable Markov Decision Process and give an overview of possible solution strategies by means of approximate dynamic programming.

1 Introduction

Deflectometry is an optical measurement technique for specular surfaces. A deflectometric setup consists of a pattern generator, like a LCD, and a camera. The LCD displays a sequence of patterns to encodes every pixel. The reflection of this sequence on a specular surface is observed from the camera and a mapping between camera pixel and LCD pixel is computed, which contains information about the local slope of the surface.

Generally, large or complex-shaped surfaces cannot be captured with a single measurement or with uniform resolution. For example, consider a convex-shaped surface and the reverse optical path from the camera to the LCD. Then light rays reflected from the convex-shaped surfaces diverge, see Figure 1. Hence, in this case, only small regions can be captured with a single measurement. The problem can be solved by making additional measurements. This raises the question of how and among which criteria appropriate sensor configurations can be selected. The configuration of a deflectometric measuring device consists of the position and orientation of a screen and a camera and possibly intrinsic camera parameters like focal length or aperture. A manual selection of the high-dimensional parameters is time-consuming and, for complex-shaped surface, a nontrivial task.

We aim to determine sensor configurations automatically so that the entire surface is covered completely with high precision and with as few measurements as possible. We use a sequential planning approach where a control loop is created, which selects a new configuration in every time step. The decision is chosen in terms of a suitable quality measure and the measurements already made. A concrete realization of this approach is obtained by means of a probabilistic framework. This allows the consideration of uncertainty, which can help to make statements about areas where a measurement is necessary. The next sensor configuration can be chosen so that the corresponding measurement result contains a maximum amount of information about the surface. This is, for example, formalized through information-theoretic quantities, such as entropy, or moment-based quantities, such as variance, in the cost function.

This report is structured as follows. Section 2 introduces two widely used frameworks for sequential planning problems with uncertainty, namely Markov Decision Processes (MDPs) and its generalization Partially Observable Markov Decision Processes (POMDPs). Next the deflectometric measurement is embedded into the POMDP framework in Section 3. Due to the complexity of the model which prevents one from applying exact solution methods, approximate methods are presented in Section 4. The report finishes with a discussion in Section 5.

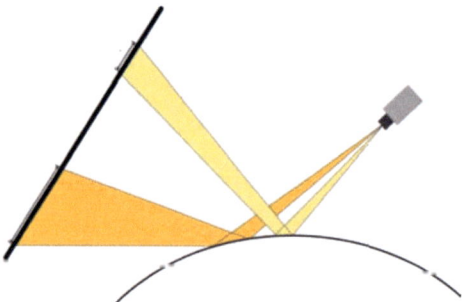

Figure 1.1: This figure illustrates a deflectometric measurement on a convex surface. Considering the reverse optical path, light rays diverge and only a small area of the surface can be measured.

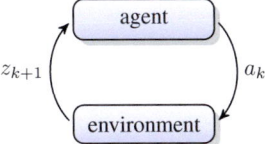

Figure 2.1: This figure illustrates the interaction of an agent with its environment. In every time step, the agent influences the environment by performing an action a_k and making an observation z_{k+1} in return.

2 Sequential Planning Problems

A sequential planning problem consists of an agent and an environment. The agent interacts with the environment to reach a goal. It can choose between different actions, which influence the environment. This happens in a sequential manner: After executing one action the agent receives some observation from the environment and decides based on this current information and the information accumulated in the past which action to take next, see Figure 2.1 for an illustration of this interaction. We are especially interested in agents which have information gathering goals. This means they take actions with the aim to get more information about the environment. Furthermore, we assume that the environment contains uncertainty. That is, actions have a nondeterministic influence on the environment and observations contain noise. The definition given for sequential planning problems so far is very general and informal. In the following, we introduce two mathematical frameworks for sequential planning problems under uncertainty, which assume additional structure.

2.1 Markov Decision Processes (MDPs)

A widely used probabilistic framework for sequential planning problems under uncertainty is the Markov Decision Process. Time is discretized and can take values from $\mathbb{N}^+$. It is assumed that in every time step k, the environment is in a state $x_k \in \mathcal{X}$, which fully describes the environment. The Markov property states that the next state depends only on the current state but not on preceding states. The agent can choose an action $a_k \in \mathcal{A}(x_k)$, which leads to a probabilistic transition from the current state x_k of the environment to a new state x_{k+1} according to the transition probability $p(x_{k+1}|x_k, a_k)$. Furthermore, the agent receives an immediate cost $g(x_k, a_k)$. The state x_{k+1} is revealed to the agent in the next time step.

A policy is function, which assigns an action to every single state. The agent chooses actions by means of a policy μ. That is, in every time step, the agent selects the action $a_{k+1} = \mu(x_k)$. It should be noted that the selected action depends on the current state. This should be distinguished from a plan, which is simply a sequence of actions. The need for a policy occurs because generally, we cannot guarantee that an action will have deterministic consequences in a probabilistic setting. There are many different methods to quantify the quality of a policy. We want to consider only the discounted sum of immediate costs

$$J_\mu(x_0) = E\left\{\sum_{i=1}^{\infty} \gamma^i g(x_i, \mu(x_i)) \,\middle|\, x_0\right\} ,$$

where $\gamma \in [0, 1]$ is some discount factor and x_0 is an initial state. Other cost functions are the finite horizon cost, which is simply the sum of all immediate costs up to a time horizon N plus a terminal cost, or the average cost. The interested reader can consult the books [Ber05, Ber07] for more details. The goal of the decision problem is to find an optimal policy, which has a minimal cost for a starting state x_0. The optimal policy $\mu^\star$ can be obtained by solving

$$J^\star(x_0) = J_{\mu^\star}(x_0) = \min_\mu J_\mu(x_0) , \qquad (2.1)$$

where $J^\star(x_0)$ is the minimal cost for the policy $\mu^\star$. $J^\star(x_0)$ can be viewed as a function, which assigns minimal costs to initial states x_0 and in this context is called the optimal cost function or optimal value function. Although the optimal policy depends on the starting state x_0 in the Equation (2.1), it is typically possible to find a policy $\mu^\star$ which is simultaneously optimal for all initial states. We give exact solution methods in Section 2.5. For many practical problems it is not possible to solve Equation (2.1) exactly. Therefore approximate methods are given in Section 4.

2.2 Partially Observable Markov Decision Processes (POMDPs)

In MDPs it is assumed that the state is fully observable by the agent. A more realistic assumption is that the state is only partially observable. This means that instead of receiving the current state from the environment, the agent receives an observation $z_k \in \mathcal{Z}$ at time step k. The observation depends probabilistically on the state and the action according to the observation model $p(z_k|x_k, a_{k-1})$. This leads to the definition of Partially Observable Markov Decision Processes. A schematic visualization of POMDPs is depicted in Figure 2.2. Before we can define a policy for POMDPs, we have to define an observable history. The agent has no possibility

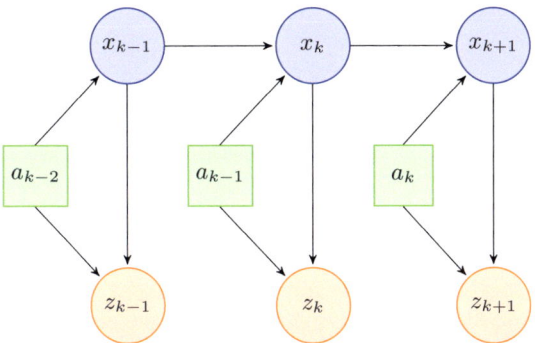

Figure 2.2: This figure depicts a diagram of a POMDP. At every time step, the environment is in a state x_k and generates observations z_k. Action can influence both states and observations.

to access the real state of the environment. The only information it receives about it is through actions and observations. An observable history

$$\mathcal{I}_k = \{b_0, z_1, \ldots, z_k, a_1, \ldots, a_{k-1}\}$$

is a collection of all the information at the agents disposal at time step k. b_0 is a prior probability distribution over the state space. It can be shown that based on $\mathcal{I}_k$ optimal decisions can be made. Therefore, the optimal policy depends on the whole observable history. In fact, the POMDP can be rewritten as a MDP by taking the observable history as the state. In this context the state is also called the information state. The disadvantage of such a formulation is that the state changes its length over time. Generally, every sufficient statistic [BMWW06] can serve as a state. A widely used sufficient statistic is the belief state which represents the available knowledge about the hidden state as a distribution over it.

2.3   Belief State MDP

One possible and formally elegant way to formulate the POMDP as a MDP is through a belief state. A belief state is a distribution over the state space $\mathcal{X}$

$$b_k(x_k) = p\left(x_k | \mathcal{I}_k\right) \ .$$

We can derive the transition function $b_{k+1} = B\left(b_k, a_k, z_{k+1}\right)$ through Bayesian inference. Bayesian inference performs two alternating steps, prediction and filtering. In the prediction step the state is estimated without taking the observation into account, merely on the basis of the transition function $p(x_{k+1}|x_k, a_k)$

$$p\left(x_{k+1}|\mathcal{I}_k, a_k\right) = \int p\left(x_{k+1}, x_k|\mathcal{I}_k, a_k\right) dx_k \qquad (2.2)$$

$$= \int p\left(x_{k+1}|x_k, \mathcal{I}_k, a_k\right) p\left(x_k|\mathcal{I}_k, a_k\right)$$

$$= \int p\left(x_{k+1}|x_k, a_k\right) b_k(x_k) dx_k \ ,$$

where the last step follows from the Markov property and the fact that x_k is independent of a_k, see Figure 2.2. In the filter step the belief is updated according to

$$b_{k+1}\left(x_{k+1}\right) = p\left(x_{k+1}|\mathcal{I}_{k+1}\right) \qquad (2.3)$$

$$= p(x_{k+1}|\mathcal{I}_k, z_{k+1}, a_k)$$

$$= \frac{p\left(x_{k+1}, z_{k+1}|\mathcal{I}_k, a_k\right)}{p\left(z_{k+1}|\mathcal{I}_k, a_k\right)}$$

$$= \frac{p\left(z_{k+1}|x_{k+1}, a_k\right) p\left(x_{k+1}|\mathcal{I}_k, a_k\right)}{p\left(z_{k+1}|\mathcal{I}_k, a_k\right)} .$$

Substituting Equation (2.2) into Equation (2.3) yields the transition function

$$b_{k+1}\left(x_{k+1}\right) = B\left(b_k, a_k, z_{k+1}\right) = \frac{p\left(z_{k+1}|x_{k+1}, a_k\right) \int p\left(x_{k+1}|x_k, a_k\right) b_k(x_k)}{p\left(z_{k+1}|\mathcal{I}_k, a_k\right)} ,$$

$$(2.4)$$

where the denominator is a normalization constant and can be computed without knowledge of $\mathcal{I}_k$. Equation (2.4) shows how the belief state b_k can be updated only from a_k and z_{k+1}.

The immediate cost of the belief state MDP can be obtained by

$$g(b_k, a_k) = \int g(x_k, a_k) b_k(x_k) dx_k \ ,$$

which can be identified as the expected cost.

2.4   Cost Functions for Information Gathering Agents

The cost function in a POMDP depends on the state. In some applications, like the one targeted in this report, it is necessary to model the cost function with direct dependence on the belief state. The objective of these application explicitly implies the reduction of uncertainty. Therefore, in [ALBTC10] the ρPOMDP is introduced, which is a POMDP where the cost function can be an arbitrary function of the belief state. In the following, we introduce possible cost functions whose objectives are to reduce the uncertainty. One can distinguish between covariance-based and information-theoretic-based cost functions. Covariance-based cost function depend on the expected posterior covariance which is defined as

$$C = \mathrm{E}_z \left\{ \mathrm{Cov} \left\{ x_{k+1} | \mathcal{I}_k, z_{k+1}, a_k \right\} \right\} ,$$

where the covariance is calculated with respect to the belief state b_{k+1}. The uncertainty can be quantified by employing different scalar functions on C. Possible functions are the determinant and the trace. The determinant measures the volume of the covariance ellipsoid. The trace, which equals the sum of the marginal variances, measures the perimeter of the rectangle enclosing the covariance ellipsoid.

Possible information-theoretic-based cost functions are differential entropy, mutual information or Kullback-Leibler divergence [Hub09]. These functions are more elaborate and capture the uncertainty of the belief state more precisely.

2.5   Exact Solution Methods

We consider solution methods for MDPs only. POMDPs are covered implicitly because they can be stated as a belief state MDP, see section 2.3. The presented algorithms all assume discrete actions and states and represent the value function as a so called table based representation. This means that for every single state, its associated value is stored in memory. For continuous values closed form solution can be found only in special cases. Otherwise, approximation methods, which are introduced in Section 4, can be used.

The algorithms for solving Equation (2.1) can be divided into three different types [BDSB10]: value iteration, policy iteration and policy search. There are also other kinds of possible solution methods like linear programming, which we do not want to consider here. Policy search solves the optimization problem (2.1) directly. This method is usually used in approximation methods by restricting the set of possible strategies. Advantages are that continuous states can be handled easily. A problem is that solution algorithms generally yield local optima.

Value iteration and policy iteration both use methods of dynamic programming. Equation (2.1) can be written as the following functional equation

$$J^\star(x_k) = \min_{a_k \in \mathcal{A}(x)} E\left\{ g(x_k, a_k, x_{k+1}) + \gamma J^\star(x_{k+1}) \right\} \qquad (2.5)$$

for the optimal value function $J^\star$ by exploiting the principle of optimality [Ber05]. Equation (2.5) is called the Bellman equation. The advantage of (2.5) over (2.1) is that the minimization is stated over a single action. By defining the operator T as

$$TJ := \min_{a \in \mathcal{A}(x)} E\left\{g(x, a, x') + \gamma J(x')\right\},$$

Equation (2.5) can be rewritten in a more compact way as

$$J^\star = TJ^\star .$$

One can show that T is a contraction mapping and has $J^\star$ as a fix point. This permits the usage of the fixed-point iteration

$$J_{k+1} = TJ_k$$

to solve for $J^\star$. This algorithm is called value iteration. It should be noted that the convergence speed depends on the order in which the values of the states are updated. This can be exploited to accelerate value iteration, see for example topological value iteration [DMW09].

For POMDPs even though the belief state is continuous, the value function has a special form in every iteration: It is piecewise linear and convex (PWLC). This allows for the use of a special solution procedure, see for example [Cas95]. For ρPOMDP this statement does not hold generally. One can show that for PWLC immediate costs, the value function is also PWLC. This property is used in [ALBTC10] to approximate a convex cost function arbitrary well with a PWLC function and then use some of the standard methods of POMDPs for ρPOMDP in a modified form [ALBTC10].

Another exact solution method is policy iteration. Policy iteration creates a sequence of policies with decreasing cost. It consists of two steps. Given a policy it evaluates the policy by calculating the value function. In the second step the policy is improved by solving the optimization problem

$$\mu_{k+1}(x_k) = \arg\min_a E\left\{g(x_k, a, x_{k+1}) + \gamma J_k(x_{k+1})\right\},$$

where μ_{k+1} is the improved policy and γ is the discount factor. One can show that this truly leads to a better policy [Ber07]. Step one can be solved either by solving a linear equation or by using a kind of value iteration

$$J_{k+1} = T_\mu J_k := E\left\{g(x, \mu(x), x') + \gamma J_k(x')\right\} . \tag{2.6}$$

3   Modeling the deflectometric measurement system

The framework introduced in Section 2 will now be applied to the deflectometric planning problem. In the following we first give a short overview of the deflectometric measurement process, then introduce a model for the sequential planning problem of surface reconstruction and afterwards generalize this model to problems of surface inspection.

3.1   Deflectometry

We give a short overview of the deflectometric measurement process, for a detailed description see [Wer11]. A typical deflectometric setup consist of a LCD, a test surface and a camera. The LCD displays a sequence of patterns to encode every pixel uniquely. The patterns are reflected on the specular surface and observed by the camera. Because the reflection of light rays on a surface point depend on the corresponding slope, the observed patterns are deformed. Based on the observed sequence of patterns an assignment l between camera pixel and LCD pixel can be computed. This mapping gives information about the normals of the surface.

A difficulty in selecting the parameters for the deflectometric measurement device is that the surface, which has to be inspected, is part of the measurement mapping. Practically, this means that the area of the surface which will be visible and the measurement quality depend on the shape of the surface. In a setting where little information about the surface is known, a planning algorithm will tend to make many measurements. The current measurement mode consists of capturing a whole series of images and is time consuming. We propose a second kind of measurement mode which captures only one image and will be used for estimating the measurement quality. Planning algorithms can then decide which measurement mode to use. In the case when a reference surface is known, it is possible to compute the observed area on the surface. Capturing a single image could possibly still be used for extracting information about the quality of the measurement.

3.2   Surface Reconstruction Problems

We model the sequential planning problem of reconstructing a specular surface with a deflectometric measurement device as a ρPOMDP. This contains defining the set of all states $\mathcal{X}$, the set of all actions $\mathcal{A}$, the set of all observations $\mathcal{Z}$, the state transition probabilities and the observation model. Then the belief state can be deduced and, based on that, the cost function defined.

The state of the environment is the shape of the surface. For our formal treatment of the subject we don't need a concrete representation and will only consider the set of all surfaces. The environment is stationary which means that the state does not change with time. The transition probability can be expressed as

$$p\left(x_{k+1}|x_k, a_k\right) = \delta\left(x_{k+1} - x_k\right)$$

and is independent of time and actions.

The actions, or in this situation the measurement configurations, consist of the position and orientation of the camera and the monitor. Intrinsic camera parameters like focal distance, aperture, etc. can be considered as well but increase the complexity of the planning problem. Additionally, like suggested in Section 3.1, we distinguish between the measurement of one pattern or a sequence of patterns. The set of all configurations is defined as the union

$$\mathcal{A} = \mathcal{A}_1 \cup \mathcal{A}_n \ ,$$

where $\mathcal{A}_1$ is the set of all configurations for capturing a single image and $\mathcal{A}_n$ the set of all configurations for capturing a sequence of images.

The observation consists of the captured images whose number depends on the measurement mode. The space of all measurements is the union

$$\mathcal{Z} = \mathcal{Z}_1 \cup \mathcal{Z}_n \ ,$$

where $\mathcal{Z}_1$ is the set of all images and $\mathcal{Z}_n = \left(\mathcal{Z}_1\right)^n$ the space of all image sequences of size n.

The observation model, in this context also called measurement model, is described by a probability distribution $p(z|S, z_{ref}, a)$, where $S \in \mathcal{X}$, $z, z_{ref} \in \mathcal{Z}$ and z_{ref} is the original pattern or pattern sequence displayed on the monitor and z is the corresponding deformed pattern. It can be expressed as

$$p(z|S, z_{ref}, a) = \begin{cases} p_1(z|S, z_{ref}, a), & \text{if } a \in \Theta_1 \text{and } z \in \mathcal{Z}_1 \\ p_n(z|S, z_{ref}, a), & \text{if } a \in \Theta_n \text{and } z \in \mathcal{Z}_n \ , \\ 0, & \text{else} \end{cases}$$

where p_1, p_n are the concrete measurement models for capturing one image and a series of images, respectively.

In the case of a pattern sequence, usually the image sequence is processed and results into the deflectometric mapping l. Probabilistically, we can model the connection between the mapping l, the observation $z \in O_n$ and the surface $S \in \mathcal{X}$ as

$$p(S|z, z_{ref}, a) = \int p(S, l|z, z_{ref}, a) \, dl \qquad (3.1)$$

$$= \int p(S|l, a) p(l|z, z_{ref}, a) dl \; ,$$

where we assume that S is conditional independent of z given l. In equation (3.1) we identify $p(l|z, z_{ref}, a)$ as the decoding function which is modeled probabilistically here.

The observable history $\mathcal{I}_k$ consists of all the information available until time step k which is

$$\mathcal{I}_k = \{b_0, z_1, \cdots, z_k, a_1, \cdots, a_{k-1}\} \; ,$$

where the belief state b_0 is a prior distribution on the surface space $\mathcal{S}$. For the belief state we get

$$b_k(S) = p(S|\mathcal{I}_k) \; ,$$

which is the estimation of the surface given all observations. This is updated according to the inference rules depicted in Section 2.3, where the prediction step (2.2) is not needed because the environment is stationary.

The cost function can be chosen as the sum of two terms

$$g_k(b_k, a_k) = g_a(a_k) - g_I(b_k, a_k) \; ,$$

where g_a describes the cost caused by the action and g_I measures the information gain and can be chosen according to Section 2.4.

The whole procedure of planning is depicted in Figure 3.1. It consists of a planning component, which selects a new sensor configuration depending on the current belief state. After the measurement, the result is used to update the belief state. Based on the new belief state, an estimate of the surface can be made and the whole procedure is repeated in the next time step.

3.3 Generalization

Additionally to the definitions in Section 3.2, we define the distribution $p(f|S, S_{ref})$, where S_{ref} is a given reference surface and f is some function which maps from the reference surface to a set depending on the problem:

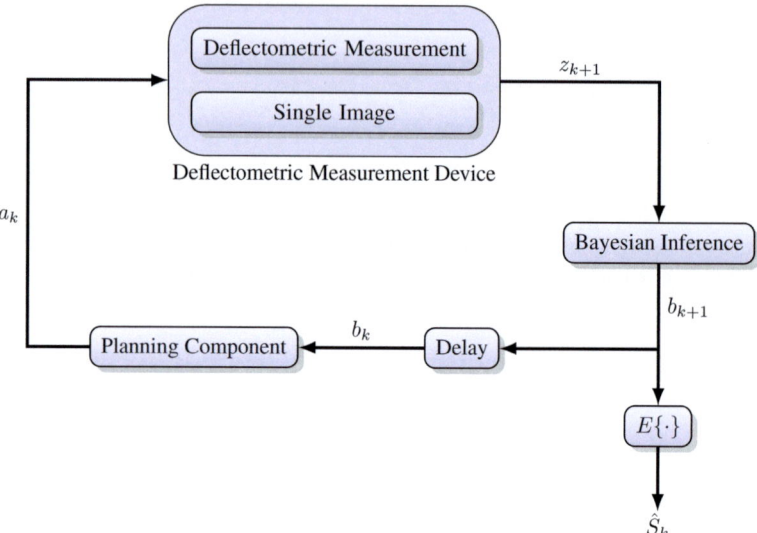

Figure 3.1: This figure illustrates the planning loop. The planning component selects a sensor configuration a_k depending on the current belief state b_k. The deflectometric measurement device creates a measurement z_k, which is used for updating the belief state. Based on the new belief state, an estimate of the surface can be made and the whole procedure is repeated.

- Surface deviation: In this setting, it is assumed that a reference surface is given. The goal is to measure the deviation of a test surface from the reference. For quantifying deviation, different values can be considered like altitude, slope or curvature deviation. The function f is chosen as $f : S_{ref} \to \mathbb{R}$.

- Surface defect detection/classification: The goal is to find defects on the surface and eventually classify them. A reference surface can be given or not. An additional problem occurs when no reference surface is given. Then it is not clear how to distinguish between defects and manifestations of the design of the surface. Therefore, some prior information of the surface must be given, i.e., smoothness properties. We will only consider the case when a reference surface is given. The function f can be chosen as $f : S_{ref} \to \{0, 1\}$ for defect detection and $f : S_{ref} \to \{1, \dots, N\}$ as defect classification.

In this setting we are interested in the estimation of the function f and not the surface S. The actions should be taken in such a way that results in information gain of f. Therefore, we take the function f to be the state of the ρPOMDP, and the belief state can be written as

$$b_k(f|\mathcal{I}_k, S_{ref}) = \int p(f|S, S_{ref}) p(S|\mathcal{I}_k, S_{ref}) dS \; .$$

The prior distribution $b_0(S|S_{ref})$ is modeled with knowledge of the reference surface. It describes the possible deviations of the test object from the reference surface. A possibly more convenient way to model the prior distribution is through a function $S = h(S_{ref}, w)$. It defines which deformations can occur depending on some random variable w.

3.4 Complexity

The deflectometric planning problem is very complex. This is because the state space, the observation space and the action space are continuous and high-dimensional. Furthermore, the measurement model is nonlinear, which makes inference intractable. The representation of the surface by probability densities is also problematic because with one single measurement it is not possible to infer a unique surface. Therefore, the belief function must be able to represent multimodal densities. For this reason, exact solution methods for the presented model are infeasible. We have to resort to suboptimal solutions.

4 Approximate Dynamic Programming (ADP)

In this section, we introduce approximation methods to solve the deflectometric planning problem. We will concentrate on the two main algorithms: value iteration and policy iteration, as presented in section 2. Both algorithms rely on exact representation of value functions. A value function assigns an optimal cost to every single state. An exact representation stores each assignment individually in memory. It is clear that for large state spaces this representation is not feasible. It should be noted that there are some special cases where a closed form solution of the value function exists, see for example [Ber05]. But generally this is not the case. A central idea which is used in ADP is to approximate value functions in a parameter space. Then, value functions can be represented compactly through their parameter.

These algorithms are sometimes called approximation in value space. There is also another family of approximations called approximation in policy space. They restrict the set of all policies and minimize the optimization problem (2.1) directly. The advantage of this methods is that they can handle large or continuous state spaces. The drawback is that they are prone to local minima. That is not true for algorithms which approximate in value space but here the convergence of the algorithms depend highly on the choice of an appropriate parameter space. We will not consider approximation in policy spaces but the interested reader can consult for example [SMSM00].

4.1 Function Approximators

We will consider parametric models for a compact representation of the value function. Let J be some value function, then we approximate

$$J(x) \approx J(x, \mathbf{r}), \quad \mathbf{r} \in \Omega \subset \mathbb{R}^M ,$$

where $\mathbf{r}$ is some parameter in the parameter space $\Omega \subset \mathbb{R}^M$ and $x \in \mathcal{X}$ is the state. We consider states which are distributions over a set of surfaces. A widely used approach is to define a set of functions $\{\phi_1, \ldots, \phi_M\}$ which map from the state space into $\mathbb{R}$ and can be interpreted as features. For convenience we write $\boldsymbol{\Phi}(x) = (\phi_1(x), \ldots, \phi_M(x))$. $J(x, \mathbf{r})$ is chosen in such a way that it only depends on the features and the parameter vector $\mathbf{r}$

$$J(x, \mathbf{r}) = f\left(\boldsymbol{\Phi}(x), \mathbf{r}\right) , \qquad (4.1)$$

where f is an arbitrary function. A widely used class are linear models. They assume that the function f is simply a scalar product and $J(x, \mathbf{r})$ has the form

$$J(x, \mathbf{r}) = f(\boldsymbol{\Phi}(x), \mathbf{r}) = \langle \boldsymbol{\Phi}(x), \mathbf{r} \rangle = \sum_{i=1}^{M} r_i \phi_i(x),$$

where, in this case, $\mathbf{r}$ represents the weights for the features. The choice of features is crucial here. The feature count should be small to allow efficient computation but at the same time contain all the relevant information, which is required for decision making. Another criterion for choosing features should be that they represent the main nonlinearities of the value function. This means that the function f in Expression (4.1) can be chosen to be linear or very smooth.

For the considered problem of deflectometric planning, the state space consists of probability density functions over some surface space. In this setting, it is important that the features should as well capture uncertainty. In particular suppose we model the surface as a Gaussian Process [Ras06] which is a generalization of the Gaussian density for function spaces and can be fully characterized by a mean function and a covariance function. In this setting we could design features which extract relevant information of the expectation but also of the covariance.

Another way of designing features is by means of heuristic policies. Let us assume we know a set of policies $\mu_1, \ldots, \mu_M$, then we can evaluate their value functions $J_{\mu_1}, \ldots, J_{\mu_M}$ and use these as features by making the ansatz

$$J(x, \mathbf{r}) = \sum_{i=1}^{M} d(x, \mathbf{r}) J_{\mu_i}(x) \, ,$$

where d is some weight function which depends on the state and is parameterized by parameter $\mathbf{r}$. This combination allows to expose the strength of every policy by choosing an appropriate approximation architecture for d and parameter $\mathbf{r}$.

If we have policies for some special surfaces like spheres etc., we could choose d as a distance between states and the surfaces. Formally, we have some reference surfaces $S_1, \ldots, S_M$ and associated policies $\mu_1, \ldots, \mu_M$. Then we choose J as

$$J(x, \mathbf{r}) = \sum_{i=1}^{M} d(x, S_i, \mathbf{r}) J_{\mu_i}(x),$$

where d now describes the distance between the reference surface S_i and the state x. It should be noted that the x and S_i cannot be compared directly because x is a distribution over functions and S_i is a concrete surface.

4.2 Approximate Value Iteration

Let $\mathcal{F}$ be a restricted function space which is defined by choosing a parameterization. Fitted value iteration is a procedure to use value iteration with function approximators and works by calculating

$$J_{k+1} = \Pi_{\mathcal{F}} T J_k \, , \tag{4.2}$$

where $\Pi_{\mathcal{F}}$ is the projector onto the space $\mathcal{F}$. Geometrically interpreted, operator T is applied to the value function J_k which leads to a new value function J'. J' generally does not lie in the restricted space $\mathcal{F}$ and does not comprise a compact representation. Therefore, in a second step J' is projected onto $\mathcal{F}$ and results into J_{k+1}. The projection can be accomplished by solving a quadratic optimization problem. A concrete realization of this algorithm, called sampled value iteration, uses samples to avoid the complete storage of $T J_k$ and the calculation of the corresponding expectation. Let $\tilde{\mathcal{X}} = \{x_1, \ldots, x_N\}$ be a number of so called base points sampled from the state space $\mathcal{X}$. With the transition probabilities for each state $x_i \in \tilde{\mathcal{X}}$ and action $a \in \mathcal{A}$ successor states $\{y_{ij}^a \big| y_{ij}^a \sim p(x_{k+1}|x_k, a), \ j = 1, \ldots, M\}$ are sampled. We can calculate y_{ij}^a through the transition function (2.4), as well. If the

action space is too large only a subset of the actions can be taken. Then the value
iteration step TJ is estimated on the points x_i by

$$v_i = \max_{a \in \mathcal{A}} \frac{1}{M} \sum_{j=1}^{M} g(x_i, a, y_{ij}^a) + \gamma J_k(y_{ij}^a) \, ,$$

which is the empirical version of the Bellman equation (2.5). In the next step, the
projection into the function space $\mathcal{F}$ is computed by solving a least-squares problem

$$J_{k+1} = \arg\min_{f \in \mathcal{F}} \frac{1}{N} \sum_{i=1}^{N} (f(x_i) - v_i)^2,$$

which can be solved iteratively with gradient methods. Unfortunately it is not
possible to combine fitted value iteration with arbitrary function approximators
because the sequence $J_1, J_2, \dots$ of values may not converge. Convergence can be
guaranteed for so called averagers [Gor95]. Loosely speaking averagers estimate
the value of a state as a weighted sum of values of nearby states. More formally
given the data $\mathcal{D} = \{(x_i, v_i)\}_{i=1}^{M}$ and weights $w_i(x, \mathcal{D})$ with the property that
$\sum_{i=1}^{M} w_i(x, \mathcal{D}) = 1$ then an averager has the form

$$J(x, \mathcal{D}) = \sum_{i=1}^{M} w_i(x, \mathcal{D}) v_i,$$

which means that the value for every state is computed as a convex combination
of the values v_i. The family of averagers contains kernel regression, weighted
k-nearest neighbors, Bezier patches or linear interpolation among others. In context
with POMDPs, fitted value iteration is often used by first mapping the belief state to
a new smaller space. Approaches for mapping are belief state compression [RGT05]
or belief state parameterization which maps the belief state into a parameterized
probability distribution space, i.e., Gaussian space [BMWW06].

4.3   Approximate Policy Iteration

Policy iteration consists of two steps, which are executed interchangeably. The
evaluation step computes the value function J_{μ_k} of the current policy μ_k and the
improvement step yields a new better policy μ_{k+1} given the value function J_{μ_k}.
In approximate policy iteration both sub steps are modified so that the algorithm
can be used for problems with large state spaces. In the policy improvement step
the minimization problem could be to complex to solve and only obtained by an

approximation. In the policy evaluation step, the value function of the current policy μ_k is only approximated by taking samples from J_{μ_k}. The samples are generally used in two different ways [Ber07]. So called direct methods estimate the value function J_μ directly by means of Monte Carlo simulation whereas the indirect methods solve an approximate form of the Equation (2.6). In the following we will only concentrate on the policy evaluation step.

4.3.1   Direct Methods

Let $\mathcal{F}$ be a restricted function space. Direct methods try to find an approximation $\tilde{J} \in \mathcal{F}$ that best matches J_μ by solving

$$\min_{\tilde{J} \in \mathcal{F}} \left\| J_\mu - \tilde{J} \right\| .$$

Here $\| \cdot \|$ is some Euclidian norm which makes the optimization problem a linear least squares problem. Generally J_μ cannot be computed exactly but is given in form of samples. Therefore stochastic iterative methods are required, for example, temporal difference (TD) methods [BT96].

4.3.2   Indirect Methods

Let the function space $\mathcal{F} = \{\Phi r \mid r \in \Omega\}$ be the space of generalized linear functions with appropriate features. The idea of indirect methods is to use an approximated form of the Bellman equation

$$\Phi r = \Pi T_\mu(\Phi r) , \tag{4.3}$$

where Π denotes the projection on the subspace $\mathcal{F}$ and T_μ is defined in (2.6) with respect to the current policy μ. Equation (4.3) is also called the projected Bellman equation. Geometrically it can be interpreted in the same way as equation (4.2).

One solution method is to find r such that the quadratic problem

$$r_J = \arg\min_{r \in \mathcal{R}^s} \left\| \Phi r - T(\Phi r) \right\|^2 \tag{4.4}$$

is minimized. Solving (4.4) directly is expensive due to evaluation of the expression $T(\Phi r)$. Least squares policy evaluation (LSPE) [Ber07] calculates the expression only for some samples and solves the equation iteratively.

5 Discussion

In this report we have presented first ideas on how to embed the deflectometric planning problem into a probabilistic planning problem. Selection of the optimal sensor configuration for visual inspection or surface reconstruction can be modeled as a ρPOMDP. The complexity of the introduced model prevents one from finding an exact solution. Therefore, we gave an overview of approximate methods for dynamic programming. There are some aspects which are not addressed in this paper and remain subject of future work:

The approximate versions of value iteration and policy iteration require both a minimization over the configuration space which is problematic because the configuration space is continuous and high-dimensional. Straight forward minimization with, for instance, a gradient method leads to local minima. In literature, the configuration space is often discretized. But for multidimensional spaces an exponential count of sensor configurations is obtained.

The presented approximation algorithms are possibly not sufficient for large surfaces. There are other methods which try to reduce the complexity of the problem by considering special structures of the underlying POMDP. For example methods in [GKPV03] exploit factorial representations of the state. Hierarchal methods are another way to reduce the complexity, for a summary see [BM03].

Finally, another important aspect not considered here is the update step of the belief state according to the inference rules described in Section 2.3. For general measurement models it is not possible to realize it in closed form or efficiently. For example, in the case of a deflectometric measurement, it is not possible to uniquely extract the surface from a single measurement but only a one dimensional solution manifold [Bal08]. Therefore the a posteriori distributions have to be multimodal and somehow represent this manifold. Approximating the a posteriori distribution with a uni-modal distribution will generally remove possible solutions and lead to wrong estimations.

Bibliography

[ALBTC10]   Mauricio Araya-López, Olivier Buffet, Vincent Thomas, and François Charpillet. A POMDP Extension with Belief-dependent Rewards (Extended Version). Research Report RR-7433, INRIA, October 2010.

[Bal08]   Jonathan Balzer. *Regularisierung des Deflektometrieproblems - Grundlagen und Anwendung*. PhD thesis, 2008.

[BDSB10]   L. Buşoniu, B. De Schutter, and R. Babuška. Approximate Dynamic Programming and Reinforcement Learning. In R. Babuška and F.C.A. Groen, editors, *Interactive*

Collaborative Information Systems, volume 281 of *Studies in Computational Intelligence*, pages 3–44. Springer, Berlin, Germany, 2010.

[Ber05] D.P. Bertsekas. *Dynamic Programming and Optimal Control, Vol. I, 3rd.* Athena Scientific optimization and computation series. Athena Scientific, 2005.

[Ber07] D.P. Bertsekas. *Dynamic Programming and Optimal Control, Vol. II, 3rd.* Athena Scientific optimization and computation series. Athena Scientific, 2007.

[BM03] Andrew G. Barto and Sridhar Mahadevan. Recent Advances in Hierarchical Reinforcement Learning. *Discrete Event Dynamic Systems: Theory and Application*, 13:41–77, 2003.

[BMWW06] A. Brooks, A. Makarenko, S. Williams, and Durrant H. Whyte. Parametric POMDPs for planning in continuous State Spaces. *Robotics and Autonomous Systems*, 54(11):887–897, 2006.

[BT96] D.P. Bertsekas and J.N. Tsitsiklis. *Neuro-Dynamic Programming.* Athena scientific optimization and computation series. Athena Scientific, 1996.

[Cas95] Anthony R. Cassandra. Optimal Policies for Partially Observable Markov Decision Processes. Technical report, 1995.

[DMW09] Peng Dai, Mausam, and Daniel S. Weld. Focused Topological Value Iteration. In *Proceedings of the International Conference on Automated Planning and Scheduling*, 2009.

[GKPV03] C. Guestrin, D. Koller, R. Parr, and S. Venkataraman. Efficient Solution Algorithms for Factored MDPs. *Journal of Artificial Intelligence Research*, 19:399–468, 2003.

[Gor95] Geoffrey Gordon. Stable Function Approximation in Dynamic Programming. In *Proceedings of IMCL '95*, 1995.

[Hub09] M. Huber. *Probabilistic Framework for Sensor Management.* Karlsruhe series on intelligent sensor actuator systems. Univ-Verl. Karlsruhe, 2009.

[Ras06] Carl Edward Rasmussen. Gaussian processes for machine learning. MIT Press, 2006.

[RGT05] Nicholas Roy, Geoffrey J. Gordon, and Sebastian Thrun. Finding Approximate POMDP Solutions through Belief Compression. *Journal of Artificial Intelligence Research*, 23:1–40, 2005.

[SMSM00] Richard S. Sutton, David Mcallester, Satinder Singh, and Yishay Mansour. Policy Gradient Methods for Reinforcement Learning with Function Approximation. In *In Advances in Neural Information Processing Systems 12*, volume 12, pages 1057–1063, 2000.

[Wer11] Stefan Bruno Werling. *Deflektometrie zur automatischen Sichtprüfung und Rekonstruktion spiegelnder Oberflächen.* PhD thesis, 2011.

Statistical inverse problem of partial differential equation: an example with stationary 1D heat conduction problem

Chettapong Janya-anurak

Vision and Fusion Laboratory
Institute for Anthropomatics
Karlsruhe Institute of Technology (KIT), Germany
chettapong.janya-anurak@ies.uni-karlsruhe.de

Technical Report IES-2011-15

Abstract:
  Local behaviour in a continuous system with spatially or temporally variable parameters is often described in terms of partial differential equations (PDEs). Given a system of PDEs, an inverse problem is to reconstruct parameters in every point given a limited number of observations or conditions. There exists a plethora of solution methods for various inverse problems, nevertheless, this is still an active field of research. In particular, non-linear systems, such as heat transfer equation, pose the biggest challenge. In this report we present a novel method based on Bayesian statistics. The parameter fields are represented in terms of some basis functions with unknown coefficients, treated as random variables. Their posterior probability distribution is then computed using Markov Chain Monte-Carlo approach. Finally, the field is reconstructed using the values that maximize likelihood. We illustrate the method with the example of the one-dimensional heat transfer equation, and discuss various choices of the basis functions and the accuracy issues.

1 Introduction

Many industrial processes e.g. thermal process or fluid process possess spatio-temporal interrelation. The spatio-temporal behavior of system is essential for analysis and control the processes. These systems are normally mathematically modeled in term of partial differential equations (PDEs). Due to their infinite-dimensionality the PDE models are not used directly for implementation. Practically these infinite-dimensional models are approximated into computable finite-dimensional model.

Han-Xiong Li and Chenkun Qi arrange and classify various finite-dimensional approximation methods in [Li11]. Modeling with preferably few finite numbers of states that keep model computation efficient and still have good a performance is an active field of research which is known as model reduction. The overview of model reduction methods can be found in [AD01].

In fact the model cannot interpret reality exactly because there are generally some unknown uncertainties in model due to incomplete knowledge. In order to keep the model close to the reality, the measurement data are used to estimate unknown parameters. Such problems are known as parameter estimation or identification problems, which can be classified as inverse problems from mathematical point of view. A number of theories and algorithm have been developed to solve these inverse problems. Recently many methods using statistical inference to solve inverse problems are proposed especially Bayesian inference method e.g. [KS05]. The statistical inverse problem has many advantages comparing to the classic deterministic solving methods [Jin06] and therefore is an interesting active field of research.

Despite of many advantages the statistical inverse problem is normally required tremendous computational efforts. Therefore the combination of model reduction and statistical inference method is the new aspect in field of modeling research as presented in e.g. [Lie09] and [Jin06]. The residuum of the discretization or the approximation always has an effect in solving inverse problem using statistical approach [KS07]. A Key to avoid such error is to choose an appropriate approximation method, which is an aim of our study.

The organization of this paper is as follows. In section 2, the background about the partial differential equation and the spatial discretization for deterministic as well as for stochastic model is presented. Section 3 is devoted to the inverse problem and their solving methods. Section 4 shows the numerical experiments of Bayesian inverse problem of PDE by means of 1D heat conduction example. Conclusions and some future works are finally discussed in section 5.

2 Partial differential equation and spatial discretization methods

Many physical phenomena can be described with the relation between some continuously varying quantities and their rates of change in some independent variables. This relation can be mathematically formulated in form of differential equation. If there is only single independent variable in the differential equation, the equation will be called *ordinary differential equation* (ODE). On the other hand the equation involving an unknown function of several independent variables and their partial derivatives with respect to those variables is defined as *partial differential equation* (PDE). In engineering the independent variables are normally time and space co-ordinate. Therefore many engineering systems can be modeled mathematically in general form

$$\mathcal{D}\left(x(\boldsymbol{r}, t) | \boldsymbol{\eta}\right) = s(\boldsymbol{r}, t) \tag{2.1}$$

where $x(\boldsymbol{r}, t) : \mathbb{R}^3 \times \mathbb{R} \to \mathbb{R}$ and $s(\boldsymbol{r}, t) : \mathbb{R}^3 \times \mathbb{R} \to \mathbb{R}$ denotes the system state and inhomogeneous term at time t and at spatial coordinate $\boldsymbol{r} = [x, y, z]^T \in \Omega$. The inhomogeneous term, the system state and its derivatives, respect to time or space coordinate, are related by means of some operator $\mathcal{D}$. The dynamic behavior and distributed properties of the system depend on the parameter of the operator, which are collected in the process parameter vector $\boldsymbol{\eta}$.

Additional conditions are generally required in order that the PDE has unique solution. In engineering view, the additional condition can be classified in 2 types relating to the independent variable, namely the initial condition relating to time and the boundary condition relating to space. The initial condition can be formulated in general form

$$\mathcal{D}_t\left(x(\boldsymbol{r}, t = 0)\right) = h(\boldsymbol{r}) \tag{2.2}$$

where $\mathcal{D}_t$ denotes a differential operator in respect to time coordinate. The function $h(\boldsymbol{r})$ describe the relation of the state $x(\boldsymbol{r}, t)$ for all spatial coordinate $\boldsymbol{r} \in [x, y, z]^T$ at the initial time $(t = 0)$. Similarly the boundary condition is formulated in general form

$$\mathcal{D}_r\left(x(\boldsymbol{r} \in \partial\Omega, t)\right) = b(t) \tag{2.3}$$

where $\mathcal{D}_r$ denotes a differential operator in respect to spatial coordinate. The function $b(t)$ describe the relation of the state $x(\boldsymbol{r}, t)$ at boundary spatial coordinate $\boldsymbol{r} \in \partial\Omega$ for all time t.

All three equations (2.1) , (2.2) and (2.3) form an *initial-boundary value prob-lem (IBVP)*, which are used as distributed parameter system models of physical phenomena in engineering and science.

2.1 Deterministic spatial discretization

The initial-boundary value problem is normally only in simple case analytically solvable. Therefore this IBVP is practically approximated from infinite-dimensional problem to finite dimensional problem. This approximation is usually applied in spatial domain and can be accomplished by transform the PDE and boundary conditions into system of ODEs. The overview of important spatial discretization methods can be founded in [Li11].

As showed in figure 2.1, the spatial discretization methods can be classified in 2 groups.

- Finite difference method (FDM): this method is an approximation of the differential operator in PDE by difference operator as

$$\frac{\partial x}{\partial r} \approx \frac{\Delta x}{\Delta r}$$

  This approximation term can be forward, backward or central difference derived often from Taylor expansion.

- Weighted residual method (WRM): It is known that a continuous function can be represented as infinite series. Based on this principle, the solution of IBVP can be expanded by a set of spatial basis function $\{\varphi_i(\boldsymbol{r})\}_{i=1}^{\infty}$ as follows

$$x(\boldsymbol{r}, t) = \sum_{i=1}^{\infty} a_i(t)\varphi_i(\boldsymbol{r})$$

  From this infinite series the solution of IBVP can be approximated in finite dimension by truncating the infinite series at N

$$x(\boldsymbol{r}, t) = \sum_{i=1}^{\infty} a_i(t)\varphi_i(\boldsymbol{r}) \approx \sum_{i=1}^{N} a_i(t)\varphi_i(\boldsymbol{r}) = \hat{x}(\boldsymbol{r}, t)$$

  This method is often used and very efficient. Based on types of spatial basis function either local or global, WRM can be classified in 2 groups namely the finite element method and spectral method. In both methods many approaches of proper spatial basis functions can be used to expand the solution into finite series. The selection of the basis functions is a critical point and always has impact to the performance of systems of ODEs.

It is noted that the FDM is an approximation of the derivatives operators in PDE, while the WRM approximate the solution of PDE.

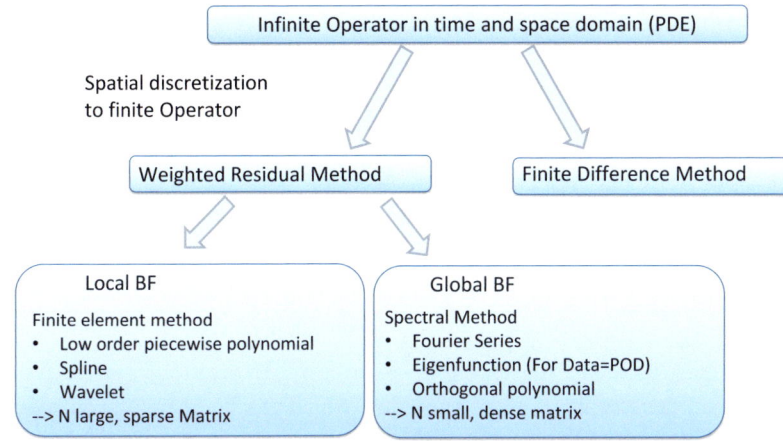

Figure 2.1: The discretization methods to approximate the PDE into system of ODEs

2.2   Discretization of random field

For some modeling aspect the uncertainty of some variables need to be considered. The state (or solution) of PDE can be modeled as random variable. In this case it will lead the PDE (2.1) to a *stochastic partial differential equation SPDE*, which represents the dynamic behavior, the distributed properties and the uncertainty of the underlying physical system.

The term stochastic process is well-known in many engineering discipline e.g in control engineering, signal processing etc. The stochastic process can be treated as functions of one deterministic argument (in most cases regarded as time) whose values are random variables. In case of several deterministic arguments (multidimensional vectors e.g. 2-dimensional space) the stochastic process can be called random field. A random field can be seen as a generalization of stochastic process. According to [SD00] the random field can be defined as:

Definition 7 (Definition of random field) Given a probability space $(\Theta, \mathcal{F}, \mathcal{P})$, a random field $H(\boldsymbol{r}, \omega)$ is defined as a curve in $\mathcal{L}^2(\Theta, \mathcal{F}, \mathcal{P})$, that is a collection of random variables indexed by a continuous parameter $\boldsymbol{r} \in \Omega$, where Ω is an open set of $\mathbb{R}^d$.

The random field can be considered as a continuous function as in deterministic case and therefore can be expanded by means of spatial basis function $\{\varphi_i(r)\}_{i=1}^{\infty}$:

$$H(r,\omega) = \sum_{i=1}^{\infty} \theta_i(\omega)\varphi_i(r)$$

This set of basis function can be either local or global as by deterministic case. Accordingly the discretized field can be expressed as a finite summation of the series:

$$\hat{H}(r,\omega) = \sum_{i=1}^{N} \theta_i(\omega)\varphi_i(r) \tag{2.4}$$

where $\theta_i(\omega)$ denotes the random variables, which can be expressed as *weighted integrals* of $H(\cdot)$ over the domain of the system:

$$\theta_i(\omega) = \int_{\Omega} H(r,\omega)w_i(r)dr$$

Various methods to random field discretization are proposed in [SD00]. All methods have the same approach as mentioned above, by truncating the obtained series after a finite number of terms. The difference between each method rely on different basis function and respectively weight function.

3   Inverse problem

In engineering and science mathematical models are mostly used to describe physical phenomena. The challenge of the modeling is to relate physicals parameters characterizing a **model** θ, to conceivable instrumental observations making up some set of **data** y. Under assumption of physical laws the relation of θ and y can be determined as a mathematical operator $F(\cdot)$ as follows:

$$F(\theta) = y \tag{3.1}$$

A forward problem is to find observable data y that would correspond to a given model θ. On the other hand the inverse problem is the problem of finding model θ given observed data y. The forward problem can normally be solved by mathematical manner because the problem is commonly well-posed. The term well-posed problem stems from a definition given by Jacques Hadamard [Had23]. He stated that the mathematical model of physical phenomena should have three properties, which are existence, uniqueness and continuous dependence of the solution on the data, in some reasonable topology.

By this well-posedness definition, an inverse problem is inherently ill-posed because the limited observation of data often inevitably implies non-uniqueness. In order to solve an inverse problem, some additional assumptions are involved to reformulate the problem. Two preferred approach are deterministic optimization and statistical inference, which be discussed in following subsections.

3.1 Deterministic inverse problem

In the deterministic setting, the inverse problem is formulated as an estimation problem of parameter $\boldsymbol{\theta}$. It is the minimization problem of an objective function $\mathcal{J}(\boldsymbol{\theta})$. The objective function is usually a normed difference between the observed data Y and the predicted output $\hat{Y} = F(\boldsymbol{\theta})$. Usually the quadratic of Euclidean norm is used, the mathematic formulation of inverse problem is to find optimal parameter $\boldsymbol{\theta}^*$, which

$$\boldsymbol{\theta}^* = \operatorname{argmin} \mathcal{J}(\boldsymbol{\theta}) = \operatorname{argmin} \left(\frac{1}{2} \|F(\boldsymbol{\theta}) - Y\|^2 \right)$$

In the absence of measurement error, the optimal parameters $\boldsymbol{\theta}^*$ are the parameters, which make the objective function equal zero $\mathcal{J}(\boldsymbol{\theta}^*) = 0$. There can be not only one parameter, which produce the data Y. The solution of this problem is still not unique, therefore this problem is still ill-posed.

In order to make this problem well-posed, the term $\beta R(\boldsymbol{\theta})$ is added in the objective function. The $R(\cdot) : \mathbb{R}^{N_\theta} \to \mathbb{R}$ is a nonnegative functional, called *regularization functional*. $\beta \in \mathbb{R}_+$ is a regularization parameter. The regularized inverse problem is reformulated as:

$$\boldsymbol{\theta}^* = \operatorname{argmin} \mathcal{J}(\boldsymbol{\theta}) = \operatorname{argmin} \left(\frac{1}{2} \|F(\boldsymbol{\theta}) - Y\|^2 + \beta R(\boldsymbol{\theta}) \right)$$

The existence and uniqueness of the solution of this problem depend on the choice of functional $R(\cdot)$. For example the Tikhonov regularization set the regularization functional as:

$$R(\boldsymbol{\theta}) = \|\boldsymbol{\theta} - \boldsymbol{\theta}_0\|^2$$

where $\boldsymbol{\theta}_0$ is some arbitrary parameter. This inverse problem with regularization is a constrained nonlinear optimization. There are no guarantees about the convexity of either the solution space or the objective function [Lie09]. The extremal problem can be solved by means of gradient method. The solution of this extremal problem is a single point in parameter space. There is no further information about the uncertainty of the solution.

3.2 Bayesian statistic formulation of inverse problem

By statistical formulation, the inverse problem is reformulated as a problem of statistical inference by means of Bayesian statistics [KS05]. The unknown parameters are modeled as random variables. The randomness of the unknown parameters describes the degree of information concerning their realizations in Bayesian statistics. The degree of information concerning these values is coded in the form of probability distributions. The solution of statistical inverse problem is the posterior distribution. This solution as a probability distribution is the main difference between the statistical approach and deterministic approach, which gives only the optimal single point solution. By statistical inverse problem the single point solution can be also estimated from the probability distribution.

The ill-posedness of the inverse problem is handled by restate the problem as a well-posed extension in a large space of probability distributions. Moreover it is allowed to add the prior knowledge that is often hidden in the deterministic regularization view. This *prior information* of unknown parameters θ can be coded into a probability density. This probability distribution called *a priori* distribution $\pi(\theta)$ represent our *a priori* knowledge of the parameters.

With joint probability density of unknown parameters θ and measurement y, which is denoted by $\pi(\theta, y)$, there is a relation :

$$\pi(\theta, y) = \pi(y|\theta)\pi(\theta) = \pi(\theta|y)\pi(y)$$

where the conditional probability $\pi(y|\theta)$, called *likelihood function*, expresses the likelihood of different measurement outcomes by given parameters θ. The conditional probability $\pi(\theta|y)$, called *posterior distribution* of θ, expresses the information of θ after realized observation y.

In the Bayesian framework, the inverse problem is expressed in following way: Given the data y, find the conditional probability distribution $\pi(\theta|y)$ of the variable θ. The statistical formulation of inverse problem can be concluded in the following theorem [KS05]:

Theorem 1 (Bayes' theorem of inverse problems) *Assume that the random variable $\Theta \in \mathbb{R}^n$ has a known prior probability density $\pi(\theta)$ and the data consist of the* *observed value y of an observable random variable $Y \in \mathbb{R}^k$ such that $\pi(y) > 0$. Then the posterior probability distribution of θ, given the data y is*

$$\pi_{post}(\boldsymbol{\theta}) = \pi(\boldsymbol{\theta}|\boldsymbol{y}) = \frac{\pi(\boldsymbol{\theta})\pi(\boldsymbol{y}|\boldsymbol{\theta})}{\pi(\boldsymbol{y})} \qquad (3.2)$$

The marginal probability density in the equation (3.2)

$$\pi(\boldsymbol{y}) = \int_{\mathbb{R}^n} \pi(\boldsymbol{\theta}, y) d\boldsymbol{\theta} = \int_{\mathbb{R}^n} \pi(\boldsymbol{y}|\boldsymbol{\theta})\pi(\boldsymbol{\theta}) d\boldsymbol{\theta}$$

acts only as a norming constant and therefore is normally neglect.

In summary, solving the inverse problem from the Bayes's point of view can be divided into three subtasks.

1. Determine an appropriate prior probability density $\pi_{pr}(\boldsymbol{\theta})$ relied on the available prior information of unknown $\boldsymbol{\theta}$

2. Construct an appropriate likelihood function $\pi(y|\boldsymbol{\theta})$ that describes the interrelation between the observation and the unknown.

3. Compute the posterior probability density $\pi_{post}(\boldsymbol{\theta})$

3.3   Inverse problem for partial differential equation

In this work, we present the inverse problem of PDEs. It means, that from the IBVP (2.1), (2.3) and (2.2) discussed in the last section, the solution of PDEs accordingly the distribution and the dynamic of state $x(\boldsymbol{r}, t)$ is normally to be founded and therefore can be seen as the data $\boldsymbol{y}$ according to the equation (3.1). The mathematical operator in this case is also the differential operator $\mathcal{D}$. The source term $s(\boldsymbol{r}, t)$, the process parameters $\boldsymbol{\eta}$, the initial condition and the boundary condition are needed in order to find the solution of PDEs and hence can be seen as a model $\boldsymbol{\theta}$.

The computation of state $x(\boldsymbol{r}, t)$ from the IBVP (2.1), (2.3) and (2.2) is forward problem. But in case the state $x(\boldsymbol{r}, t)$ is known or observable and the others are unknown. Typical inverse problems of PDEs is normally the problem of:

- Source location : find $s(\boldsymbol{r}, t)$

- Parameter estimation : find $\boldsymbol{\eta}$

- Boundary reconstruction : find $b(t)$

- Initial reconstruction : find $h(\mathbf{r})$

In the statistical inverse problem the unknown variable is casted as a random variable. In case that the distribution (e.g. source distribution $s(\mathbf{r}, t)$) is sought, the sought distribution has to be approximated by discretization, because it is impossible to find the total distribution in infinite space. The distribution can be discretized by means of a set of basis function as showed in section 2. In this case the coefficients of the basis function is the unknown to be found and therefore are modeled as random variables.

As discussed in the last subsection there are three tasks to be worked on to solve the Bayesian inverse problem. Firstly the unknown parameter prior density are commonly modeled by Gaussian density for solve such inverse problem of PDE, which can be formulated in following form.

$$\pi_{pr}(\boldsymbol{\theta}) = exp\left(-\frac{1}{2}\beta(\boldsymbol{\theta} - \boldsymbol{\theta_0})^T S^{-1}(\boldsymbol{\theta} - \boldsymbol{\theta_0})\right)$$

where $S \in \mathbb{R}^{n \times n}$ denotes covariance matrix of random variables $\boldsymbol{\theta}$ and $\beta \in \mathbb{R}_+$ is some arbitrary constant. Under the assumption of additive white noise in the measurement and giving the forward model $F(\boldsymbol{\theta})$ the likelihood function is:

$$\pi(y|\boldsymbol{\theta}) = exp\left(-\frac{1}{2\sigma^2}\|F(\boldsymbol{\theta}) - Y\|^2\right)$$

where σ denotes the standard deviation of the measurement noise. More information about both formulation can be found in [CO10],[Jin06] and [KS05].

Finally we have to find the method to compute the posterior distribution π_{post}. For large dimension, the integration over space $\mathbb{R}^n$ cannot be done with numerical quadrature. One effective class of technique to compute the integration in large dimensional space is known as *Markov Chain Monte Carlo (MCMC)* simulation. The MCMC method use a set of point from the given distribution, a *sample*, to approximate the Monte Carlo integration. The sample ensembles are generated by using the Markov chain random walk algorithm, for example *Metropolis-Hasting algorithm* or *Gibbs sampling*. There are also some modifications of this algorithm for better performance and computation such as *Delay rejection (DR)* or *Adaptive Metropolis-Hasting (AM)* [HLMS06]. The MCMC realizes the computation of the posterior distribution and its estimation of expected values.

4 Numerical study of Bayesian inverse problem of PDE with the 1D heat conduction example

In this work, the estimation problems of heat source in one dimensional stationary heat conduction serve to illustrate the use of Bayesian statistic to solve the PDEs inverse problem. One dimensional stationary heat conduction, for example heat conduction in rod, can be described with PDE as follow.

$$\frac{\partial}{\partial x}\left(Ak\frac{\partial T(x)}{\partial x}\right) = -Q(x)$$

where $T(x)$ is the temperature distribution in considered domain. $Q(x)$ is the heat source distribution function. A is the surface area of the rod. k is the heat conductivity of the material. Normally in heat transfer literature, this problem is formulated to find the temperature distribution $T(x)$ by given boundary condition and the other fixed parameters. This formulation is the forward problem as equation (3.1). In contrast, our heat conduction inverse problem example can be formulated as follow. By giving temperature T at measure point d_i, the heat source distribution $Q(x)$ is to be estimated under the conditions that the boundary condition and parameters Ak are known (see figure 4.1).

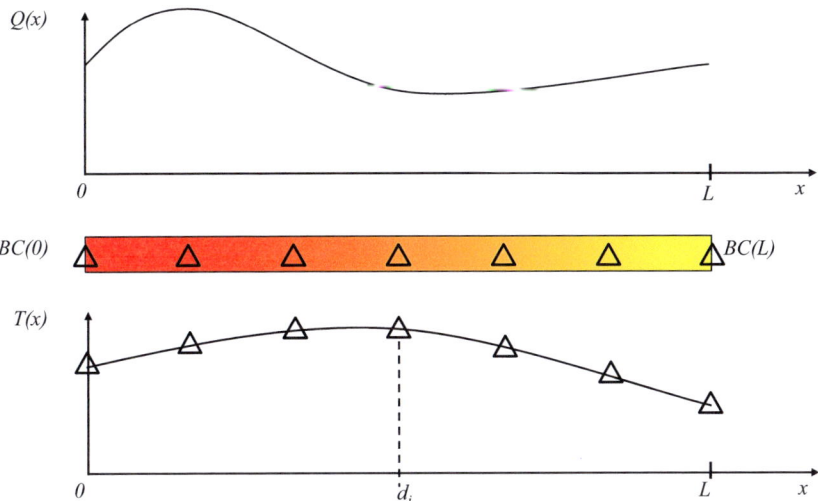

Figure 4.1: the inverse problem in 1D stationary heat conduction as an example

For simplification the parameters A and k are supposed to be constant. In our work the boundary conditions are set to be Neumann boundary condition on the left end and Dirichlet boundary condition on the right end as following equation (4.1).

$$\frac{\partial T}{\partial x}(0) = b_1(const.)$$
$$T(L) = b_2(const.) \tag{4.1}$$

Because the estimation total heat source distribution $Q(x)$ in the whole infinite space directly is impossible, it has to be discretized in finite space with some spatial basis functions in order to keep the unknowns in finite number. In this work we present three type of spatial basis function which we go in detail in the following subsection.

- linear local basis function

- quadratic local basis function

- global basis function

4.1 Linear local basis function

Suppose we have the temperature measurement data $T(d_i)$ at sensor position $d_i = \{0, 0.1, ..., 5.9, 6\}$ as shown in the figure 4.2. The ground truth of heat source distribution function $Q(x)$, which is afterwards estimated , is piecewise linear. In this example it is discretized in 4 elements with 5 nodes by linear local basis function. The approximation of heat source distribution for example in first element is:

$$\hat{H}_I(\xi) = \theta_1\left(1 - \frac{\xi}{l_I}\right) + \theta_2\frac{\xi}{l_I}$$

where ξ is the local coordinate in the element and l_i the length of the i-th element. Transform the local coordinate ξ to the global coordinate x, the heat source distribution for total domain is:

$$\dot{Q}(x) = \sum_{i=I}^{IV} \hat{H}_i(x) = \hat{H}_I(x) + \hat{H}_{II}(x) + \hat{H}_{III}(x) + \hat{H}_{IV}(x)$$

Instead of estimation source distribution of total domain, we need to estimate only 5 variables $\theta_1, ..., \theta_5$. By using the Bayesian statistical method as shown in section

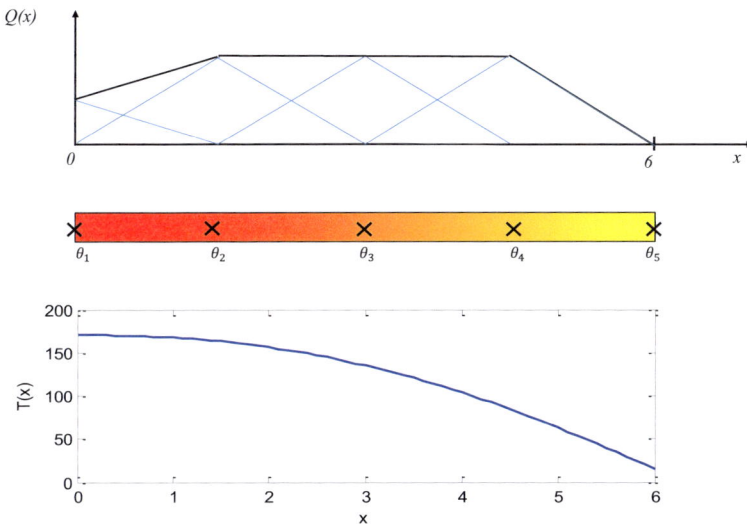

Figure 4.2: shows the example in 4.1. The ground truth of heat source distribution function $Q(x)$, the position of the variables θ and the temperature data

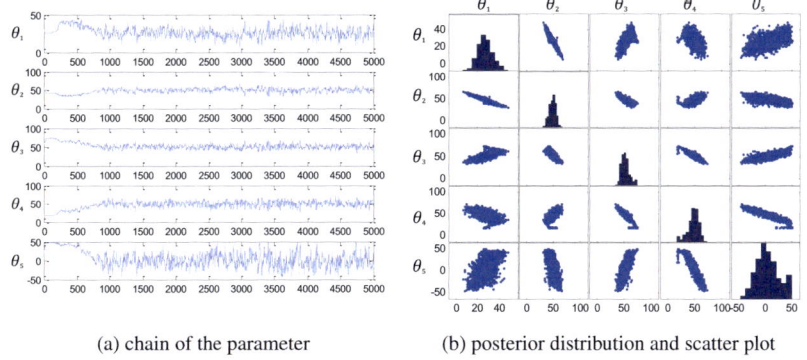

(a) chain of the parameter   (b) posterior distribution and scatter plot

Figure 4.3: The result distribution of unknown parameter $[\theta_1, ..., \theta_5]$ from MCMC simulation in the example 4.1

3.2 these 5 unknowns are casted as a random variable. The MCMC simulation results the chain of parameters as shown in figure 4.3a. The posterior distribution and the scattering plot, which present the probability and the dependency of each parameters, are shown in figure 4.3b.

The estimated heat source distribution $\hat{Q}(x)$ in total domain can be reconstructed by using the expected values from the posterior distribution as a coefficient of basis function by using equation (2.4). The expected value of the parameter can be estimated with *Maximum a Posterior (MAP)* or *conditional mean (CM)* from the posterior distribution. The figure 4.4 shows the plot of the reconstructed heat source distribution, which are satisfyingly accurate. Only at the right boundary one can see that there is a large deviation. The scattering plot also shows that the variable θ_5 is quite independent from the other variables. Because of the Dirichlet boundary condition at the right boundary, the variable θ_5 has a little effect to the solution of the forward model. This shows how the Bayesian statistic handle the ill-posed problem.

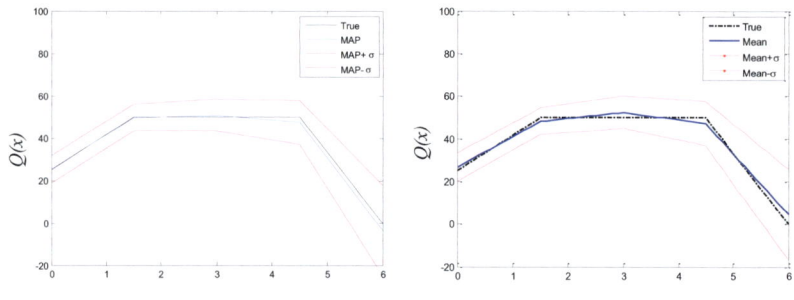

(a) reconstructed source distribution with MAP   (b) reconstructed source distribution with CM

Figure 4.4: the reconstructed source distribution using linear local basis function in the example 4.1

4.2   Quadratic local basis function

In some case the linear local basis function cannot reproduce original function accurately. Compare to the quadratic local basis function the linear local basis function need more nodes to keep good accuracy. The figure 4.5 show that at the same number of variables the quadratic local basis function can approximate the original function better than the local basis function. The quadratic local basis function need 3 coefficient in 1 element as shown in equation (4.2).

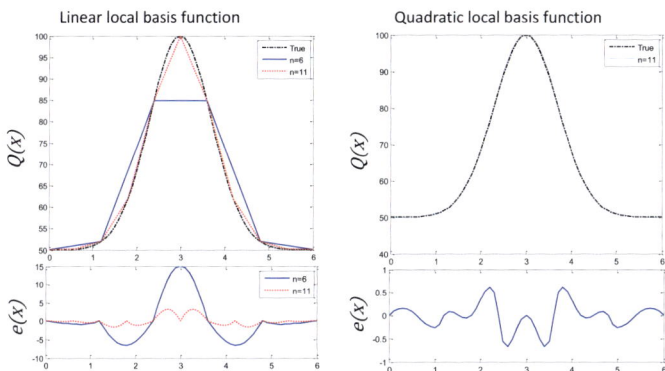

Figure 4.5: comparing the reconstruction of $Q(x)$ using linear basis function and quadratic basis function

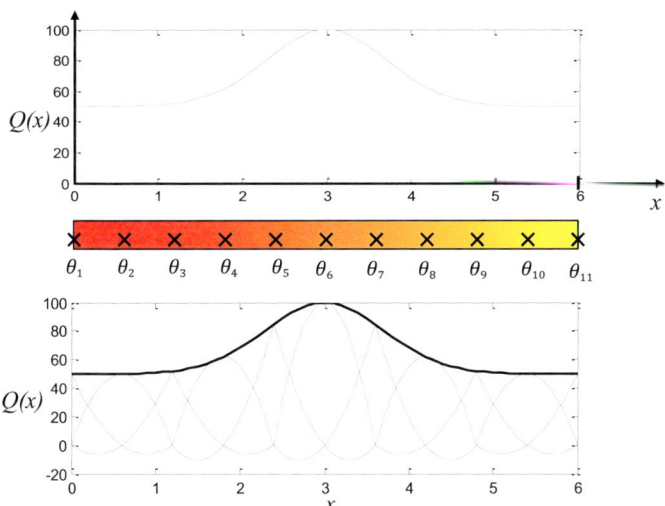

Figure 4.6: shows the example 4.2. The ground truth of heat source distribution function $Q(x)$, the position of the variables θ and the temperature data

$$\hat{H}_I(\xi) = \theta_1 \left(1 - \frac{\xi}{l}\right)\left(1 - 2\frac{\xi}{l}\right) + \theta_2 4\frac{\xi}{l}\left(1 - \frac{\xi}{l}\right) + \theta_3 \frac{\xi}{l}\left(2\frac{x}{l} - 1\right) \quad (4.2)$$

The approximation of heat source distribution is the summation of all local element after transformation the local coordinate to the global coordinate system.

$$\hat{Q}(x) = \sum_{i=I}^{N} \hat{H}_i(x)$$

The figure 4.6 shows the ground truth of the heat source distribution and its discretization with the quadratic local basis function. In this example the ground truth of heat source distribution is determined as follow

$$Q(x) = 50(1 + e^{(x-3)^2})$$

The MCMC simulation results the posterior distributions of all unknown coefficients (11 variables in this example). The reconstructed heat source distribution with the MAP- and CM-estimators are shown in figure 4.7

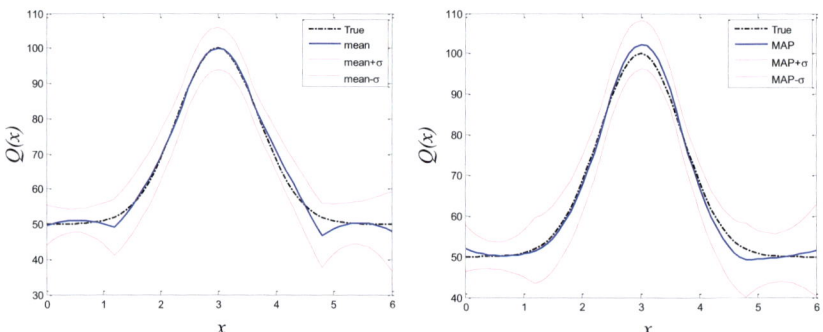

Figure 4.7: the reconstructed source distribution using quadratic local basis function in the example 4.2

4.3   Global basis function

The quadratic local basis function can give a satisfactory result but it need a lot of coefficient to reconstruct the original function. Sometimes it can lead to the curse of dimensionality. As we discussed in the section 2.1, the global basis function can be also used to reconstruct the original distribution. There are a plenty of type

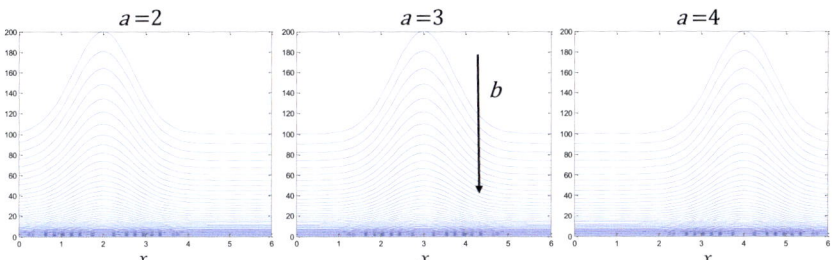

Figure 4.8: set of the assumed possible heat source distribution functions

of global basis functions as aforementioned discussion. In this work we use the *Proper Orthogonal Decomposition* or short POD-Basis function. This POD-method is also known *Principal component analysis (PCA), Kahunen-Loeve transform (KLT)* or *Hotelling transform*. This technique uses some given empirical data to extract a basis function, which hold the important feature from the given data set. More information about POD-basis function can be found in [Ast04] and [New96]. Suppose we possess a set of possible heat source distribution function data as shown in the figure 4.8. These data are described with the equation

$$Q(x) = 100e^{-b}(1 + e^{(x-a)^2}), \text{ for } a = \{2, 3, 4\}, b = \{0, 0.1, ..., 6\} \quad (4.3)$$

which we presumably do not know. These data represent known learn input

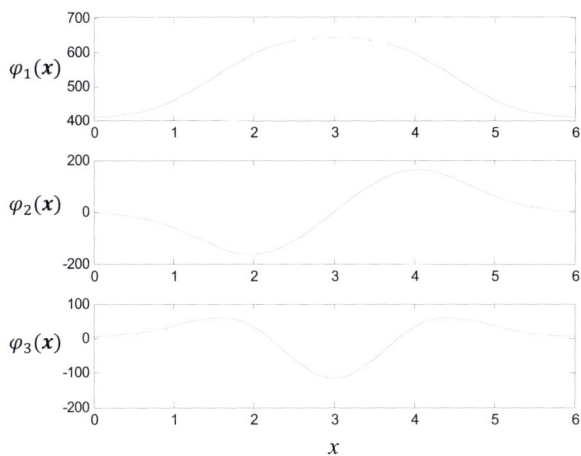

Figure 4.9: the first three POD-basis function

data. From these data we can extract the global basis functions by using POD-method. According to the equation (2.4) this possible source distribution can be approximated by using the first three important basis function as shown in figure 4.9.

With this three global basis function, we need to estimate only three unknown parameters. In this example we test our approach with 4 heat source distribution as following equations .

$$Q(x) = 50(1 + e^{(x-3)^2})$$
$$Q(x) = 50(1 + e^{(x-4)^2})$$
$$Q(x) = 50(1 + e^{-\frac{1}{2}(x-3)^2})$$
$$Q(x) = 50(1 + e^{(x-3.5)^2})$$

The figure 4.10 shows the reconstruction of heat source distribution functions with the POD-basis function. It can be seen that the estimation is very accurate for cases a) and b). There are also no large deviation on the right boundary due to the property of the global basis function. On the other hand these three basis functions cannot reconstruct the heat source functions of case c) and d) satisfyingly. The reason is that both heat source functions in case c) and d) do not belong to defined possible heat source distributions (equation (4.3)).

5 Conclusion and Future work

In this report, the solving PDEs inverse problem using Bayesian statistical inference method is presented. The unsolvable infinite dimension problem is approximated into finite dimension problem with different type of spatial basis functions. Using MCMC simulation the posterior distribution the unknown variables are computed from the prior informations and the likelihood functions. The Bayesian inference method is illustrated by heat source estimation problems in one dimensional sta-tionary heat conduction as study examples. From the examples, it is found that choosing spatial basis function has a considerable influence in the solution. Using the local basis function is simple, but it needs a high number of unknown variables. The global spatial basis function such as POD-basis function can reconstruct the heat source distribution function with only a low number of variables, but it also need a set of learn data to generate the basis function. Each type of spatial basis function has different advantage and disadvantage in different situation. The exact effect of spatial basis function in this method will be further researched in the future work.

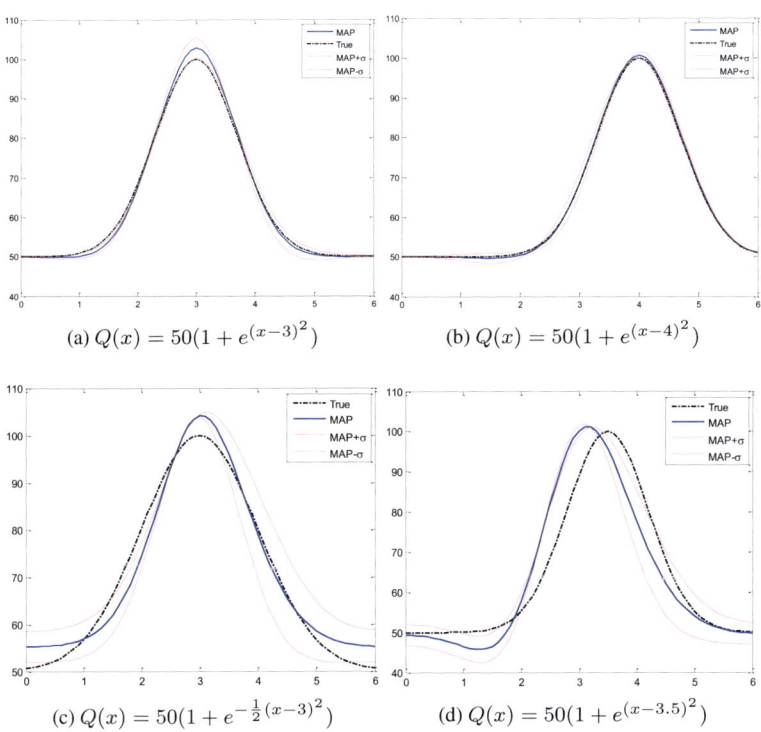

(a) $Q(x) = 50(1 + e^{(x-3)^2})$

(b) $Q(x) = 50(1 + e^{(x-4)^2})$

(c) $Q(x) = 50(1 + e^{-\frac{1}{2}(x-3)^2})$

(d) $Q(x) = 50(1 + e^{(x-3.5)^2})$

Figure 4.10: the reconstructed source distribution using POD basis function in the example 4.3

Bibliography

[AD01]   A.C. Antoulas and D.C. Sorensen. Approximation of large-scale dynamical systems: An overview, 2001.

[Ast04]   Patricia Astrid. *Reduction of process simulation models: a proper orthogonal decomposition approach*. Technische Universiteit Eindhoven, Eindhoven, 2004.

[CO10]   Karen Willcox Chad Lieberman and Omar Ghattas. Parameter and state model reduction for large-scale statistical inverse problems. *SIAM Journal on Scientific Computing*, 32(5):2523–2542, 2010.

[Had23]   Jacques Hadamard. *Lectures on Cauchy's problem in linear partial differential equations, by Jacques Hadamard,..* Yale University press, New Haven, 1923.

[HLMS06]   Heikki Haario, Marko Laine, Antonietta Mira, and Eero Saksman. Dram: Efficient adaptive mcmc. *Statistics and Computing*, 16:339–354, 2006.

[Jin06]   Jingbo Wang Ph. D. *Bayesian computational techniques for inverse problems in transport processes*. 2006.

[KS05]   Jari Kaipio and Erkki Somersalo. *Statistical and computational inverse problems*. Springer, New York, 2005.

[KS07]   Jari Kaipio and Erkki Somersalo. Statistical inverse problems: Discretization, model reduction and inverse crimes: Applied computational inverse problems. *Journal of Computational and Applied Mathematics*, 198(2):493–504, 2007.

[Li11]   Han-Xiong Li. *Spatio-tenporal modeling of nonlinear distributed parameter systems: A time/space separation based approach*. Springer, [S.l.], 2011.

[Lie09]   Chad Eric Lieberman. *Parameter and state model reduction for Bayesian statistical inverse problems*. 2009.

[New96]   Andrew J. Newman. Model reduction via the karhunen-loeve expansion part i: An exposition. Technical report, Tech. Rep. T.R. 96-32, Inst. Systems Research, 1996.

[SD00]   Bruno Sudret and Armen DerKiureghian. *Stochastic finite element methods and reliability: A state-of-the-art report*, volume 2000,08. Dept. of Civil Engineering Univ. of California, Berkeley, 2000.

Karlsruher Schriftenreihe zur Anthropomatik
(ISSN 1863-6489)

Herausgeber: Prof. Dr.-Ing. Jürgen Beyerer

Die Bände sind unter www.ksp.kit.edu als PDF frei verfügbar oder
als Druckausgabe bestellbar.

Band 9   Thomas Bader
          Multimodale Interaktion in Multi-Display-Umgebungen. 2011
          ISBN 3-86644-760-8

Band 10   Christian Frese
          Planung kooperativer Fahrmanöver für kognitive Automobile. 2012
          ISBN 978-3-86644-798-1

Band 11   Jürgen Beyerer, Alexey Pak (Hrsg.)
          **Proceedings of the 2011 Joint Workshop of Fraunhofer IOSB and
          Institute for Anthropomatics, Vision and Fusion Laboratory.** 2012
          ISBN 978-3-86644-855-1